A DIVINE REVELATION OF SATAN'S DECEPTIONS & SPIRITUAL WARFARE

2-BOOKS-IN-1

A DIVINE REVELATION OF SATAN'S DECEPTIONS

&

SPIRITUAL WARFARE

BEST-SELLING AUTHOR
MARY K. BAXTER

WHITAKER
HOUSE

Publisher's note: This book is not intended to provide medical or psychological advice or to take the place of medical advice and treatment from your personal physician. Those who are having suicidal thoughts or who have been emotionally, physically, or sexually abused should seek help from a mental health professional or qualified counselor. Neither the publisher nor the author nor the author's ministry takes any responsibility for any possible consequences from any action taken by any person reading or following the information in this book. If readers are taking prescription medications, they should consult with their physicians and not take themselves off prescribed medicines without the proper supervision of a physician. Always consult your physician or other qualified health care professional before undertaking any change in your physical regimen, whether fasting, diet, medications, or exercise.

A Divine Revelation of Satan's Deceptions & Spiritual Warfare
Two-Books-in-One

Mary K. Baxter
marykbaxter1@yahoo.com
www.marykbaxterinc.com

ISBN: 978-1-64123-544-0
Printed in the United States of America

Whitaker House
1030 Hunt Valley Circle
New Kensington, PA 15068
www.whitakerhouse.com

1 2 3 4 5 6 7 8 9 10 11 28 27 26 25 24 23 22 21

CONTENTS

A DIVINE REVELATION OF SATAN'S DECEPTIONS

CONTENTS

Prologue:

Keys to the Kingdom

Upon this rock I will build my church; and the gates of hell shall not prevail against it. And I will give unto thee the keys of the kingdom of heaven: and whatsoever thou shalt bind on earth shall be bound in heaven: and whatsoever thou shalt loose on earth shall be loosed in heaven.
—Matthew 16:18–19 (KJV)

Jesus said, "Look, listen, and learn. I've given you the keys to the kingdom. I want you to take a key in your hand in the spirit." All at once, I looked at my hand, and there was a spiritual key in it. "What do I do with it, Jesus?" I asked. He said, "Come with Me." Then we were standing in front of one of the large, transparent, glass-like cages. Something that looked like a white glow was moving in it. I said, "What is this, Lord?" He replied, "Take the key and put it in the lock and, in My name, Jesus Christ, Emmanuel, Yeshua, open that door."

So I took the key. In the name of Jesus Christ, Emmanuel, Yeshua, I put the spiritual key in the lock and turned it. The lock broke open, and out flowed the most beautiful presence. Jesus had dropped to His knees, and He said, "My Spirit will once again flow over the earth and bring the people on the earth to conviction. My Spirit will again begin to draw people unto Me, child, by the thousands."

INTRODUCTION: A REVELATION FOR TODAY

As I have related in my previous books, Jesus Christ appeared to me in human form in 1976. I was an ordinary mother and homemaker, with a houseful of little children, who loved God with all her heart. Prophets and apostles had told me my calling, saying, "God's going to visit you and show you strange things that will shake the world." And God has fulfilled, and is fulfilling, that word.

When Jesus appeared to me, I had not died, and I was not dreaming; I was fully alert. By His power, for thirty nights, three hours a night, Jesus took me in spirit form into hell so that I could see its reality firsthand and warn people of the consequences of rejecting God the Father and His offer of forgiveness through His Son Jesus Christ. God is holy, and human beings were created in His image to be holy, also. But ever since the first man and woman turned their backs on God and disobeyed Him, people have been born with a sinful nature. To be restored to God, we must be cleansed by the blood of Jesus, who came to earth as a baby and grew into a man to die on the cross for us. He became our Substitute, receiving the punishment we deserved, and then He was gloriously resurrected from the dead by God the Father. Our part is to believe in Him, to repent of our sins, and to receive His sacrifice on our behalf so that we can be forgiven of all our wrongdoing and live a new life in Him.

Since the time when God first gave me revelations of hell, followed by ten days of revelations of heaven, I have spent my life ministering around the world, warning people of the reality of heaven and hell and telling them of God's extraordinary power to save us and equip us to do what He has called us to do. But God has recently taken me back to those first revelations. In 1976, when the journey of the thirty nights in hell was concluded, Jesus said to me, "I will close up your mind, and you will not remember some of the things I have shown and told you. But I will reopen your mind and bring back your understanding in the latter days. Then I will open up your remembrance and reveal to you the things I want put on paper. You will write a new book about hell. And I will raise up others who have seen hell and others who know about hell, and they will be witnesses to what I have shown you. For this purpose you were born, to write and to tell the things I show and tell you. There is much the world needs to know, for there is a beginning and an end to everything."

Jesus has brought many of those experiences back to my memory, and this book contains scenes from hell that I have not related in my other books. He opened up my mind and began to show me and tell me these things so that the world could know them now. These things are not pretty. I'm so glad Jesus Christ didn't allow me to remember everything at that time, because I couldn't have handled it then.

This revelation is for the times in which we now live. Through this book, I must tell these things that Christ has brought back to my remembrance for the world to understand. In addition, a movie will be made that includes some of these experiences. I want it to be an excellent film that will clearly show the truth about hell. The Lord Jesus told me, "This is a book that will make the power of God shake this nation. You are a key, a key in the midst of a great revival I am going to bring." My response was and is, "Glory to Your name, Father. Spirit of the living God, have Your way."

We human beings have a dangerous adversary named Satan, or the devil. But we have a much more powerful God who is able to save and deliver us from any of his deceptions and attacks! Satan was once an archangel of God, but he wanted to usurp heaven's throne, and so he seduced a third of God's angels to rebel against Him. Satan and his angels were expelled from heaven. Yet the devil still seeks to seduce human beings, who are God's highest and most beloved creation. He wants us to rebel against our Creator so that we will fall further and further away from Him and ultimately be judged and sent to hell. Hell was prepared for the devil and his fallen angels; it was not intended for human beings. But it has become the destination of all who reject God.

Our God wants us to know that, in His power, we can stand against Satan's traps! *A Divine Revelation of Satan's Deceptions* is a call to recognize Satan's devices that keep people separated from God, prevent them from receiving Christ, and destroy them in hell. It contains revelation of how Satan has stolen and held captive the blessings that God has given to His people to accomplish His work in the world—blessings of anointing, gifts, resources, and more, which we must reclaim in these latter times. To do this, we need to obey God, renew our love for Him, and use specific "keys to the kingdom" that He has given us. God has called us to this so we can minister salvation, deliverance, and healing to the millions in the world who are dying and facing eternal judgment. These keys are described in the pages that follow.

We cannot allow Satan to deceive and rob us any longer. The Lord told me that this is a time for the judgment of demons. Satan and his forces of darkness can be defeated. We must fight back and reclaim our spiritual inheritance in the power of God.

My heart is full of new revelations that God has given me to tell the church. My heart is full of things that God has shown me, told me, and "downloaded" into me for many years. My heart is full of a desire to talk about the things that Jesus has revealed to me. There are truths of revelation that we need to understand. God said, *"My people are destroyed for lack of knowledge"* (Hosea 4:6). Therefore, I have tried my best to relate to you through this book some things that Christ first showed to me many years ago but has now revealed to the world. Jesus' words are not necessarily verbatim but do convey the messages that He gave to me.

God has given each believer a spiritual gift or gifts in order to build up the body of Christ. We all need one another if we are to grow more Christlike and be equipped to minister in His name to each other and to the world. Revelation and prophecy are the particular spiritual gifts that God has given me.

I have dedicated my life to communicating God's revelations. With His help, I will continue to do so for you and your family, for myself and my family, and for all the people of the world. We must come to a realization of the truth. The scales need to come off our eyes, and our ears need to be unstopped, so that we can see and hear what God is saying to us today. As I now relate some of the graphic details of hell, as well as the spiritual authority God has given us, get ready for a ride in the Spirit, for you'll never be the same.

Part One:

RECOGNIZING SATAN'S DECEPTIONS

1

THE REALITY OF HELL

When Jesus Christ took me into hell, I was in my spirit form, while my body remained on the earth. Jesus, however, was in human form. He looked about six feet four inches tall, and He was wearing a long white robe with a golden belt and sandals. His hair flowed to His shoulders, and He had a trimmed beard and mustache. He had beautiful blue eyes, and looking into those eyes was like looking into eternity. Everything about Him was so holy, pure, and precious. He was full of glory and of the fruit of the Spirit. (See Galatians 5:22–23.)

THE DEPTHS OF AN ETERNITY WITHOUT GOD

I looked down at Jesus' feet and saw large nail holes, and real blood seemed to be flowing from them. He took my hand, and my hand felt warm, even though I was in the spirit form. Blood from the nail hole in Christ's hand filled my hand and dripped to the ground. I screamed and said, "Oh, Jesus, why is this happening to You?" I looked at Him and saw big tears coming down His face. He said, "Child, for all these souls I died and shed My blood, but it is too late for them. But in this book you are doing—and it will be made into a movie—people shall see and know and understand the depths of eternity and of being lost without Me. The world needs to know this truth of an eternity without God. People need to understand the suffering and the pain that thousands and thousands are going through, while they go about life upon the earth, even as I call them to repent. This is a warning to the world to repent and to come back to the Lord Jesus Christ."

> *Repent therefore and be converted, that your sins may be blotted out, so that times of refreshing may come from the presence of the Lord.*
> —Acts 3:19

"IF I HAD ONLY KNOWN"

While Jesus and I were walking together in hell, it was a time of sorrow, of such sadness and grief, as I saw the millions of suffering souls. They looked like skeletons, and some of them were missing arms, legs, or other body parts. All of them had what looked like a dirty mist inside their ribcage—this was their eternal soul.

I looked around me as Jesus and I walked up a hillside. We were on a dusty, rocky, dirty road. Along the way, demons would run from Jesus, because He caused light to shine. They would scream, "What do we have to do with You?"[1] And then they would run away.

We walked for a long time, and I smelled odors and saw flames in many areas. There were dark shadows in the mountains and caves. I heard souls screaming, "Let us out; let us out! Is there no

1. See Matthew 8:29; Mark 1:24; Luke 4:34.

more hope? There's no life down here, but yet I cannot die. Help me; help me!"

Around the top of the mountain, I saw high flames. Down below, in a valley full of dead men's bones, there was an army of thousands of skeletons, burning and screaming, "Let us die; let us die." As we walked past them, I could hear a multitude of voices crying such things as this: "Why didn't someone warn me? Why didn't someone tell me about this horrible place? I would have chosen the Lord and not lived such a wicked life, if I had only known." I looked at Christ as tears came down His face, and I had pity and great compassion for Jesus.

The ground was all smoky and black, and there was an evil-looking darkness everywhere. But Jesus caused a light to shine, and the darkness went away for a while. He sat down on a big rock that overlooked a valley of high flames, and I sat by Him, very scared. We were far up on a mountainside, and I was so tired from hearing all those cries of regret, all that grief and sorrow.

As we sat, I looked over into the valley. About half a mile down, there was a greenish-yellow mist hanging over some fires. Christ was crying. I kept looking at His feet and wanting to wipe the blood away. I thought, *Thousands and thousands are here, and more are coming. What can I do, Lord? What can I do?* He put His arm around me and pulled me close to His side.

Then Jesus looked at me and, calling me by my middle name, said, "Katherine, you see all of this?" He waved His hand, and as He did, the fog and mist moved back, and I could see thousands of skeletons burning and screaming, "Let us die; let us die. We cannot die. We cry for death, and death doesn't come." I looked at them and said, "Jesus, please get them out. Please give them flesh and bone and make them new again, Lord." But Jesus said, "It's too late. This is the judgment of My Father upon the sins of the flesh. I was manifested to destroy the works of Satan[2] so people would know and understand how he deceives. People are doing the wicked things of the world—cursing, lying, cheating, hating, refusing to forgive; committing adultery and fornication; practicing witchcraft and sorcery. Satan deceives people, child. God has rules and laws and regulations concerning these things, and the key is to repent. Tell the people to repent and to ask Me to forgive them, come into their heart, and save their soul, and I will."

> *If you confess with your mouth the Lord Jesus and believe in your heart that God has raised Him from the dead, you will be saved. For with the heart one believes unto righteousness, and with the mouth confession is made unto salvation.*
>
> —Romans 10:9–10

I looked at Jesus' face, so stern and so sad, and I put my arm around Him and fell onto His chest, crying; yet no tears came from me, because I was in the spirit form. I remember thinking about my home—my children and other family members. I looked at the Lord and said, "Jesus, what can I do? I am a mother, and I have children. I never want my children to come here, Jesus. Promise me they won't." I looked up at His eyes, and He said, "Child, ahead of you is greater horror and great sorrow, but I will give you the strength to go through this. I will give you the anointing to go through this, and it will help thousands come unto Me."

Jesus spoke to me with deep compassion and great love, saying, "Child, I'm walking you through hell to show you the depths, degrees, and levels of torments. I'm showing you the truth. My leaders on the earth are lying to people. Yes, many are telling the truth, but many others tell people that there is no hell and that they can live in whatever way they want. They say that God is good

2. See 1 John 3:8.

and therefore would never send anyone to an eternal punishment. But My Father is a righteous Judge. My Father is a holy Judge. In the Holy Bible, it tells you not to commit the sins of the flesh once you come to the knowledge of repentance and truth.[3] My Word will stand forever. Child, it's too late for all of these, but I want you to hear them."

AWAKE, AND SEEK THE LORD

I looked down at the Lord's feet and again saw the nail holes with the blood flowing out. I began to think about the Holy Scriptures, which describe how Jesus was beaten for me and for all other people so we wouldn't have to go to hell, if we would only believe that He is the Son of God, that He came to earth and died on the cross to save us from eternal damnation, and that His blood will wash us clean as we repent of our sins and begin to live for God.

I looked again where all the flames were coming from, very high at the end of the massive army of skeletons that were burning and screaming and gnashing their teeth. Every so often, I would see something like corrupt flesh grow on the skeletons' bones, and then the flames would burn it off, and the bones would be dry, and worms would crawl out of them. I thought about the masses of people in the world who need the Lord—now, in this very hour.

I saw demons who had eyes of red fire and skin that was like black coal. They had horns on their heads, with fire coming out of them. They had wings full of maggots. And they had an odor that was beyond belief. It smelled like rotten flesh, like sewers and dung, like burning oil.

We resumed walking, and I saw that as Christ walked, He left blood on the ground. I screamed, "Jesus, where are we going?" He said, "I am going to show you this, and then you will return home.

3. See Hebrews 10:26.

Then again, tomorrow night, we will come back to the same place." I said, "Jesus, I don't know if I can do this." He answered, "I will give you the strength and the courage to do this." I clung tightly to Jesus' hand and noticed that there was no blood there now. I looked at His feet, and they, too, were dry. We continued walking, and I kept crying, although no tears came. My heart was breaking, and I was thinking about the earth. *There is so much manipulation and so much sin and so much evil and so much death. Will the world listen to me? Will people understand that there is an eternity without God for those who do evil and reject Him? The world has many theories and many lies; and so many preachers are telling people one thing or another that is not true. Awake, awake, men and women of God; seek the Lord while He can be found.*

> *Seek the* Lord *while He may be found, call upon Him while He is near. Let the wicked forsake his way, and the unrighteous man his thoughts; let him return to the* Lord*, and He will have mercy on him; and to our God, for He will abundantly pardon.* —Isaiah 55:6–7

THERE IS HOPE IN JESUS

I then began to think of the love of God and of hope in Jesus Christ. From the mountaintop, I turned around and looked right into the eyes of the Lord, and He said to me, "There is hope in Me. There is deliverance in Me. Warn the people to return unto Me; tell them that once again I want to raise up the fivefold ministry[4] where the people need hope. They need to know that I am their Anchor, and that they can put their trust and their hope in Me, the Lord Jesus Christ."

---

4. See Ephesians 4:11–12.

We are in the midst of a precarious world situation today, as you well know. But if you turn to the Lord Jesus Christ, there is hope. He wants us to look to Him. He wants to heal us. He wants to stop the evil. He wants to stop the wars. He wants us to live with Him forever. There is hope for us and for our families and for the generation of our children and grandchildren. There is hope in Jesus Christ. Turn to Him with all your heart, all your mind, all your soul, and all your strength. (See Matthew 22:37; Luke 10:27.) Jesus will make you an overcomer.

> *Blessed be the God and Father of our Lord Jesus Christ, who according to His abundant mercy has begotten us again to a living hope through the resurrection of Jesus Christ from the dead, to an inheritance incorruptible and undefiled and that does not fade away, reserved in heaven for you, who are kept by the power of God through faith for salvation ready to be revealed in the last time.* —1 Peter 1:3–5

RECOGNIZING SATAN'S DECEPTIONS:

Satan tries to deceive us into thinking that it will be a long time before we die, so we can put off receiving Jesus Christ and serving God. Don't be caught in that trap. If you don't know Jesus as your Savior, or if you have fallen away from God, you can be restored to Him right now by praying the following prayer and making a commitment to love and serve Him. Please say this prayer:

> Heavenly Father,
>
> I believe in You and in Your Son Jesus Christ, who came to earth to die on the cross for my sins. I believe that You raised Him from the dead and that He is alive forever, so that everyone who believes in Him can receive eternal life. Because of what Jesus did for me, I ask You to forgive

all my sins and to come into my heart and save my soul. Fill me with Your Holy Spirit, and help me to live for You from this day forward. Thank You for saving me and giving me a new life. In Jesus' name, amen.

2

MULTITUDES OF EVERY NATION

The next night, Jesus spoke, and I was again walking with Him in hell. He said, "Come on, child, I want to show you something in the jaws of hell. Hell has a body. Remember that in the middle of the earth there are degrees of fire, torment, and judgment of God. And at the great white throne judgment, when death and hell are brought up out of here to stand in the galaxies, those here will be judged out of the books that were written—which say that they never repented of their sins and that their sins were never washed in My blood—and they'll be thrown into the lake of fire, My daughter, because their names are not in the Book of Life."[5]

All at once, we went into another area, and I could feel the earth move under my feet. As we walked, Jesus said, "God made the soul of man and woman to live forever. This is the judgment of My Father on sin. Their judgment is set." Then He repeated, "They will be here till the great white throne judgment of God, and then they'll be put in the lake of fire." I felt so helpless. Jesus

5. See Revelation 20:11–15.

told me, "I am the way, the truth, and the life, Katherine."[6] I heard the cries of the dead get louder and louder, and I knew that they had been there for years—years of sorrow, years of grief, years of pain, years of weeping and gnashing of teeth, years of burning yet not burning up.

Jesus knew my thoughts, and He said, "Child, if a person is blind in one eye and then dies and comes to hell, he is blind in hell. If someone comes to hell who has had cancer, the cancer is ten times worse; the pain is that much worse. The flames come over them, the worms crawl through them, and they feel the excruciating fire of the eternal judgment of God. My Father sent Me so that people would not come here, child. But they have mocked Me on the earth; they've made fun of Me, child. They've said that I'm not real. They tell all kinds of lies about My holy Word. And God has a plan. He planned for you, My daughter—a mother, a housewife—to come and see all these horrible things, to write books and make records of what's in the middle of the earth. This is your mandate; this is your calling. And you will know and understand in the days ahead how much more I have for you."

During my time in hell, I learned that demons also give bottles of acid to those who were alcoholics on earth; when they drink it, the acid burns them, and they scream. Those who murdered people are stabbed by demons over and over again, but they cannot die. Those who raped little children have their bones torn apart by demons. (See Psalm 50:22.) World, wake up; wake up! Hell is your fate if you do not repent. (See Luke 12:40–48; Matthew 24.) May the Lord God have mercy on the world.

"THEY WOULD NOT LISTEN"

We kept on walking. I wanted to run. I wanted to cry. I wanted to pull the people out of the fire and put flesh on them, but I couldn't do that. I had no power. It was horrible. I thought, *I*

6. See John 14:6.

hope I don't see anybody I know, because I knew many people who had died without Jesus. The dead were screaming, "Let us die. We know we've sinned against God. Oh, can you forgive us now, Jesus?"

The cries of the dead were getting worse and worse, and I screamed, "Oh, God, is there nothing You can do?" There were multitudes and multitudes of voices of every nation. The demons would come up and stab people with something and say, "Shut up! Satan is king here." And they would put more fire on the souls.

Some of the skeletons were in holes, some in caves, and some behind rocks. Others were in vats of fire, salted with fire, bobbing up and down. And on the vats was written "The abominations of desolations." I said, "Oh, God, what is that in the jaws of hell?" He said, "Child, they are those who used to preach My Word, but they lied. They mixed a perverse spirit with My Word and made it seem like I was a phony God. I've loved them, My daughter, but they would not listen. And they caused many to go to hell. You have seen them in our walk through hell. So, My Father judged them. The Father is a holy God, a righteous God, a sincere God. He knows all things, Katherine."

It is appointed for men to die once, but after this the judgment. —Hebrews 9:27

Death was all around, but no one dies in hell. They just keep burning and burning and burning. They cry and scream from unbearable pain. There is no relief; they cannot sleep, and they cannot pass out.

I knew about my heavenly Father's judgment on sin, and I looked down at Jesus' feet and saw the blood flowing. But I noticed that when He walked, the blood disappeared immediately. I thought about how many times on the earth I had pleaded His precious blood—the covenant of God—over me, my family, and other people for healing and protection. As I looked at Jesus, I said, "Lord, this is covenant; Jesus is our covenant. We have to bring the ark of the covenant [the Holy Word of God] back. Jesus is the One who was sent to deliver us from eternal damnation."

The Lord said, "Katherine, I'm going to raise up—and I have already risen up—many others who have seen hell, and it's going to be a witness to what I've shown you. And there shall be a day, My daughter, when this movie will be made, and I the Lord will put a great anointing upon it; I will make the people listen. For you and others have suffered greatly to write this, to tell this, if they'll just listen. For Satan does not want the people to listen to the truth. Satan wants the people to have 'fun' in evil ways, perverse ways, unclean ways. But My Father said, 'Be ye holy, for I am holy.'[7] And if the people do sin, tell them to repent. For they have an Advocate now through Me. I will travail to the Father for them. And I will forgive them if they will be real and call on Me, Katherine. I'm showing you all of this so that you and your family will be saved, and masses of others."

I thought of various family members, friends, and others who did not believe that God created the world with His word (see Psalm 33:6) and did not acknowledge everything He has done for us. Hell was made for the devil and his angels (see Matthew 25:41), but hell has enlarged itself to hold lost souls—the souls of those who would not listen to God and repent (see Isaiah 5:14).

My little children, these things I write to you, so that you may not sin. And if anyone sins, we have an Advocate with the Father, Jesus Christ the righteous. And He Himself is the propitiation for our sins, and not for ours only but also for the whole world. —1 John 2:1–2

---

7. See, for example, Leviticus 11:44–45.

I thought, *Jesus, it hurts so bad to see a skeleton burning that used to have flesh and hair and organs, that was alive on the earth having a good time while the sun was shining and they were enjoying the fresh air and beautiful things. And to think they died in their sins, and when their soul came out of their body, demons brought them down here to give them the punishment related to the sin they committed the most during their lifetime.* When I looked at Jesus, He said, "Child, it's too late for all of these you see burning and screaming and weeping, because they would not listen. They wanted the world and the lusts thereof more than Me and the Father's commandments. I do not want you to fret or worry, because I have so much power, daughter; I have all power in heaven and earth and in between.[8] I'm giving you this testimony to tell the world so that people do not come here. If the world would repent of their sins and look to God, He would hear them.

"Hell is a holding place till the great day of the great white throne judgment, when their books, which are all in hell, will be brought before the throne of God and opened. Their books were never washed in My blood. My people—those who love Me and try their best to keep the commandments of God—will not be judged, My daughter; they've been washed in My blood and cleansed and saved from eternal damnation. My commandment is 'Love you one another as I have loved you.'[9] Katherine, help Me to win the lost. Tell the people what is here. I will anoint the message with truth and the fear of the Lord. Also, I will keep those who turn to Me. If they would repent of their sins and ask Me to forgive them and come into their heart and save their soul, I would. I'm going to raise up many young people to preach the gospel."

There is therefore now no condemnation to those who are in Christ Jesus, who do not walk according to the flesh, but

8. See, for example, Matthew 28:18.
9. See John 13:34; 15:12.

> *according to the Spirit. For the law of the Spirit of life in Christ Jesus has made me free from the law of sin and death.*
>
> —Romans 8:1–2

"MY FATHER, HAVE MERCY"

Jesus said, "This place is so horrible and sad. This place is so hot and evil. This place is so demonic." Fire was burning. Snakes were crawling around. Rats weighing from one pound to seventy pounds were biting the souls. There was grief, fear, and sorrow. There was hatred in many places. The cries of the dead were everywhere. They were the cries of men and women of every nation. Some souls were blaspheming God, some were crying, and some were saying, "Is there no more hope?" These souls had the pleasures of sin for a season. Some had enjoyed hurting people. Now they were in hell.

We came to another rock and sat down. I was so exhausted, yet I was grateful that my family members were in their beds, asleep, and that God's angels were all around them, watching over them. I knew that almighty God would take care of me; He would watch over me and my family.

I had all my faculties—my thoughts and my emotions. I knew exactly what was going on; I knew exactly what I was seeing. I knew that this was Jesus Christ. I knew that I knew that almighty God was showing me this revelation to help everybody understand the reality of what is hidden and invisible. I began to get angry at the devil. As Jesus and I had walked in hell, I had seen the burned ground and the thousands and thousands of skeletons burning and screaming. I had seen the sections in hell where liars were kept; the sections where abusers of men and women were held; the sections for those who been in pornography; the sections for those who had practiced perverse sins and unclean sex acts, and whose souls were burning and screaming and running to try to put out the fires that were burning their bodies, but could not.

Every so often, Jesus would let me see real flesh grow on the skeletons. For a little while, they would look the same as human beings on earth, but then all at once their flesh would melt down like hot lava, and worms would teethe on their bones and cause them great pain. They would scream, "Help me. Doesn't anybody care for me? Why didn't somebody warn me?" And Jesus said, "Katherine, tell My people to read the Bible. Tell My people to listen to worship music. Tell My people to find good churches to go to."

I said, "Jesus," and then I sat on a rock. Jesus said, "Come and sit with Me." He had on the white robe and sandals, and the golden belt around His waist. Jesus put His hands on His face and began to pray, "My Father, My Father, have mercy, have mercy." As He began to pray and travail, hell shook. Words came out of Him from the depths of His soul. And I knew He understood that souls are eternal. So many liars on the earth will tell you that you don't have an eternal soul. You do. And I could hear Jesus screaming, and suddenly hell shook at the violence of it. The fires died down. Some of the souls who were in the pits fell over on the sides. For some of the skeletons, the pain stopped for a few minutes. And Jesus' face was covered with tears. His love is so strong. His acts were of love, and He grieved so over everything He was showing me.

He said, "Child, come sit." I was feeling so helpless, so afraid. I thought, *Oh, God, what if I had died when I was backslidden from You? What if that was me when I was in sin, Lord? What if You had not saved me? When I had my car wreck, I could have died. The doctors took my spleen out, and I was in the hospital for days. God, I could be here with the rest of them. I thank You for Your mercy. Thank You for Your grace.* I was so afraid.

Jesus said to me, "Peace, be still." I remembered that He had said the same words to many of the skeletons when He had talked with them, just as we will see in later chapters. He would go up to one of them and ask, "O man, what are you doing here? What is your name?" I remember the skeletons telling Him the things they had done on the earth, and that they did not want their family to come there. He'd say, "Peace, be still," and the demons would run away from Him and scream, "Don't say that word here!"

When Jesus told me, "Peace, be still," immediately, a peace came over me. And Jesus said, "I will direct your steps. These things you will write and you will tell. I will have you write books about hell and heaven, My daughter."

I became scared again. I'd been walking such a long way before we sat down. I was very tired, but I could not sleep. I was hungry, but I could not eat. I was thirsty, but there was no water. I was sad, but I could not cry. My only hope was in Jesus, being next to Him. And Jesus was so very close. He took my left hand and said, "I'm leading you, and woe be to those who hurt you or judge you, for I am the Lord who loves thee. You've given your life for Me. I want the world to know. And yes, you'll be mocked, you'll be laughed at, you'll be scoffed at, but that's okay. Satan is going to fall, his kingdom is going to fall. I took from him the keys of death and hell, daughter.[10] There are many mysteries to Satan; there are many things that haven't been told yet; there are yet many more revelations. But I say, 'Come on, little one, come on.'" He pulled me close to His side, and I felt such peace.

WHAT IF THAT WAS YOU?

And then I heard the cries of the dead again, and they began to curse God in all things. I said, "Lord, this is horrible." I looked below, and a large circle of fire came up in the air. I thought, *All things were created by God.* He had created the souls of the people

10. See Revelation 1:18.

who were now in the flames down there burning and crying out to die but being unable to. Think about it. What if that was you? Imagine being thrown into hell so that you never slept again, never ate again, never got to pray again, never even got to do anything wicked again. You would simply be burning and burning and remembering.

Yes, the dead remember their life on earth. In Jesus' parable of the rich man and the beggar named Lazarus, the rich man was aware that he was in hell. That could be you or me, if it had not been for God's grace. He wants to save you. You do have an eternal soul. That's why I am pouring out my heart to you, so that you will listen and hear the truth about hell. Go to God and receive His offer of forgiveness in Jesus right now.

There was a certain rich man who was clothed in purple and fine linen and fared sumptuously every day. But there was a certain beggar named Lazarus, full of sores, who was laid at his gate, desiring to be fed with the crumbs which fell from the rich man's table. Moreover the dogs came and licked his sores. So it was that the beggar died, and was carried by the angels to Abraham's bosom. The rich man also died and was buried. And being in torments in Hades, he lifted up his eyes and saw Abraham afar off, and Lazarus in his bosom. Then he cried and said, "Father Abraham, have mercy on me, and send Lazarus that he may dip the tip of his finger in water and cool my tongue; for I am tormented in this flame." But Abraham said, "Son, remember that in your lifetime you received your good things, and likewise Lazarus evil things; but now he is comforted and you are tormented. And besides all this, between us and you there is a great gulf fixed, so that those who want to pass from here to you cannot, nor can those from there pass to us." Then he said, "I beg you therefore, father, that you would send him to my father's house, for I have five brothers, that he may testify to them, lest they also come to this place of torment." Abraham said to him, "They have Moses and the prophets; let them hear them." And he said, "No, father Abraham; but if one goes to them from the dead, they will repent." But he said to him, "If they do not hear Moses and the prophets, neither will they be persuaded though one rise from the dead."

—Luke 16:19–31

RECOGNIZING SATAN'S DECEPTIONS:

Satan tries to deceive us into thinking that God doesn't exist or that we don't need Him; we can just enjoy the pleasures of sin without worrying about the consequences. Don't fall into this trap. Romans 14:12 says, "So then each of us shall give account of himself to God." *What account of your life could you give to God right now?*

3

HELL IS NOT YOUR HOME

As I walked with Jesus along the pathway high in the mountains of hell, every so often, I would feel a hot wind blow. It seemed as if there were certain places in hell that were so cold and yet so hot. And winds would blow through and make the flames hotter.

THE RESPONSIBILITY OF A PROPHET

I was thinking about my life ahead, about my family and friends, and about eternity, and I thought, *Surely, Jesus Christ, the Son of God, has all power in heaven and on earth and everything in between. What Christ is showing me is a big responsibility.* Without a doubt, what my Father has commanded me to do has been a great responsibility. I was awakened to an immense reality when God sent His Son Jesus to actually translate me to the bowels of the earth to walk among the dead in hell. I had an obligation to record what I saw and to find a publisher and complete the book, so that the world could know that hell is real but that God has provided forgiveness for us through Jesus Christ.

As I was thinking about this responsibility, the Lord Jesus said to me, "Katherine." I answered, "Yes, Lord." He continued, "I have brought forth many others in the last few years to confirm what I have shown you down here and in heaven. I will bring others yet, My daughter. As I see the Father do, I do."

I looked at the King, and He was wearing a crown and holding a scepter in one hand. He is my King, and I must obey Him. He never promised me it would be easy. When God calls you and chooses you for a mighty work, you truly pay a price. You often go through a lot in life to prepare for such a calling and to carry it out. And even though you do rely on your fellow believers for prayer and encouragement and other things, you must ultimately seek God's counsel and wisdom rather than man's.

> *And Jesus came and spoke to* [His disciples], *saying, "All authority has been given to Me in heaven and on earth. Go therefore and make disciples of all the nations, baptizing them in the name of the Father and of the Son and of the Holy Spirit, teaching them to observe all things that I have commanded you; and lo, I am with you always, even to the end of the age." Amen.* —Matthew 28:18–20

THE KING OF THE LIVING

I opened up my mind, my heart, and my spirit to the Lord Jesus. I looked up again, and He was no longer wearing the crown or holding the scepter. He said to me, "Child, I do not want to be a King of the dead. I want to be a King of the living. You are going to bring life to many through this responsibility. And I give you a promise: For those who try to harm this work or to take it from you deliberately and willfully, the judgment of the Lord will be swift and quick upon them. Those who do it innocently will be judged differently. Now come; let's go. The covenant of God stands for you and your family, and I will bring them all unto Me, daughter, I promise you."

As we began to walk on this dark and ugly mountain of black soot and burned rocks, I heard growls that sounded as if they were coming from huge animals; I did not know what these sounds were. I held tightly to the Lord's hand, and strength came into me as I kept walking with the King.

Then, much light appeared around Jesus and me. The sirens of death were around me, too, the cries of men and women, some of them screaming, "Have mercy; let me die," and others blaspheming and screaming cries of regret, such as "Why didn't someone warn me?" Again, I felt such responsibility.

I heard a growl, and ahead of me was a large, ugly demon with a face like a lion and a body like a serpent, with clawed feet and a long tail full of fire. I saw that it had many arms, and then I noticed it also had other heads. I said, "Jesus, what in the world is that?" Jesus spoke to the demon and said, "You will remove yourself from this pathway, for I adjure you in the name of God Almighty." The demon fell down on the ground and withered into a small worm. Christ stepped on it, and fire and blood came out of His feet, destroying the demon. I looked at the Lord, and He looked at me and said, "I am your King. I am able to destroy many things, for it is the time of the judgment of many demons to be destroyed in the earth and in the galaxies."

I said, "Lord, is that another mystery, another revelation?" He said, "Yes, My daughter, yes. In My holy name, the Lord Jesus Christ, Emmanuel, Yeshua, I will begin to release teaching and wisdom and knowledge on that revelation, for in My name, great things are done. Come."

He continued, "I never want you to have a divided heart—a heart that loves Me one day and a heart that doesn't love Me the next day. I know your heart. I made your heart. I have been with you through all those dilemmas. And now, let's look ahead." We kept walking, and the King no longer spoke. Everything became quiet, even the voices of the dead. We were so far away from them, I could barely hear them.

You shall love the Lord your God with all your heart, with all your soul, with all your mind, and with all your strength.

—Mark 12:30

SATAN'S THRONE

"What's ahead of me, Jesus?" I asked, and I pulled on His hand. He replied, "My child, Satan is very, very evil. His days are numbered. And this is a place where the blood of many whom he has killed falls down like a waterfall. Remember, he is a fallen angel. Remember, he knew many secrets of God. Remember, he understood about the blood covenant—that I gave My life for the world. I am going to show you evil things that he has done. I will give you the strength to see them, the strength to record them, the strength to tell about them. You will receive more wisdom and knowledge concerning the revelation of hell, and others will, too, child, through the new book you will write."

The King and I were standing at the top of a mountain of darkness. I looked into the darkness, and Jesus raised His hand; He was holding a scepter again. A flame shot out, and the darkness became light. He said, "Child, I am using a different scepter down here. This is the Scepter of Revelations. And now, as you are looking at this next scene, this will help to open the eyes of thousands of people as you tell about it or write it. My angels are with us."

Before me was a huge opening, larger than the Grand Canyon. What I saw in this opening was very clear and detailed. In different sections were many demonic beings and skeletons. There was also a wide, foul-smelling stream of flowing blood, at least a mile wide, which came off a high part of another mountain. It flowed down, and then it went into something like a cavern and finally to a river. Jesus told me that this stream was really an illusion manufactured by Satan to symbolize the death and destruction that he had inflicted upon the earth. There were times when the flow of blood was visible, and times when it would vanish. This cascade of blood was fed by at least three smaller falls/streams that flowed into it, each one related to the spiritual state in which people had died.

The Lord said, "This is the blood of many, My daughter, who have died without Me, as well as the blood of the innocent people Satan has killed." After seeing this stream of blood, I understood why I saw blood flowing in hell at times.

The Jesus said, "Look over there." I looked, and there was a room with gold walls, such as a king would have, which was wide open in the front; it seemed to be about half a mile long. There was also a gold ceiling with chandeliers. Everything looked so immaculate and beautiful.

And then I saw a throne—and there sat Satan! He was facing the blood that was flowing down. I can't really describe it as a waterfall, but it was full of blood, all blood. And Satan was laughing about it.

On either side of the throne was a large demon. One of the demons was standing next to the devil, holding a scroll. He was perhaps thirteen feet high and very round, with three heads, a hairy body, six arms, and about six legs. He looked as if he weighed two thousand pounds. Opening up the scroll, he held it to the devil's face, saying, "O King, we will win against God. The list has increased of those who have lost their souls."

The devil was very large, as well. He had a big face and huge horns; his countenance was like the face of a man, although part of his head was crushed. He had a wide chest, about four feet across, and huge, muscular arms. He also had very large, muscular legs. And he had webbed feet and claws. Sometimes his body appeared to be red, and sometimes it appeared to be brown.

As he sat there, he turned into a good-looking man wearing a suit. Satan stood up and said, "I know the secrets, because I was in heaven. I know what temptations to send a man through women and other lusts of the flesh to destroy him. I know that my voice has not yet been destroyed, but if my force of evil was ever shut down, I would not be able to seduce so many people. And I am letting all you demons hear this and know this."

I noticed that there was an opening at one part of the vision. But then Jesus corrected me, saying, "It is not a vision, My child; it is real." He knew my thoughts.

ALMIGHTY GOD IS GREATER THAN SATAN

Standing in an area in this valley were what seemed like a million demons. Satan turned to them and said, "It is your job never to allow this revelation of my strength and my courage and my power to be revealed to the prophets or the apostles or the people; for there truly is a judgment on me, and I will be thrown in the lake of fire one day because God has said so. But I've taken the wisdom I learned in heaven and the wisdom I've learned of man as my own wisdom and knowledge, and I've seduced thousands and thousands into hell through the lust of their flesh, which they desired more than God's commands; and the bloodfall there is a result of my wisdom." I trembled and said, "Oh, God, how can this be?" Jesus looked at me and said, "Listen, child."

I watched and listened again as Satan sat back down on the throne and returned to his original appearance. He laughed and said, "I have the power to change my form anytime I want, and I have given that power to some of my demons that are going to be roaming the earth. I have many plans of evil. I will seduce many people so that they will not follow Jesus Christ."

We are in a war against Satan and his powers of darkness. We must seek God, pray, and take a strong stand against the devil on behalf of the lost.

For Satan himself transforms himself into an angel of light.
—2 Corinthians 11:14

Another demon came over carrying a different scroll that said "The Deeds of Evil of Satan." I saw the writing. And I heard unspeakable things, earthshaking things. Jesus said to me, "What he speaks shall not be, for in My name, the name of the Lord Jesus Christ, I rebuke all these things he has spoken and has written, Katherine. The Father, the Holy Spirit, and I agree together that this shall not be.

"Now, My child," said Christ, "we will go to another part of hell, and you will see more unspeakable, horrible things that Satan does to souls. These souls used to preach My gospel, but Satan seduced them, tempted them to backslide, and caused them to die. I spared many such souls before they died, but I want My prophets, My apostles, My preachers, My evangelists, and My chosen to hear this. I have called them. Clean out your hearts, your minds, and your souls. Come forth to Me and tell Me the truth. I will understand. I will forgive you and wash you clean. Don't think you will have tomorrow, because sometimes tomorrow never comes." I just hung my head and thought of my own weaknesses. I remembered things that I have had to repent of, and I said to myself, *Oh, God, oh God, how can we—*

But Jesus didn't let me finish my thought. He said, "You will overcome by the blood of the Lamb and the word of your testimony; and I am able to make all My people overcome if they will listen to Me. Satan does not know everything. He thinks he does, but he does not. My Father is greater, and He has greater plans than Satan could ever think of. My Father could erase that knowledge from him in a second, My child. And eventually, He will do that. But man has a will, and at this point in time, God wants that will to be toward Him, and Satan wants that will to serve him. This is definitely a war, a spiritual war. But greater is almighty God. Remember, He created Satan. There are many mysteries and much knowledge you will never understand, and other people won't, either, because God doesn't want them to. But I say, 'Look up, look up, My child, and trust Me.'" And with that, we were leaving hell, and I was going back to my home.

> *And they overcame him by the blood of the Lamb and by the word of their testimony, and they did not love their lives to the death.* —Revelation 12:11

RECOGNIZING SATAN'S DECEPTIONS:

In what ways does Satan appear as an "angel of light," making things that are evil appear to be good so that people will be ensnared by them? Is there anything in your own life that many people would say is acceptable but is actually contrary to God's Word or His plan for your life? Don't allow yourself to fall into this trap. Repent of any sin and be reconciled to God. You were saved by His grace, and He will welcome you back.

After you have been restored to God, make a commitment to no longer yield to the desires of the sinful nature, or the flesh. Learn to control those desires. Jesus said that we must deny ourselves, take up our cross, and follow Him. (See, for example, Mark 8:34.) If you find yourself yielding to those desires, repent immediately and maintain a close relationship with God.

4

SEDUCING POWERS

DEMONIC DECEPTION AND DESTRUCTION

Jesus said, "Now we have to go to another place here in hell, child. And this is a place that is so horrifying. It's how Satan works on the earth to bring deception to the people through lust. There are seducing powers out there that pull people into great lust and perversion and demonic activity. Demon powers have also caused many people to commit suicide, and God has great mercy on these souls, Katherine.

"There are times and seasons when God's power moves on the earth. You're going to need My power, child. You're going to need My anointing. And many others are going to need it to bring back the ark of God [the holy Word of God, His covenant with us]. For Satan is running rampant in the earth, bringing forth much witchcraft, much occult on television and in the movies, much demonic activity, but My Word can counteract him and deliver people from his destructive grasp.

"And I'm telling you, little children are being raped, beaten, and murdered by demonic powers operating in people whom they have possessed. Little children who are innocent and pure. And My Father is grieved over this. There are absolutely no babies, no little children, in hell. My Father is merciful. He takes them to heaven when they die. He gives them new bodies, and there is great joy in heaven over them. They're taught; they go to school in heaven. Some of them grow up in heaven; some of them stay small until their mother and father come to heaven, and then they meet them at the gates of glory, and they grow up in heaven with them.

"My Father has so much in heaven—golden streets; body parts in storehouses, ready to be poured on the earth where Satan has mutilated people. God is getting ready to bring an avalanche of miracles to the earth. He sees the suffering of the saints. He sees that you're living in times like those in the book of Daniel, where many are so afflicted by the enemy, and He sees how the saints pray and travail, and how there seems to be no end to the sorrow. But the Lord has sent mighty angels to help you and many other saints to know Him and to obey Him, Katherine."

I said, "It's my greatest desire, Lord." Jesus wants us to heal the sick, raise the dead, and allow the Holy Spirit to draw people to God through us!

Are not all angels ministering spirits sent to serve those who will inherit salvation? —Hebrews 1:14 NIV

DEMONIC CREATURES

When I looked at Jesus, I saw such compassion. He said, "Come and see this place." And we went to a very black area in the middle of the earth where I heard snakes hissing. The demons there were twelve feet high and twenty feet high. They had three heads and ten arms and ten feet. And oh, were they ugly! They had worms coming out of their wings. And they were everywhere.

I said, "Dear God, what are these?" Jesus told me that what I was seeing was a mixture of illusions of demonic beings and actual demons that attack people. These demons are described in the book of Ephesians as *"principalities,...powers,...rulers of the darkness of this age,...spiritual hosts of wickedness"* (Ephesians 6:12). The evil principalities, powers, rulers, and spiritual hosts work with Satan to lie to people and to deceive them, causing great harm to those who do not know the power of the name of Jesus. The demons seek to destroy Christians by encouraging them to yield to their sinful nature. Whenever we give in to our fleshly desires, we open the door to allow such demons to influence and attack us. But we have power in the name of Jesus and in His blood to counteract these forces of darkness and to stop their evil purposes. We are protected by Jesus' blood as we die daily to our fleshly desires and diligently put on the *"whole armor of God."* (See Ephesians 6:10–18.)

Jesus told me, "You have power to speak My blood over these demonic beings. They're here for a season. As I said, the Father is grieved over the murder and rape of little children, and some of these demons in hell have caused these things and have entered people and possessed them on the earth. It's a horrible thing, My child, but it's all in the hands of God. The people need to know and understand that what God says is true."

As we walked, I heard the Lord say to an evil creature, "Peace, be still." This demonic being looked something like a seal—except that it had about ten legs—and it was rolling in some dust and running. I screamed, "Oh, my God, what's in the middle of the earth?" I hung on to Jesus' hand, and He said, "We're getting close to the abyss." There were slithering snakes there, and I smelled sewage coming down from the earth; the odor reeked of dung and rotten flesh. And again, I heard the cries of multitudes. Over in a black mist with flames of fire, I saw hideous things. I was so afraid. But Jesus was with me and held on tightly to my hand. He said, "Fear not. Nothing will harm you, because you're with Me." About two feet of light appeared around Him, and He pierced the darkness, but I could still see the evil creatures along the wall. They were screaming out blasphemous words to God. I thought, *What in the world?*

The Lord showed me hidden treasures. He moved His hand, and there in the jaws of hell were gold and silver, stacked up like a mountain. He also showed me rivers of blood mixed with fire, in which skeletons were chained together and screaming, "Let us die," and "Help us!" Above them, it said, "Men loving men and women loving women, with no fear of God or His judgments."[11]

Further on, I saw another horrible-looking being with a round face, teeth, and a whispering voice. There were about twenty-five of these creatures. Jesus explained that they planned to go on the earth and cause people to commit suicide, and He told me, "Listen to them." One of them said, "This is what we're going to say to them: 'Oh, nobody loves you. Nobody cares for you. Look at your family—they've abandoned you. Look at your friends—you're not good enough for them.'" The demons were discussing how they could weaken people both emotionally and mentally so they would take their own lives. They are lying spirits (see, for example, 2 Chronicles 18:21), and they can cause people to believe deception and delusions. These demons can even make themselves appear and disappear to people, causing these vulnerable people great fear and torment.

Be sober, be vigilant; because your adversary the devil walks about like a roaring lion, seeking whom he may devour. Resist him, steadfast in the faith. —1 Peter 5:8–9

---

11. See Romans 1:24–27; 3:18.

"HELP ME TO WIN THE LOST"

I have come to the realization that before God's chosen children understand what He has called them to and where they're supposed to be and what position they are to hold, many of them are severely attacked by the enemy. The demons try to get rid of the prophets and apostles and others whom God is raising up. I'm praying that God will bring forth leaders who can explain this deception of Satan to believers and also show them how to prepare for it.

Jesus said to me, "My name, the name of Jesus, and My blood will stop them, Katherine. Tell the people to use My name and renounce suicide demons. Tell them that if they have thoughts of suicide, they should call people who can help them. They should call people to pray for them. Tell them to not be ashamed, for it is not they who are thinking these thoughts; these suicidal ideas are in the airwaves. And tell them I love them and I will help them if they will call on Me."

Jesus turned to me and said, "Katherine, help Me to win the lost. Tell the people what is here. I will anoint the message with truth and the fear of the Lord. Also, I will keep those who turn to Me."

This place was so evil, horrible, and sad. I thought again, *What if it had been me who was brought to hell for eternity, with no more hope, no more destiny, burning forever in pain without being able to sleep or eat or die?* There was no sunlight or rain in hell, just fire and smoke, along with sorrow, grief, fear, and hatred. Men and women from every nation were crying for help, for release, even while realizing they would be in hell forever. Deep sobs of sorrow came from so many. I heard a woman screaming, "I had so many chances to receive Jesus Christ, and I made fun of Him and mocked Him. Then one day I was killed in a car wreck, and I came here. I had the pleasures of sin for a season. Now, it's so sorrowful."

Jesus said, "Tell the people of the earth about this place; tell them to repent before it's too late." Once more, I thought, *Oh, Lord, I hope I don't know any of these souls.* I saw the form of a man. His bones were red and black from burning. He was a very tall skeleton, and in his hands was a book on fire. Jesus stopped and said, "Peace, be still. O man, what are you doing here?" The skeleton turned his head toward Jesus. He had hollowed-out eyes, and snakes were crawling through him. He screamed, "Jesus, can You forgive me now?" And Jesus said, "O man, what did you do?" He answered, "I was called at a young age to preach Your gospel. And I did go to church. I learned a lot about You. But I never really loved You as I should have. I wanted the world, and I wanted what it could give me, so I lied about You. I told men that men could marry men and that You would love them and understand them, and they would go to heaven. I told people that prejudice was right. I told people we should hate people of other nationalities. I lied. I built a great congregation."

"I WANT TO REFINE MY PEOPLE"

As I looked at this preacher, Jesus said to me, "I want to send the fire that is spoken of in the book of Malachi to refine the people.[12] I want to help them, Katherine, so they'll not end up here like this preacher full of lies who died in his sins. Some of the people you pass by were tricked by him." The refining fire of God is different from the fire in hell. The first is a fire of holiness, which purifies God's people; the second is a fire of punishment.

> [God] *will sit as a refiner and a purifier of silver; He will purify the sons of Levi, and purge them as gold and silver, that they may offer to the* Lord *an offering in righteousness.*
>
> —Malachi 3:3

---

12. See Malachi 3:1–3.

"Now, listen," Jesus said. "Come." We began to move out of the jaws of hell and back to my home. Jesus told me, "Katherine, I want to refine My people. I want to send the fire of the Holy Spirit upon them to refine them, the Refiner's fire. That fire will burn off, destroy, many things of darkness. They don't need to understand it but just believe it. There is coming a time, someday soon, when My children will be more equipped than ever; there is soon coming a day when the movie related to this book will be out, and thousands are going to come to Me, child. I will cause fire to come on My people—not to burn them on the earth but to love them, cleanse them, and bring correction to them and convict their hearts. And they will repent. There are many things I want to do, child."

Jesus continued, "The earth is so big, My daughter, and thousands are dying and going to hell. I am the Waymaker. I am the One who will keep people from a burning hell if they will only turn to Me and repent of their sins. My Father made it easy. Where you saw those wicked demons, and where you saw the valley, and where you saw the river of blood and fire and vapors of smoke,[13] where you saw the demons tormenting those who are dead but yet alive, Satan knows all about this. The prince of the power of the air,[14] the rulers of demon darkness, the spiritual wickedness in high places—tell the people to use My name, Yeshua, the Lord Jesus Christ, Jesus Christ of Nazareth, to come against those things in My name; tell them to plead the blood, My precious blood, over them, and renounce them. I want the youth to arise and to do a book, *How to Cast the Devil Out in Jesus' Name*. I want the youth to understand who I am and what I'm doing. My daughter, this life is as short as the twinkling of an eye, as you well know. The devil is going to release thousands of souls, and I am the Lord your God who is telling you these things."

Thank You, Lord!

---

13. See Acts 2:19.
14. See Ephesians 2:2.

> *"For behold, the day is coming, burning like an oven, and all the proud, yes, all who do wickedly will be stubble. And the day which is coming shall burn them up," says the* Lord *of hosts, "that will leave them neither root nor branch. But to you who fear My name the Sun of Righteousness shall arise with healing in His wings; and you shall go out and grow fat like stall-fed calves. You shall trample the wicked, for they shall be ashes under the soles of your feet on the day that I do this," says the* Lord *of hosts.* —Malachi 4:1–3

My reader, I love you so much. I do not want you to burn forever in hell with no way out. There are no exits in hell. There are no doors that lead out of hell. When you're there, you stay there, and everything around you is fire, pain, sorrow, grief, and doom, accompanied by the ceaseless cries of souls who want to get out.

Satan wants us to sin with our bodies, so he wars against our hearts and our thoughts. He tempts us to act upon the desires of our fleshly nature instead of living according to God's ways. We must take authority over him and rebuke him in Jesus' name. (See, for example, 2 Corinthians 10:4–6.)

It is time for us to turn back to God. It is time for us to hear what He is saying to us. We don't seem to realize the reason our Savior, Jesus Christ, gave His life on that cruel day in which He was beaten and put upon a cross. He died to keep us from the eternal damnation that I am revealing to you through this book.

Do you care about yourself and other souls? Do you really care? If so, do something about it. Receive Jesus as your Lord and Savior. Tell somebody else about Jesus and how they can be saved through Him. Pray with other people. Satan doesn't want you to open your mouth and speak God's truth. Don't let him stop you. Speak it anyway.

Let us talk about salvation in Jesus Christ! Let us lift up Jesus Christ. He said, "*Now is the judgment of this world; now the ruler of this world will be cast out. And I, if I am lifted up from the earth, will draw all peoples to Myself*" (John 12:31–32).

RECOGNIZING SATAN'S DECEPTIONS:

Satan wants to deceive people into thinking that things would be better if they took their own life. In reality, he wants to separate them from God and destroy them. The devil also wants people to believe partial truths so they will think they are following God when they are actually being led into error that will pull them away from their heavenly Father. Make sure that you regularly read God's truth, the Bible, and keep your mind focused on what is right and beneficial.

> *Whatever things are true, whatever things are noble, whatever things are just, whatever things are pure, whatever things are lovely, whatever things are of good report, if there is any virtue and if there is anything praiseworthy—meditate on these things.* (Philippians 4:8)

5

POWER IN THE BLOOD OF JESUS CHRIST

CALL UPON JESUS AND BE CLEANSED

I remember a church service many years ago in which teenagers between the ages of fifteen and eighteen came up to the altar. I preached on drugs and what sin will do to you, and as I spoke, these young people moved toward the front. They were repenting and crying because they were on drugs and doing sinful things. I felt such love and power from God as the teenagers came. It was beautiful.

As they were making their way forward, someone took a picture of them. Later, when I got the film developed, the picture showed something above the teenagers that looked like a reddish blanket coming down out of the ceiling; the red (which I believe symbolized

Jesus' blood) became something like water, washing them clean. The Word of God is true. Jesus' blood has never lost its power.

One night, when I was walking with my King down below in hell, the Lord Jesus revealed to me truths about His powerful blood. "My blood was shed upon Calvary to wash away every sin, every evil thing anybody ever committed, the past that was wicked and dirty. If people would repent before Me, I would wash them clean and save their soul, Katherine. But there is something that men, women, and children who know and understand the gospel must do. They must ask Me to forgive them of all their sins and to come into their heart and save their soul. Then My precious blood will wash them clean. When they call upon Me, the angels in heaven know it, and it is exactly as I've said."

> *If we walk in the light as He is in the light, we have fellowship with one another, and the blood of Jesus Christ His Son cleanses us from all sin. If we say that we have no sin, we deceive ourselves, and the truth is not in us. If we confess our sins, He is faithful and just to forgive us our sins and to cleanse us from all unrighteousness.* —1 John 1:7–9

As Jesus and I began to walk in hell, I looked down at Christ's feet, and the blood was there again. He said, "Child, all of these people we have been seeing would not be here in hell today if they had only believed that My power is still alive today, that My blood is still real today. If they had repented, I would have washed them clean from all their sins and put joy back in their heart and their life; if they had only believed that I am the Son of God." Then He said, "Come and see."

Jesus took me to another place up on the burned path and hillside. Then He raised His arm, and a large door appeared in the atmosphere. Inside, it depicted the lives that many of the burning skeletons had lived on earth. I saw a lot of them in churches, in schools, in towns, and in their cars; they were young people, living everyday lives. "It was the past," Christ said.

Then I heard pastors preach to them in church services, and many of the young people were drawn by the Spirit of God. But when they were out on the street again, they would shake their heads and walk away, not realizing that Satan had a plan in the days ahead to cause them to be in an accident or to die. As I watched this, I saw that many of them didn't have parents who were believers and that they were confused about the teaching they had heard. I said, "Oh, God, it is so simple; You died on that cross to forgive us of all our sins, to heal our broken bodies. You took it all, Jesus. If only they would believe."

Then I saw a few people accept Christ and shout with joy, and the blood of Jesus came down and washed them clean. But I saw others go back into their very sinful ways. And I saw death come to them through car wrecks or other accidents or through gang violence. When I would see them die, I would scream.

One young person died in a motorcycle crash. I watched his soul leave his body; a white mist came out and went up into the air. I saw the outline of his soul, and then I saw black forms come and grab it. And I heard the screams of this soul. The evil spirits pulled it down a gateway into hell, into the fires. They took this soul before the devil, who was sitting on his throne. The devil talked to the demons and showed them on paper where to place the soul in the burning hell.

TELL PEOPLE ABOUT JESUS

I watched similar scenarios over and over, and then I cried out to Jesus, "I can't take it anymore. I can't stand this anymore, Jesus. Help them; do something." He turned to me and said, "Child, what are you going to do? Are you going to tell people about My blood, that if they would repent, it would wash them clean? For you know that in this hour and this time, many are dying and going to hell with false teachings. There is a phantom in the land, My daughter, of people not teaching the truth about My blood, My crucifixion, and My life-giving to save people from eternal damnation in hell. Stand tall and tell them about My blood and about how I gave My life. Tell them how My Father raised Me from the dead. Tell them, tell them, tell them."

At another time, Jesus had showed me skeletons clothed in fire, and He told me, "This is the judgment of the youth who have died on the earth in the last few years." There are absolutely no babies or little children in hell, but there is an "age of accountability" in which young people understand who God is and are capable of making a decision to believe in Him or not. Black chains were wrapped around these skeletons, and they were screaming, "Is there no relief? Can I not die?" They would grit their teeth and say, "Why didn't I listen to my mother? Why didn't I listen to my father? Why didn't I listen to the preacher?" One screamed, "Why didn't my neighbor take me to church? Why didn't somebody tell me about eternal damnation?" Another screamed in a man's voice, very loudly, "The preacher lived right next door to me and never came and told me to repent. I was mean, I was wicked, but no one told me to stop." Then I heard the voice of a young girl who said, "I was demon possessed; I served the devil, and then one day I was killed and came here, and I've been here ever since. Why didn't I listen? I heard about Jesus, and I didn't believe like other people believed. But I served Satan because I believed Satan. Oh, let me die, let me die."

> *Now the Spirit expressly says that in latter times some will depart from the faith, giving heed to deceiving spirits and doctrines of demons, speaking lies in hypocrisy, having their own conscience seared with a hot iron....* —1 Timothy 4:1–2

PRAY FOR YOUR FAMILY

The blood of Jesus Christ can save your soul from eternal damnation if you will only repent and believe that He shed His blood and died to make you whole. We all come into this world as innocent babies, and we need Christian parents who can teach us about the Lord. But many parents aren't Christians yet. They need to attend a good church, learn about Jesus, and be saved. Then they can teach their children how to be saved.

Pray for your own family. Warn your children, your parents, and your grandparents about hell. Tell them of spiritual realities that they don't know about, and let the Spirit of God draw them to salvation. Don't just ignore their spiritual state and allow them to die without Christ and go to hell.

RECOGNIZING SATAN'S DECEPTIONS:

Satan wants people to think that just knowing about Jesus and what He did for us on the cross is enough. Yet we have to personally respond to Him and His sacrifice for us in order to be saved. We must believe that He died for us and that His blood is real and powerful and able to cleanse us from all our sin. If you have not yet done that, you can do so right now by praying this prayer:

Dear Jesus,

I believe that You died on the cross for me. I repent of every sin I have committed. Thank You for shedding Your blood to cleanse me of all my wrongdoing. Thank You for washing me clean by Your blood. I believe that God the Father raised You from the dead, and that You have given me new life in You. Fill me with Your Spirit and help me to live for You. In Jesus' name, amen.

6

JESUS TALKED WITH THE DEAD

When Christ and I were walking together in hell, I was very much afraid, especially when He would go to different levels, different degrees of fire, and talk with various skeletons, who looked like the skeletons you see at Halloween. Many of these souls would get on their knees and beg and cry, but without tears. They would tell Christ things like, "Oh, Jesus, if only I had repented before I died. Now there's no more hope. There's no more destiny for me except eternal damnation."

ETERNAL REALITIES

One time, when I was watching Jesus talk with one of the skeletons, I was thinking hard about eternity. Many people on earth continue to go their own way, serving their flesh—their sinful desires that go against God's laws and truth. They keep rejecting

God's commandments to repent and be born again through Jesus Christ. Instead, they laugh and mock God. But one day, death will come to them, and if they have not made their life right with God, they will be eternally punished.

Chapter 5 of the book of Galatians talks about the lusts of the flesh. Here is a passage from that chapter:

> *For you, brethren, have been called to liberty; only do not use liberty as an opportunity for the flesh, but through love serve one another. For all the law is fulfilled in one word, even in this: "You shall love your neighbor as yourself." But if you bite and devour one another, beware lest you be consumed by one another!* (Galatians 5:13–15)

Those who practice the works of the flesh without repenting will not inherit the kingdom of heaven; they will inherit hell. (See Galatians 5:19–21.) I remember being with Jesus in many sections of hell where multitudes were screaming to die but could not. Jesus would turn to me and say, "Child, if they had only listened. I am the way, the truth, and the life." Many of the souls would blame other people—they might have been talking about you or me—for not warning them about hell, not telling them about Jesus, not sharing how they could be saved.

THE STORIES OF THE DEAD

As I walked with Jesus one night, He said, "Come, child, I'm going to show you some things I've not revealed to you yet. They are very sad and horrible, and they break My heart, child; it hurts to see these things, but they must be told so that the earth will awaken and come back to God."

The ground was cracked, burned, dry, and hot—so hot that there were molten rocks on the sides of the pathway. Demons were hiding behind rocks and making awful sounds. Most of the time, these evil spirits were very visible in hell, unlike on earth, and I pondered that fact. After a while, Christ said to me, "Child, look." We were in a place that appeared old, rusty, dirty, and black. The cries of the dead—the moans, the groans, and the gnashing of teeth—were all around us. And Christ said, "I'm going over here to talk to someone. Come with Me."

We walked over to a walled area and soon came upon a small compartment, or cell; then we came to another, and another. It was a very long line of cells built by demons. Each one had black bars with a big lock on the outside. The floor consisted of dirt and filth. Jesus went up to one of the cells, and I heard the cry of a man's voice. He came over to the bars with his chains rattling. I thought at first that the noise was his bones clinking, but it was the chains, which were wrapped all around him. Where his eyes should have been, there were burned sockets. Part of his foot was missing. He put his bony hands on the bars and cried, "Jesus, Jesus." As he spoke, I saw his greyish-black soul move up and down inside his ribcage. Jesus said, "O man, what is your name and what have you done to be here?" He answered, "Jesus, if I had only, only listened to the gospel. I wanted the world more than I wanted You. I did evil things in the world. I was very wicked. I harbored hatred and unforgiveness, and I killed several people. And I was told on the earth by preachers and other people that You would forgive me, but I didn't believe them. Oh, if I'd only believed. Oh, if I'd only believed. One day, I went to do something, and I was captured by these other wicked people. They put chains around me, and I died in the chains, Lord. They left me tied up in the woods. And here I am in hell with the chains still upon me, and I cannot die. I died on the earth, but when my soul came out of my body, demon powers brought me down a gateway, and I've been here for so many years, Lord. But I can remember every time the gospel was preached to me. I remember every time I heard the good news."

He who believes in Him is not condemned; but he who does not believe is condemned already, because he has not believed in the name of the only begotten Son of God. —John 3:18

I looked at Jesus and saw great tears fall down His face. And I heard the moans of another man who was in the next cell. We walked over there, and Jesus said to this skeleton form, the same as He had to the other soul, "O man, what is your name and what have you done to be here?" The voice was deeply sorrowful as it said, "Jesus, I'm here because of lies and deceiving people to get their money. I'm here because I heard the gospel many times and rejected it and loved my life of sin." As he talked, written words appeared around him in the air. They read, "Deceiveth their own self, deceivers and being deceived."[15] The man continued, "Jesus, I had so many chances to repent. I knew the gospel, but I also knew that as long as I lied and manipulated people, because they were so stupid, I could make myself millions of dollars. But the day came when I was killed in a car wreck. I didn't have time to repent. My soul came out of my body, and demons brought me here. And oh, how I've suffered for my sins. And there's no end to it, my God. I know there's no more hope for me." The skeleton shook with a great cry of pain.

I walked on with Jesus, and I felt so sad for all these souls who had loved wicked things and done things that are unspeakable, and I kept on thinking, *Dear God, when will this ever end?*

Do not love the world or the things in the world. If anyone loves the world, the love of the Father is not in him. For all that is in the world—the lust of the flesh, the lust of the eyes, and the pride of life—is not of the Father but is of the world.
—1 John 2:15–16

15. See 2 Timothy 3:13.

I couldn't stop crying. Christ was holding my left hand, and He said, "Come on, child." I looked down at His feet, and every so often where the nail scars were, blood would gush out, and then it would quickly disappear. I thought, *Oh, Jesus, You hurt, You bled, You died for these people, and Your Father raised You from the dead, and You are alive evermore to give us life eternal. If people would only believe the gospel, they would not come to this horrible place.*

There were innumerable cells, with moans and cries coming from every one of them. I said, "God, this is unbearable to me. Can we just please leave?" Jesus looked at me with great tenderness, "There is more I have to show you."

I looked around and wept, and we continued walking among cells. We came to the voice of a woman who was screaming, "Jesus, Jesus, Jesus, I'll now do what is right, if You'll let me out of here. Jesus, Jesus, come hear my story." Jesus walked over to her and said, "Peace, be still. O woman, what are you here for?" When He said, "Peace, be still," the demons that were nearby fled backward. Light would appear wherever Jesus was talking to someone, and the demons would flee from it. But I knew the word *peace* had also driven them away. The demons didn't ever hear such a word in hell; it scared them, so they ran from it. There is no peace in hell.

This woman said to Jesus, "I was a seller of fine clothes. I bought and sold fine clothing for women. But I had a team of people, too—in the secret, in the dark—that worked witchcraft and spells on the innocent. I used the clothing line only to work my magic. And my magic came back on me. A lot of the Christians know about the power in Your name, Jesus, and the power of the blood that You shed as the Lamb of God. I was no fool. I understood. But my heart was deceived. As I served Satan, I kept thinking he would give me a kingdom. I kept thinking that if I practiced magic and wizardry on the innocent, I would gain more power with the devil, because I enjoyed seeing people suffer."

I looked closely at this soul as she talked to Jesus. Her skeleton seemed afloat, but her chains held her down. Inside her carcass, her soul was a black, dirty mist, but she could move her skeleton mouth as she spoke. Snakes came out of her eyes and through her skeleton form, and worms teethed on her bones, as they did on the bones of all the other souls.

As I listened to her, I thought, *How can this be? She's still thinking of serving the devil as she's burning in hell.* Then, suddenly, fire came around her feet; it shot up over her like a torch, and she screamed, "Stop, O Satan, stop. I served you faithfully on the earth, and this is what you give me?" Her cell actually shook, and Jesus and I walked away. I said, "Jesus, she's still trying to be evil in hell!" The Lord said, "She was highly deceived, mightily deceived by the devil. I would have forgiven her if she'd only come to Me and really meant it. But she didn't really mean it, child. She wanted to play games with Me, games with the devil. And the day came when I stopped drawing unto her. For it says, 'My Spirit will draw them unto salvation.'[16] But there's also a day when a line is drawn, and the judgment of My Father comes."

I walked on with many unanswered questions, really puzzled. And Jesus turned to me and said, "Child, you will understand someday. Right now, I must show you hell."

Do not be deceived, God is not mocked; for whatever a man sows, that he will also reap. For he who sows to his flesh will of the flesh reap corruption, but he who sows to the Spirit will of the Spirit reap everlasting life. —Galatians 6:7–8

BEFORE IT'S TOO LATE

We traversed a narrow pathway and came to a flat area where the ground was full of hot smoke. Over it was something like dirty,

16. See John 6:44.

mucky water—it wasn't really water; it was like dung, and there were nasty, filthy smells. The odor was horrifying; it was like the smell of burning plastic, animal dung, and pollution, and it seeped down from the earth. From a distance, I saw infernal, blazing fires. I saw a slow fire creeping on the ground and burning things up. I thought perhaps that some of this fire was for the purpose of purifying the ground. I don't know; there were some things I never got answers for.

Jesus said, "Come, child." He caused light to shine, and we began to walk on big, smooth stones across that disgusting place. When we got to the other side, Jesus said, "I want to show you a monster." I thought, *Oh, God.* But He said, "I have you by the hand. I'm with you; fear not." He held my hand with His right hand, and He raised His left hand over the mucky, evil place that we'd just crossed, and the whole thing rose up in the "air" of hell. As it did, I saw that it was actually a huge, ugly monster with enormous eyes, a long tail, and fire coming out of its mouth. It looked like a long dragon with old scaly skin like an alligator's.

I was trembling as I stood next to Jesus, and again He said, "Fear not. It cannot touch you. But in the days ahead, not many will understand that after My church is raptured out, this thing will come up out of hell and roam the earth. But, according to God's Word, it cannot be released until the time spoken by God.[17] For God is the Creator of all things; God is the One."

I still trembled, and I walked close to Jesus. We climbed the hill, and the monster laid back down in the muck. I thought, *Hell is in the middle of the earth. It's the abode of the dead; there are demonic beings, talking skeletons, burning flesh, smells of dung, corruption everywhere.*

I looked up and saw dark objects falling through an opening, falling way down into a valley, and demons were laughing and hurrying

17. See 2 Thessalonians 2:1–12.

toward them. Jesus said, "Child, those are souls who just died on the earth and came down some gateways, and they're going to be picked up by the demons and put in their place of torment. If they were liars, they will be put with liars; if they were murderers, they will be put with murderers; if they were haters, they will be put with haters; if they were unforgiving, they will be put with the unforgiving; if they were drunkards, they will be put with drunkards. They will be placed with thousands such as they. They'll be in pain and sorrow and grief and crying, and they won't be able to get out of here. If they had returned to Me, I would have forgiven them the sins of the flesh. That's why I am showing you hell, to make people turn around and come back unto Me before it's too late, before they reach the everlasting fire."

Jesus was sad, and I was sad. Jesus' hands and feet were bleeding, and He said, "I died for all of these, but it's too late, too late." He looked up and prayed, "My Father, My Father, have great mercy." And hell shook again.

I clung to Jesus and said, "This could have been me when I was backslidden from You, Lord. I was backslidden at one time and did things I shouldn't have. But I repented and came back to You." He looked at me and said, "Child, we are going to go to another place. And in this other place, you're going to see people who kept putting Me off, saying, 'Not yet. Tomorrow, tomorrow.' But tomorrow never came."

Come now, you who say, "Today or tomorrow we will go to such and such a city, spend a year there, buy and sell, and make a profit"; whereas you do not know what will happen tomorrow. For what is your life? It is even a vapor that appears for a little time and then vanishes away. Instead you ought to say, "If the Lord wills, we shall live and do this or that." But now you boast in your arrogance. All such boasting is evil.

—James 4:13–16

We left that place and went around a bigger corner at the bottom of the hill. There were smoldering fires and heat like you would not believe. There was the smell of rotten, burning flesh and dung. There were rats running everywhere. There were snakes, which fled from the presence of Jesus. There were also little bitty things full of hair that were bouncing on the ground; I didn't know what they were, but I was terrified of them.

It is my responsibility to warn you to turn back to God if you have not yet repented of your sins and received Jesus, because the Bible says that if you see the sword coming against the land and you don't warn the people, their blood will be on your hands. (See Ezekiel 33:1–6.) So, I'm telling you like it is. Repent, O earth, repent. Because Jesus is coming back for a church that has no "*spot*"—meaning that we must be cleansed from sin and begin to obey God—"*or wrinkle*"—meaning that we can't just do anything we want to with no fear of God or His commandments. (See Ephesians 5:27.)

You need to read your Bible, and you must hear what the Spirit is saying to the churches. I urge you to faithfully attend a good church that will teach you the truth of God's Word. We must bring back the "ark of the covenant," meaning the holy Word of God, for hell is getting fuller every day with those who have rejected God, those who have rejected Jesus Christ and the truth of the gospel. Hell is expanding itself while some preachers on earth are lying about the truth. I'm warning the preachers, too: You must repent and turn back to God and help to save people from judgment in hell. If you're not being truthful with them about God's Word, if you're not being real with them, then you're sending many of them to eternal condemnation.

As I continued walking with the Lord, I was becoming angry with the devil, and so was Jesus. I kept thinking, *For all of these down here, there's no tomorrow except for burning pain. All of these down here will be thrown into a lake of fire. Oh, my God, have mercy, have mercy*. I was thinking of all these people. I looked behind me, and there were fires, the screams of the dead, and echoing chambers of horror. I remembered those who had died with diseases and were suffering from them ten times worse in hell, screaming to die from the pain.

A GREAT MOVE OF GOD'S SPIRIT

Jesus said, "Come, I want to show you something." We came to a place where there were a great number of men. They were skeletons, but I knew that they were all men because they were screaming in men's voices in languages of every nation. Jesus said, "Look, these all died as alcoholics; they loved strong drink more than they loved Me. They loved to party; they loved to get drunk. They enjoyed their life; they did not really care about anybody but themselves and what made them feel good. There are thousands of alcoholics in the earth yet today. They need to turn back to Me. I'll forgive them and deliver them.

"I'm going to begin to send My Spirit into the earth, Katherine, in a stronger way; I'm going to begin to give chances to many people who are being prayed for by their parents and the church. I'm going to begin to pour out My Spirit of drawing unto them, for the goodness of the Lord draws man unto salvation.[18] I'm going to begin to pour out My Spirit in a unique way that will amaze many people. For hell is getting so full of the people's sins of the flesh that this must be preached about again. People must know that I will deliver them from every sin of the flesh, if they will ask Me. Sometimes I deliver them even if they don't ask, daughter, I truly do, because of My great love for humanity. There is a time and a season coming soon when there will be a great move of My Spirit to bring people unto Me. There'll be a time coming soon when there will be a great avalanche of healings again in the earth, a great revival. And part of the revival will be

18. See Romans 2:4; Hosea 11:4.

brought about through what I'm telling you, and a movie will be made out of this book. I will do it, and it is time for this, saith the Lord. It is time for the world to awaken so that people will not come to this horrible place."

Then Jesus said to me, "It's time to go back now. We have been here for quite a while." And I was so glad, because I was very tired and scared. But from time to time during the night, Jesus had touched me and said, "Peace, My child," and great peace had flooded over me. Now, Jesus said, "Let's go," and in the twinkling of an eye, I was out of hell. Jesus moved so fast; He had so much power, and He came down outside my home, and I was still in the spirit. He made sure by His power that I was back in my bedroom, and then He left. I sat up in bed in my human form, and I began to weep.

It is difficult for me to talk about what I experienced in hell. It is hard to describe it. Because of this difficulty, I ask you to pray for me that this truth might go around the world. And if you do not know the Lord Jesus Christ as your Savior, may you truly repent now of your sins and ask Him to forgive you, come into your heart, and save your soul. Give your life to Him and ask Him to baptize you with His Holy Spirit.

God's Spirit will help you. When you're tempted to commit a sin of the flesh, the Holy Spirit will give you the strength to resist. Call upon God when you are tempted and in trouble, and He will deliver you. If you should fall, He will pick you up again. Do not be afraid to go back to your heavenly Father, and do not harden your heart. Return to Him, and He will forgive you.

Call upon Me in the day of trouble; I will deliver you, and you shall glorify Me. —Psalm 50:15

RECOGNIZING SATAN'S DECEPTIONS:

Satan deceives some people into thinking that if they serve him and worship him, he will reward them with good things in this life and with a kingdom in the next life. His promise of a kingdom is a lie; it is merely an imitation of Jesus' promise that our heavenly Father will give us His kingdom. Satan just wants to use people for his own purposes before discarding and destroying them. They will not receive any "special treatment" from Satan in hell but will suffer eternally. If you have been involved in the occult or if you are currently a follower of Satan, go to God immediately and repent. He will forgive and cleanse you in Jesus. Only God fulfills His promise to give us His kingdom.

> *But seek the kingdom of God, and all these things shall be added to you. Do not fear, little flock, for it is your Father's good pleasure to give you the kingdom. Sell what you have and give alms; provide yourselves money bags which do not grow old, a treasure in the heavens that does not fail, where no thief approaches nor moth destroys. For where your treasure is, there your heart will be also.* (Luke 12:31–34)

Part Two:

RECLAIMING THE KEYS AND GIFTS OF GOD

7

KEYS TO THE KINGDOM

SOUND THE ALARM

I was walking with Jesus again in the middle of the earth where hell is. Christ was wearing the long white robe, with sandals on His feet. He had the most beautiful, sweet anointing about Him, and such love flowed from Him. But there was a very sorrowful look on His face, and there was deep grief in His eyes. To His left, down in a valley, skeletons on fire were screaming. Straight ahead, there were some pits and cells where skeletons were burning and screaming. Demons were laughing at them and jeering, "We deceived you; we deceived you."

I held tightly to Jesus' hand. We kept walking until we came again to that parched, burned, dry mountain that was very wide and rocky and had many paths on it. Jesus would always make a light shine to show me something. He raised His arm, and we stopped when a large opening appeared in the darkness to our right. Jesus said, "Child, warn My people. Sound an alarm in My holy mountain. Warn them of this place. Tell them what I am showing you and telling you. My Word will back it all up. These are revelations given from My Father to you that you can tell the world. And now, look, listen, and learn."

> *Blow the trumpet in Zion, and sound an alarm in My holy mountain! Let all the inhabitants of the land tremble; for the day of the Lord is coming, for it is at hand.* —Joel 2:1

BIND THE ENEMY

In the large opening, I saw many demons. They were of various sizes, from about two feet tall to fifteen feet tall. Some of the tall demons had horns on their heads; big, broad faces; and large teeth and fangs. They had huge, hairy bodies and long, clawlike hands, with something like razorblades on the back, and large legs and feet. Some of these demons had three heads. Some demonic beings had six feet, some had three, some had two, and some had one. Some had one arm, some had two, and others had six. Some demons had six wings, while others had ten. Some were shaped like a long, slinky tail with what looked like sharp razorblades. Some were in the shape of a snake and had wings that looked like a snake's head; they had evil-looking eyes and fangs, and fire came out of their mouths.

I shivered and said, "Jesus, why are You showing me this?" He said, "This is Satan's kingdom, child. He works in darkness; he seduces. He sends out demons to bring drugs and alcohol and abuse to families. That is why I gave you My name, the Lord Jesus

Christ—so that you could take authority and bind these things; and they shall be bound in chains."

As I watched one of the demons, a big black fiery chain came out of nowhere and bound it. The demon screamed and fell over and could not move. The other demons ran away. Jesus said, "One of My children on the earth is binding this demon with My name, the name of Jesus Christ." The chained demon became covered with flames, and it was reduced to ashes. I said, "Lord, it was cremated." He said, "Yes, and I want them all cremated. But come." We walked past the ashes of that evil demon, and a hot wind came and blew the ashes away. (See Malachi 4:3.)

> [Jesus] *said to them, "I saw Satan fall like lightning from heaven. Behold, I give you the authority to trample on serpents and scorpions, and over all the power of the enemy, and nothing shall by any means hurt you. Nevertheless do not rejoice in this, that the spirits are subject to you, but rather rejoice because your names are written in heaven."*
>
> —Luke 10:18–20

I kept walking with my King, but I was weary. I was thinking of all the demons I had seen, and I shivered again. The cartoon artists that depict demons don't even know what they are drawing. There are so many seducing powers upon the earth.

Jesus said, "Look, listen, and learn." He raised His arm again, and a large opening appeared, but this time I could see on the earth. I saw the inside of a large grocery store with people pushing shopping carts. I saw families there. All at once, large demons materialized around some of the people. One of them took a woman over to the liquor section; it kept whispering in her ear, "Get this; you know you want this. It would make you feel good to drink it." She would shake her head no and keep on walking. Then a larger demon stood in front of the cart, stopped it, and whispered to her some other things. She went back and bought the liquor. Jesus told me that these demons work in ones, twos, threes, fours, fives, and sixes—different ones at different times to seduce people to get into sin and to destroy their lives and their families.

Then Jesus showed me another part of the vision in which a lot of cars were backed up on a freeway. He zeroed in on one man's car in which there were three demons. One demon whispered, "Well, just drive around them and get out of this mess." In another car, a larger demon was laughing and telling the driver, "Well, I would like to just run over every one of them and kill them." And then I saw the two cars pull out and collide. The cars flipped over, and the drivers died. I thought, *Oh, my God, the seducing power of these tongues of darkness, these words of evil.* I said, "We must obey the laws of the land. Our world would be chaos if we didn't have laws of the land."

Then I was taken in the Spirit with Jesus. We seemed to be at a bar on the earth. Jesus let me see inside to the barstools. Demons were sitting around in the darkness, and they were whispering to the men, "Buy more alcohol and get arguments going." These demons appeared to go in and out of some of the men, and I wondered why. And there were women there, too. Jesus said, "They've opened the door to the enemy to do whatever he wants to with them." I thought, *Oh, my God.* Then He said, "They will all end up in hell, My daughter, if someone doesn't warn them. They need to repent and turn to Me, and I will deliver them and protect them by My Word and My covenant and My blood."

Again, I would challenge you to attend a good church that teaches you the holy Word of God and to keep yourself from evil.

After this, Jesus and I were walking in hell on ground that was very cracked and burned. We stopped, and I saw many flames shooting up, as well as cells. Jesus said, "Look." When I looked at the cells, I saw the people who had crashed their cars on the freeway. I saw the woman who had been in the grocery store. I also saw people from other scenes that I had watched. For a few minutes, those souls seemed to have flesh so that I could recognize who they were. Then the flesh turned into bones, and there were worms on the bones, and I heard the screams of these dead souls. They were saying, "Why didn't somebody warn me? Why didn't somebody tell me of this place?"

The Lord looked at me and said, "Katherine, you are to warn people. You are to tell them of this place called hell. Many demonic devices are used against people. And I have given you the authority to bind the devil, to loose My power upon the people, to set the captive free. I am anointing you with a new anointing to share this new revelation. I'm anointing you with more power, My daughter, to set the captive free."

> [Jesus said,] "*The Spirit of the* LORD *is upon Me, because He has anointed Me to preach the gospel to the poor; He has sent Me to heal the brokenhearted, to proclaim liberty to the captives and recovery of sight to the blind, to set at liberty those who are oppressed.*" —Luke 4:18

My heart goes out to people who are being held captive by the devil. I looked at Jesus and said, "Thank You, my Lord, thank You, thank You." We kept walking, and I was thinking, *Well, Jesus, I've made mistakes. How can You even use me?*

All at once, the Lord stopped, looked at me, and said, "Katherine, My Father has chosen you, and I have chosen you. You are washed in My blood; you are cleansed by My blood. You are clean through My Word. I do not want you to be concerned about the past, for it is gone. We must look at tomorrow and have hope, My daughter, great hope."

KEYS FOR RELEASING THE CAPTIVES

Jesus said, "Now I want to show you a place of different layers and degrees for different torments of souls for the various works of the flesh they committed upon the earth. Some of them were murderers. Some were thieves. Some were robbers. Some were liars. I can make people overcome these things if they would accept Me as Lord and Savior, if they would give Me their heart and would love Me with all their mind, their soul, and their strength. There is much that I have for the people, Katherine. I am showing you the abode of the dead and the reasons they are here, and I am showing you that I am the way, the truth, and the life. If any man comes to Me, I will in no wise cast him out.[19]

"I am showing the people through revelations how to pray and use My name and pull down strongholds and shut doors of evil. Many years ago, My daughter, I appeared to you in a burning bush in Guatemala. There are so many things I want to teach the people about the keys to the kingdom. The keys to the kingdom are: 'Whatever you bind on earth is bound in heaven. Whatever you loose on earth is loosed in heaven.'[20] And there are many other keys." I said, "Thank You, Jesus, for those teachings. Thank You for this revelation. Thank You, Lord."

Jesus gave us the keys to the kingdom so that we could take dominion and authority over the powers of darkness and thereby set the captives free. Many times, I have been ministering in a service when God's anointing has come in very powerfully, and people have been screaming and seeking Christ. The people have told me that God touched them and set them free. I open up this revelation knowledge so that people can understand how to use the keys to the kingdom to release the captives.

In a mighty supernatural visit, the Lord revealed to me further keys to the kingdom. The more I think about them and study

---

19. See John 6:37 (KJV).
20. See Matthew 16:19; 18:18.

them, I believe that the keys to the kingdom are similar to the various fruits of the Spirit of God. (See Galatians 5:22–23.) In addition to the keys of binding and loosing and using the authority of Jesus' name, some other keys are:

- Obedience—obeying God and doing whatever He tells us to do. If we fail, we are to get right back up, repent, ask for forgiveness, and keep going.
- Compassion—showing true concern for the lost, sick, and oppressed.
- Humility—having a humble spirit before God.
- Love—loving other people as God has loved us.

As we obey God, have great compassion on people, humble ourselves in God's sight, and love others, then miracles, signs, and wonders will occur.

Then Jesus went about all the cities and villages, teaching in their synagogues, preaching the gospel of the kingdom, and healing every sickness and every disease among the people. But when He saw the multitudes, He was moved with compassion for them, because they were weary and scattered, like sheep having no shepherd. Then He said to His disciples, "The harvest truly is plentiful, but the laborers are few."

—Matthew 9:35–37

The Lord said to me, "Katherine, many souls would not be in hell if they had listened and used the keys to the kingdom. If many of My ministers would take heed to their lives, stop doing the things the world is doing, and turn unto Me with all their heart, their mind, their soul, and their strength, thousands would be saved from this place. Truly, there is more teaching on the keys to the kingdom. But let's move on, daughter."

QUICKSAND IN HELL

Jesus and I began to walk again, and we came to a very large area that was full of different degrees of fire, with skeletons of every size. There was weeping and gnashing of teeth. Worms were coming out of the skeletons' bones. I watched the souls scream and pull out some of the worms.

When we arrived at this group of skeletons—there must have been two thousand of them—I saw that they had black chains around their ankles, and that they were also chained to one another. Flames came around them, engulfed them, and went over their heads. The flames would die down and then come again. The skeletons were standing on something like quicksand, because every so often, some of them would sink below the surface and then bob back up again.

As the flames burned their bones, the skeletons would scream and cry, "Help me; does anybody care about my soul? Help me; I cannot die. Why was I not warned of this place? Why was I not told of this place of eternal damnation?"

I watched in horror as demons stood around this large place. The area seemed to be like a dried-up lake, but it was moist and damp where the skeletons were. I looked more closely and saw that some skeletons would sink to their waist before they came back up, while others would sink to their neck before rising again. Their screams and the cries of the other dead were beyond belief.

I thought, *Oh, my God, what terrible things drugs and alcohol, perversion, uncleanness, and all the works of the flesh do to people; and yet these fires are God's eternal judgment, the fires of God that will never go out.* (See Mark 9:43–48.) I watched in shock as other demons would drag souls to a high cliff and throw them in the quicksand, which added to the cries of the dead. I wondered, *Oh, my God, what torment is this? What torture is this, Jesus?* Jesus looked at me and said, "My daughter, behold, I gave My Word, I gave My name,

I gave My blood. I gave instructions in My holy Word. I have great preachers and leaders in the lands. And yet, many people still love their evil ways—their carousing, fighting, drinking, swearing, blaspheming, and speaking evil of all things and all men. I plead with them and plead with them to stop, but they do not. And this is the end for some of them; this is the place of the judgment of God for some men and women who have gone a different way. They loved the lust of their own flesh more than God's commandments. Men loving men and women loving women.

"Many cries have come out for people in the earth to repent, as with Sodom and Gomorrah; some have and some haven't. But, if you notice, as these souls come up out of the quicksand, they are chained together, and they are hitting each other and screaming at each other with their bony arms and hands. They are nothing but skeletons full of dead men's bones. They scream because of their sins, yet they still desire to do evil; but they cannot."

Woe is the man who will not listen to God's Word, I said to myself. *Woe is the woman who will not take heed to correction.* As I looked again at these masses, over two thousand or more souls clothed in fire and being sucked down into the quicksand, I thought, *Oh, my God, we need to warn people; we need to tell them of this awful place.* I remembered that the book of Romans says that God gave people over to a debased mind because they rejected Him and did not want to retain a knowledge of Him. (See Romans 1:18–32.) As I watched, I thought of how many thousands of people in the world were in that state.

Today, certain laws in our lands have changed greatly for the worse. The truth of Jesus Christ must be preached more and more to save people from a horrible hell. I believe we must love people, counsel them, and guide them, so that perhaps they will turn from their sins and call out to God. We must stand firm for the counsel of God and try to win even murderers to Him. People must understand the role and deceit of demons, although self-willed people sometimes do wicked things even when no demons are involved. We must use the keys to the kingdom to set people free.

I bow in my heart to Jesus. I love Him, and I know there is a price to pay to be alone with Him, for the enemy does not want us to spend time with Jesus, learning from Him, believing in His Word, and coming to understand His supernatural power.

I looked up at my Savior, and the expression on His face was one of great pain. As He observed the judgment of His Father upon lost souls, His eyes were so sad. Jesus said to me, "If only they had listened, they would not be here. If only they had understood that I did everything for them so they could have life eternal in heaven with Me. Come on, child, I want to show you something else."

> *God so loved the world that He gave His only begotten Son, that whoever believes in Him should not perish but have everlasting life. For God did not send His Son into the world to condemn the world, but that the world through Him might be saved.*
> —John 3:16–17

DEVOURING SERPENTS

We began to walk along a curved pathway, and I could hear the cries of the dead far into the blackness. I wondered where Jesus was taking me, and I held His hand tightly. I was so afraid. I thought about my family on the earth, wondering, *How are they going to believe me?* I thought about passages in the Bible that talk about how God will protect us and watch over us.[21] I thought about how I wanted Jesus to return to earth very quickly.[22] Yet, as I walked there in hell among the dead, I also thought about the millions of

21. See, for example, Psalm 139:7–10.
22. See, for example, Revelation 22:20.

people on the earth who didn't know Jesus and how I had a big responsibility to release this deep revelation of hell to the world.

When we came to a high cliff, I looked around. There was darkness, then light, and then fire below us. After that, I saw what looked like another mountain, like a volcano getting ready to erupt. It was red and bulging, and its base looked like charcoal. I looked at the Lord and said, "Jesus, is that going to be an earthquake?" He said, "Yes, child, at the appointed time. My Father is in control of all these things. And He said He wants man to repent and turn unto Him, child."

Then Jesus told me, "Look over this way." I was standing on His right side, and I looked far down a high cliff. I was very afraid of heights like that, so I clung to Him and said, "What is this, Jesus?" He replied, "Keep looking in the darkness." I looked far down. As Jesus spoke, light appeared, and I could see a valley in which there were snakes the size of a train. Some were curled up, and others were stretched out. I screamed, "Jesus, what is this?" He said, "These serpents shall be released after My church is caught out.[23] They will be destroyed, but they will devour many before this happens, My daughter." *Oh, God. Oh, God.* I said, "Please stop it; please abort this awful thing." He looked at me with tears in His eyes, and then He moved His arm back, and darkness covered the serpents again. But I could hear snarls, hissing, and even some blasphemy coming from them. I thought, *Oh, my God, how I hate snakes!*

Jesus said, "You have to go home now. I'll take you back now, but tomorrow night I will bring you here again, and I will show you and tell you some things that are very important to the body of Christ and to the world."

RECLAIMING THE KEYS AND GIFTS OF GOD:

So far, we have noted these keys to the kingdom: (1) binding and loosing, (2) using the name of Jesus, (3) obedience, (4) compassion,

23. See, for example, 1 Thessalonians 4:15–17.

(5) humility, and (6) love. Read Galatians 5:22–23 and write down in what ways you think these keys of the kingdom correspond to the fruits of the Spirit. Begin to focus on one particular fruit of the Spirit that you will cultivate in order to better prepare yourself to use the keys to the kingdom.

8

GLASS-LIKE CAGES

GIFTS IN CAPTIVITY

The next night, after Jesus had brought me back to hell, He told me, "Listen, child, there are things that must be unlocked and released from here. Take the keys to the kingdom and unlock these doors with Me." Jesus had many keys with Him. I said, "Okay, what do I do, Lord Jesus?" He said, "Look, listen, and learn."

We walked what seemed like miles around an area that had heaps of skulls and was filled with bad odors. Christ told me to call this area the Cave of Debris. This cave was a revelation; for example, even the dung on the walls represented the corruption of mankind. There was also a large number of containers—perhaps a thousand of them—that looked as if they were made of solid glass.

Suddenly, we stopped walking. I looked more closely at some of these glass containers, and I wondered why the glass looked so clean and why the things inside them looked like holy objects, such as golden horns, drums, robes, crowns, music sheets, and books. I said, "What is this, Lord Jesus?" He said, "These were gifts I gave to My church and to My people to spread the gospel; the book of First Corinthians talks about the gifts of God."

> *There are diversities of gifts, but the same Spirit. There are differences of ministries, but the same Lord. And there are diversities of activities, but it is the same God who works all in all. But the manifestation of the Spirit is given to each one for the profit of all: for to one is given the word of wisdom through the Spirit, to another the word of knowledge through the same Spirit, to another faith by the same Spirit, to another gifts of healings by the same Spirit, to another the working of miracles, to another prophecy, to another discerning of spirits, to another different kinds of tongues, to another the interpretation of tongues. But one and the same Spirit works all these things, distributing to each one individually as He wills.* —1 Corinthians 12:4–11

One glass container had something like pure, beautiful smoke rising from it and then disappearing. Another had fire inside it. I learned that in these containers, each of which had a lock on it, were "trophies" of Satan—things related to the Lord that the enemy had stolen. (I faintly remember having read something similar to this years earlier from someone else who had seen hell, but I don't remember the details.)

RELEASING GOD'S TREASURES

I was so tired that I leaned on the Lord and said, "Oh, Jesus, what can I do?" He said, "Look, listen, and learn. I've given you the keys to the kingdom. I want you to take a key in your hand in the spirit." All at once, I looked at my hand, and there was a spiritual key in it. "What do I do with it, Jesus?" I asked. He said, "Come with Me." Then we were standing in front of one of the large, transparent, glass-like cages. Something that looked like a white glow was moving in it. I said, "What is this, Lord?" He replied, "Take the key, put it in the lock, and in My name, Jesus Christ, Emmanuel, Yeshua, open that door."

So, in the name of Jesus Christ, Emmanuel, Yeshua, I put the spiritual key in the lock and turned it. The lock broke open, and out flowed the most beautiful presence. Jesus had dropped to His knees, and He said, "My Spirit will once again flow over the earth and bring the people on the earth to conviction. My Spirit will again begin to draw people unto Me, child, by the thousands."

Like a mighty wind, that beautiful presence went up and out of hell; I saw it break through the earth and shout up into heaven. And Jesus said, "It is going to My Father, so that He can purify and cleanse it. The angels will take care of it." We walked toward the next one. I said, "Oh, Jesus, this is going to take forever." And He said, "No, you will see in a few moments."

On top of the next glass cage, which held a crown, was written "The Trophies of Satan." The crown seemed to be alive; it was moving in the air, and it had jewels in it. The Lord said, "This is all spiritual and natural, child. I want to crown My people with glory and with righteousness, but the enemy has sent demons by the thousands, and he has blocked so much of My grace for My people. And I want you to cut away the debris."

As I looked at this beautiful crown, Jesus said, "Take this." And again, a spiritual key appeared in my hand. Then He said, "You do that in My name, Jesus Christ, Yeshua, Emmanuel." I declared, "In the name of Jesus Christ, Yeshua, Emmanuel, be loosed from this place." When I said that, the door of the cage opened. A wind came around the crown, and the crown shot up through hell and straight into the sky above the earth. And I saw God's angels take it and bring it into glory.

We went to a final cage. Due to the fire of Jesus, the ground all around us was being cleansed; the debris was burning away. I was so happy because I no longer smelled foul odors. This last cage also said "The Trophies of Satan." Inside were flaming swords, and a Bible was over them. They were moving as if they were alive. Jesus said, "Here is another key. Now do the same with this one." I said, "In the name of Jesus Christ and Emmanuel, Yeshua's name, I open up this door for the glory of God, in Jesus' name." The door swung open, and then a wind swirled around Christ and me, and we were raised up out of hell, into the sky above the earth, and into the galaxies.

The wind belongs to Jesus. I saw that the flaming swords were suspended in the galaxies. I thought, *Oh, my God, the swords are on fire, and the Word was over them. What is this?* Jesus told me, "It is My Word. My Word will come back again. The flame, the swords, represent the fire of God. The fire will permeate the darkness and the demons, My daughter." All at once, angels came and took the swords up to heaven. Jesus said, "They will all be cleansed and purified."

> *Above all, taking the shield of faith with which you will be able to quench all the fiery darts of the wicked one. And take the helmet of salvation, and the sword of the Spirit, which is the word of God; praying always with all prayer and supplication in the Spirit, being watchful to this end with all perseverance and supplication for all the saints.* —Ephesians 6:16–18

I looked at the Lord and thought, *Jesus, who am I that You would do these things through me?* He answered, "Because I have chosen you, little one. I love you, and I am going rebuild your youth. I am going to strengthen you and heal your body. People are going to be amazed at the sign you will be on this earth." I said, "Oh, thank You, God. Thank You. I am so tired, Lord. Oh, Lord, I love You so." Jesus said, "You are going home now, and tomorrow we will come back to the cave, My daughter." Then I was back in my home again.

Jesus had revealed to me that what I had seen that night represented the spiritual and the natural; I was using supernatural keys to change the state of things on earth. I knew that what Satan had brought into captivity must be loosed in the mighty name of Jesus Christ with the keys to the kingdom. From walking with the King, I knew how important it was to listen to every word He said. As I was thinking about all these things, I understood that the devil had brought much heartache and depression to people, causing them to give up their gifts and permitting him to take the gifts captive. Now these gifts had to be loosed again on the earth.

RECLAIMING THE KEYS AND GIFTS OF GOD:

What gifts has God given you to build His church and to reach the lost? Are you using them? If not, why? If you have become discouraged, depressed, or even lazy to the point of allowing your gifts to slip away from you through disuse, ask God to forgive you and to restore these gifts to you. In Jesus' name, loose them from the stronghold of the enemy. Then, ask God how He wants you to use these gifts for His glory.

9

GOD HAS RESCUED HIS GLORY

The next night, Jesus Christ appeared to me and said, "Child, let's go." We returned to the horrible cave where I had seen the glass cages containing the gifts that Satan had stolen from God's people. As I looked around, I thought about how I had laid down my own gift at times. I hadn't listened to God; I hadn't prayed; I hadn't written. The Lord had shown me and told me many things that I had never recorded or related to other people. I thought, *It is so important to let God use you to the fullest.*

THE RESTORATION OF GOD'S GIFTS

Jesus and I now looked at another glass cage. Like many of the others, it was labeled "The Trophies of Satan." In it, books and pens were suspended in the air. The pages of the books would open, and I could see that they contained revelation knowledge and wisdom from God. The covers of the books would change from gold to silver. These were books that God wanted people to write, books that were meant to be award winners.

I watched as Jesus told me, "Take the spiritual key." Again, a spiritual key appeared in my hand. He continued, "Now open this gate in My name." So I put the key in the lock and turned it in the mighty name of Jesus; I commanded the door to open in the name of Yeshua, Emmanuel. When I unlocked the door, again the wind came, and the door flew open. The wind carried the books right out of hell and straight up like a tunnel into the sky. I knew the angels would catch them, cleanse them, and take them to the Father.

I was so excited to know that God was setting free from captivity the gifts that He had given to the church for preaching the gospel of Jesus Christ, for telling people about heaven and hell, and for announcing His coming. I wept a little in my soul, and I thought, *Oh, my God, I am going to be more obedient so that the devil cannot steal the gifts of God.*

I knew that God was going to repair and restore His gifts to His people and that many demonic powers were going to be cremated by God, for it is their judgment time, so that the Word of God can spread over the world and God's glory can return in greater measure to the earth. I *knew* this. The Holy Spirit is my Guide and Teacher, and He is right here with me as I record these revelations for you.

We went to the next glass cage, and I thought, *What is in this one?* Jesus said, "Katherine, what do you think is in here?" At first, I couldn't see anything inside it. Then, when I did see something, I couldn't make out what it was, but it resembled a cloud. So I asked, "Jesus, what is in this glass cage?" He said, "The reason it is in glass and it is transparent is so that Satan doesn't come down here and rejoice when thinking about what he has done with the gifts of God. But this day, they are going to be set free and come back up on the earth, and My Father will purify them."

When I looked into the glass cage, its contents disappeared again, and then I saw something like a blackness and then a whiteness. I thought, *What in the world is this, Jesus?* He told me, "Child, look again, but rebuke that darkness in My name." So I said, "Father, in the mighty name of Jesus, I rebuke this darkness." Suddenly, the darkness fled.

Jesus said, "Child, this is the gift of discernment. Real discernment has been stolen from the earth. This gift is very important to the body of Christ so that people will not be seduced by the devil. This gift is operated by the Holy Spirit, but it was stolen, and the enemy has mixed falsehood with it. He mixes things to bring delusions to people. Now, take a spiritual key and open this door."

I turned the key in the lock and said, "In the name of Jesus Christ, in the name of Emmanuel, in the name of Yeshua, I open this door and loose this gift from this place." The door opened up, and a wind came as before. It was as if there was a gentle breeze around this gift of discernment, and it shot straight up out of the top of the cage and into the sky. Angels gathered it into something like a large glass vase with a cover. I said, "Lord, that is so remarkable." He replied, "It is not by might, nor by power, but by My Spirit, saith the Lord;[24] and I will not allow My Spirit to be mixed with anything false. I am saying that the Spirit of Truth, the Spirit of Revelations, the Spirit of the Gifts of the Spirit will return to the church and to the earth." I let out a big sigh and went on to the next glass cage.

> *There shall come forth a Rod from the stem of Jesse, and a Branch shall grow out of his roots. The Spirit of the Lord shall rest upon Him, the Spirit of wisdom and understanding, the Spirit of counsel and might, the Spirit of knowledge and of the fear of the Lord.*
>
> —Isaiah 11:1–3

---

24. See Zechariah 4:6.

"Lord, what is in this cage?" I asked. He showed me shiny gold and silver guitars. In all, there were twelve cages of musical instruments. Jesus said, "Satan has stolen the real praise of God, the real music. It has to come back. So take the key and open these." I took the spiritual key to one cage and said, "In the mighty name of Jesus, Emmanuel, Yeshua, I loose this." When I turned the key in the lock, the power of God came out, and these musical instruments shot up out of hell into the earth above, and the angels gathered them. The same thing happened with the others, until all twelve cages had been opened by spiritual keys. Sometimes, I said, "In the name of Jesus Christ, Emmanuel, Yeshua, I loose this gift to go back to the Father to be repaired." Jesus would prompt me what to say. He told me, "Child, you are loosening these gifts from the bondage of Satan, and they are going to go back and be replenished." I replied, "Praise ye the Lord. Praise God."

We continued walking and came to many other glass cages; there were so many that they seemed to be without number. I would take the keys and speak what Jesus told me to say. We came to one in which a beautiful satin robe was floating. It was florescent white with gold trim, and red would appear on it at times. It was adorned with diamonds and every other type of precious stone imaginable, as well as pearls. I took the key and said, "In the name of Jesus Christ, Yeshua, Emmanuel, I loose this from the captivity of Satan." After I unlocked the door, the robe shot out, and Jesus shouted! As it went up, there seemed to be a dove flying with it. Jesus told me this was the robe of righteousness. Many of God's people had sold out to sin and fleshly pleasures, and they were not living godly lives, but righteousness would now be restored to the church.

As we went along, we came to a glass cage that held the robe of salvation. In another cage was something that looked like a dove, crying. After we loosed these, we went to a cage containing an outline that looked like the spirit of a person humbly bowing his head and crying. God would not tell me what that was. But Jesus loosed it, and, like all the others, it shot up and out of the top of the cave in a mighty whirlwind, and the angels received it in the air.

For several days, Jesus and I walked among these glass cages. He put the spiritual keys in my hand, and I gladly unlocked the doors. One cage was full of gold and silver, and Jesus said, "Child, Satan has bound up the finances, the money, of many, but My Word is true. I said I will bless; I will restore My people and bring wealth to them so that they can preach My gospel. Take this spiritual key." He put a spiritual key in my hand, and I said, "In the name of Jesus, Emmanuel, Yeshua,..." This time, Jesus told me to add, "...to God be the glory, and to loose this." When I turned the key in the lock, the door flew open. The glory of the Lord is so powerful. A wind came and picked up all the gold and silver and carried it through the top of the cave and into the sky, where there were something like horses with chariots that had a holding place for all this gold and silver. There were riders in the chariots, and they shouted, "To God be the glory!" I thought, *Oh, my goodness, what a vision, what a revelation. The earth needs to know that God is truly setting free His glory.*

For the earth will be filled with the knowledge of the glory of the Lord, as the waters cover the sea. —Habakkuk 2:14

"THE THIEF HAS BEEN CAUGHT"

I don't know how to put it into words, but when I looked at Jesus, He appeared to have "more." He is full of wisdom and understanding, but somehow He looked even more steadfast. I looked inside another cage and saw that suspended in the air were Bibles from all nations. The Lord said, "Satan has watered down My Word. The thief has been caught, Katherine. With a revelation that I am going to release to the earth, people will know how evil the devil is, and they will begin to cry to Me and look to Me again. Satan has taken their eyes off of Me, and he has brought distorted words."

Jesus gave me a spiritual key, and with that key to the kingdom I unlocked the door in the name of Jesus Christ, Yeshua, Emmanuel. The door flew open, and the wind came and took those Bibles right out of hell and into the sky above the earth. Angels came to retrieve them, just as they had with the contents of all the other cages; the angels had beautiful small glass containers, and they put each Bible inside a glass container and then went up to heaven. The Lord said, "Child, this day, saith the Lord Your God, as you are writing this and recording this in 2013, great revivals shall begin to break out in the earth because this is being revealed."

We went on to the next glass cage, which was full of fire. Jesus said to me, "Child, all through My Word, it talks about God as a consuming fire. All through My Word, it talks about the Holy Spirit fire, the Holy Spirit presence. It talks about the fire to cleanse things, to purify things. Also, in Malachi, it says that the wicked shall be ashes…." He told me, "Say, 'Ashes.'" I said, "Ashes." Then He continued, "…under the souls of your feet. My saints have not sought Me on that revelation. I gave them the keys. I gave them the fire through the Holy Spirit baptism. In the book of Acts, the fire of God was even enclothed in tongues above the disciples' heads.[25]

"Now, My child, this fire in here has been kept secret. It says 'Trophy of Satan,' for although there are many people in the earth, few have grasped this revelation; but this is the mightiest gift to My children, and the gift of love. And your hearts must be pure; you must live right to be able to use this fire. My daughter, now I will release it, saith the Lord your God, and it will go all over the earth, and it will bring revival. It will burn off the droughts. It will burn up the demon powers. This is their time of judgment; it is

25. See Acts 2:1–4.

now because I went to the cross and shed My blood. Many do not understand this revelation, but they can use My name and ask the Father to send the fire to cremate the darkness, and the Father will."

Jesus paid the high price of being mocked, taking the sins of the world on Himself, suffering death on the cross, and defeating Satan and his demons so that we could use His name, the name of the Lord Jesus Christ, to defeat the enemy. Yet we have neglected to use His name; and we have not understood the power of God's fire to destroy the works of the enemy. We must ask the Lord to send His fire to burn up the forces of darkness.

I said, "Oh, Lord, forgive me for not understanding." He said, "The glass cage in which we saw the smoke and the darkness and the light that was released, My daughter, was also for understanding." When I looked at Him, I saw His face light up, and I asked, "Oh, Jesus, You are very happy over this?" And He said, "Yes, take this spiritual key in My name and open this up." I took the key to the kingdom that He had given me, and, in the name of Jesus Christ, Yeshua, Emmanuel, I unlocked the door to this fire, and the door flew open. A high wind came, and it caught up Jesus, me, and the fire, and we went up through the top of the cave, into the earth, above the earth, and into the galaxies, with the earth far below us. Jesus said, "Behold, behold, angels." There were many angels shouting, and they were dancing in fire. Then other angels came and put the fire from the cage into a container.

God makes His angels spirits, His ministers a flame of fire.
—Psalm 104:4

I saw something like a stairway going up to heaven. And Jesus said, "I must go now, and you have to go home. But I want to tell you something: Very soon, I am going to take you up this stairway to see heaven and to come back and report. It will not be your time to leave the earth. I am going to take you there just for a visit and then bring you back. But now I must go with My angels to My Father and present this before My Father." I thought, *Oh, I'm so happy. This is truly God.* With His finger, Jesus wrote in the sky some Hebrew words I didn't understand. Then I was back in my home, and daylight was coming. I thought, *Oh, my Lord, how beautiful.*

Jesus had said, "The thief has been caught." That meant that the devil had been caught with his trickery, his mockery, his seducing, his taking the gifts of God and mutilating them and mixing them with corruption. But Jesus said that God's fire was being released to burn up much of the enemy's darkness and to give His saints understanding of how to use the fire of the Holy Spirit, the fire of the presence of the Lord. Praise the Lord!

The fire brings cleansing. God has a spiritual fire to destroy the darkness. He has weapons against Satan. He has swords. He has His mighty Word. And we must learn about His gifts and weapons for us. We have to study them and, in the name of Jesus Christ, keep moving forward with them to defeat the enemy. Therefore, read the Bible and study the passages that refer to the spiritual fire of God. (See, for example, Exodus 13:21–22; 24:17; Deuteronomy 4:24; 9:3.) *"For our God is a consuming fire"* (Hebrews 12:29).

THE SLEEPING GIANT

The book of Proverbs says that a thief must return sevenfold what he stole. (See Proverbs 6:30–31.) I think the same applies to what Satan has stolen from the church. God has given us spiritual keys to open spiritual locks and to release what the devil has robbed from us. So, with the wisdom of God, I just want to say this: It is time for us to take back these "trophies" of Satan. It is time for us to arise and use our gifts. It is time for us to stand up with the keys to the kingdom.

We must recognize that we have been far too lazy and apathetic about the things of God. Although the Lord has given us many gifts, we don't want to use them. Sometimes, we are afraid that we will offend somebody if we exercise a gift. My friend, God wants you to arise and serve Him, no matter whom you offend. I prophesy that you will rise up with the gift that He imparted to you, the one that has been buried. I prophesy that you will be as bold as a lion and have the courage to complete the job God has given you to do, because thousands are dying and going to hell—the very hell that I have been describing. There are many souls suffering in eternal punishment today who wish they had been born again, who wish they had obeyed God.

The Lord asks you to unite with Him in defeating the enemy. You must wake up, shake the dust off yourself, and start praying and doing what He has called you to do. There are people reading this book right now who are running from the gift God has given them. Stop, repent, and claim that buried gift in Jesus' name. God wants you to rejoin His army. He will heal your wounds, and He will mortally wound the forces of darkness. I am not referring to people receiving a mortal wound but rather the devil and his demonic spirits. It is time for the church to arise as a powerful army for God in the earth. Let this "sleeping giant" arise in the mighty name of Jesus. Amen!

RECLAIMING THE KEYS AND GIFTS OF GOD:

Are you running from the gifts God has given you? Are you afraid of offending someone if you use a particular gift? If so, move past your fear by focusing on the ways in which your gift will help other people to grow in their faith, to be healed or delivered, to be comforted, to be spiritually refreshed, and so forth. Commit your gifts to God and then begin to exercise them in faith. Start using them in small ways, and as you learn how to exercise them under God's guidance, you will gradually be able to use them in greater ways.

We must always remember, too, that our spiritual gifts are to be used in conjunction with the gifts of other believers. We need to work together in Jesus' name to accomplish God's purposes. It takes a corporate anointing to break yokes of demonic bondage off of people. God desires a restoration of unity in the body of Christ. (See, for example, 1 Corinthians 12:12–31.)

10

ARISE

In this chapter, I want to talk more about awakening the sleeping giant. The giant is God's people, His army, all over the earth. We've been slumbering for too long. The church must be stirred up again, and its leaders—prophets, apostles, pastors, and others—must pull themselves together, because there are millions of spiritually lost and oppressed people who need us. We have to comprehend the reality of heaven and hell and the significance of our calling to share the gospel. We have been too lazy as time has slipped by and hundreds of thousands have gone to hell.

What if you had just died and, having rejected Jesus Christ, were slipping into hell right now? God has shown me the horrors of eternal punishment, and He has shown those horrors to others, too. He will continue to show them, because He is trying to shake believers awake. I am very serious about this. We must *"fight the good fight of faith"* (1 Timothy 6:12).

THE CHAMBER OF DEATH

Jesus Christ appeared to me again and, by His power, took me with Him down a gateway to hell. This time, we ended up in an area that was even darker than any I had been in before. Jesus said, "Behold, child, we are in the right arm of hell." He raised His right arm, and a great door appeared in the darkness. Then He spoke, and light shone everywhere. I was able to see things that would just astonish you. They astounded me, and I grabbed the Lord's hand.

Jesus was again wearing a white garment, which was shining and brilliant, a golden belt around His waist, and sandals. His hair was beautiful, and His skin was olive-colored. His eyes pierced through my soul. As I looked at Him, I began to weep, and I said, "Lord Jesus, You died and gave Your life and Your blood to keep us from this place. And what I behold with my eyes is horrible."

I stood close to Him and just cried. He put His arm around me to comfort me and said, "Child, you don't even realize how important you are to My kingdom. You don't realize, do you?" I said, "No, Lord." He said, "I'm glad you are like a child, with a humble spirit of compassion; that you can tell of these things you see without greed, without wanting money."

I looked where Jesus had opened the door in the darkness, and it seemed as if I could see very clearly for a hundred miles. The area inside that door was called the Chamber of Death. I thought, *Oh, my God, all hell is death.* Jesus said, "Yes, daughter, but look at the top of the chamber and see what is written." At the top of that chamber, which had the appearance of copper and bronze, there was a huge sign with the words "Trophies of Satan." I said, "Lord, I thought the things in the cages were his trophies." Jesus said, "Behold and look." As I looked into one part of the chamber, Jesus said, "I told you we are in the right arm of hell. The right arm of Satan is very evil, whereas My right arm—as well as the Father's right hand and arm—is very gentle."

[God said,] *"I drew them with gentle cords, with bands of love, and I was to them as those who take the yoke from their neck."*

—Hosea 11:4

I saw what looked like a huge python; it was as large as a train and twenty-five to thirty miles in length. This snake was green and yellow with bright colors. And it was alive. At first, it was coiled up, but it uncoiled itself and moved in a circle. Then it curled up into its original position again before uncoiling once more and making a circle. I screamed when I saw large doors open up on the sides of the serpent. I counted twelve of them. Jesus said, "Keep counting." When I got to fifteen, He said, "Wait." There were fifteen open doors, and five more that were shut. Then I saw that there were many rattlers on the snake's tail. I had thought it was a python, but it was actually a rattlesnake.

As I looked at the serpent, Jesus said, "Child, behold and look. Remember that the right arm has power. Remember the right arm; when people shake hands, they shake with the right hand." I saw one door open, and Jesus said, "We are going to go down there, and we are going to look in that door." I said, "Oh, Jesus, what is it?" He said, "What did the sign say? 'Trophies of Satan.'"

Jesus illuminated the area, and the light spread out in a big circle. Behind the rattlesnake were rows and rows of demons holding pitchforks and other things. Many of them also had chains around them and held large keys in their hands. They screamed and ran from the light of the Lord Jesus. The Lord raised His left hand, and fire shot out into the darkness, cremating the demons; they turned into ashes right before my eyes, and smoke arose from their remains. I said, "Oh, Jesus, thank You, thank You." Little snakes were crawling around, but when Jesus pointed toward them, they, too, were cremated.

Jesus said, "My Father gave Me the commandment that I could do this. Child, look, listen, and learn. Things I have shown you and told you, thousands would want to do, but I cannot trust them. Some I can't. Now look."

I saw that where the demons had once been, there was dry, brown ground, with many cracks in it. However, the snake appeared to have grown larger.

THROUGH DOOR 1

Jesus explained, "We are going to go down there and go through each door. The snake will not be able to do anything." Then the Lord spoke, and we went down a very rocky hill. We walked through the entrance of a large circle called "Trophies of Satan." Door 1 on the side of the serpent was wide open. It was at least ten feet wide and twelve feet high. I thought, *What is this, Lord?* He said, "Look, listen, and learn." (As the Lord recalled this scene to my memory, I remembered that years after He had taken me to hell, while I was praying during a prayer meeting, I had seen a vision of an enormous serpent with doors, similar to what I saw here.)

We walked through the doorway into a large room, and I saw that it contained some very beautiful things. All the rooms we later went into seemed extremely large, though it's hard to estimate their dimensions. This room contained things that Satan had stolen from people to keep them from prospering and to cause them to become discouraged and stop serving God. All around, there were shelves and shelves of beautiful things such as the "rich and famous" would have in their homes—adornments, sheets of beautiful colors, and so on.

I turned around, and Jesus said, "Look above one of these." I saw many gold bars stacked up, so I asked, "What is this?" He said, "Satan's trophies—the money he stole from the church." *Oh, my.* There were stacks and stacks of bars, worth perhaps billions of dollars. Then I looked over at the next shelf, where many books with gold and silver covers were piled up. They seemed to glow. I said, "What is that, Lord?" He replied, "The devil has taken the writings, the truth. He has deceived many in the earth with false teachings, with lies. He has watered down My Word."

The room was like a large warehouse. Jesus showed me all kinds of expensive cars that Satan had stolen. Then He showed me clothing that had been stolen. And accessories. And shoes. All stolen. Jesus stopped in front of the shoes and said, "What do you think these are, Katherine?" "I don't know, Lord, unless You give me the understanding." He said, "These are the 'shoes' of My people, of prophets and apostles, the fivefold ministry. They have stopped walking for Me; they have stopped talking for me. They have laid down and wept; they have given up. Tell My people not to give up but to keep on walking. Don't let their shoes be stolen by Satan. Don't let Satan block them and knock them down. If he does, they must get up and fight him with My Word. I gave My Word to set the captive free."

There were many other shelves. One was full of computers. Another had money floating in it. Jesus said, "This money belongs to My saints. But in My name, it shall be loosed; and in My name, it shall go back up on the earth, and My Father will answer from heaven. Let the people reading this book understand: Do not let the devil take your gifts." Then I began to comprehend about the gifts of the Spirit and how we become lazy when God tells us to do something. We don't want to do it, so we put it off or refuse to do it altogether. Day after day, we procrastinate and don't do what we're meant to do. I've been guilty of that.

See then that you walk circumspectly, not as fools but as wise, redeeming the time, because the days are evil.

—Ephesians 5:15–16

Then Jesus said, "Look in this room." I understood that Satan, the old dragon, had come and seduced us and deceived us. Jesus shook His head and said, "Yes, it is true what you are thinking." I followed Him to another room where there were a large number of swords of the Spirit. The Word was there. It was written on a large sword that was suspended in the air and full of fire.

Jesus said, "In the book of Daniel, it says that My truth was cast down to the ground.[26] The angel Gabriel talked to Daniel,[27] and I sent Gabriel to you, Katherine, a year ago. I sent Him to you, and he gave you some secrets. This is part of the secrets. As I am opening up your mind in remembrance of these things, the Angel of Revelation is there with you, and the Holy Spirit."

Then Jesus showed me things that contained the blessings of God for people's bodies. Satan had stolen them with lies, deception, and seduction. The Lord said, "Yes, there are powerful demons out there. When people are in sin, he seduces them. They love the flesh; they love to please it. They do the things they should not do because evil is in them. Evil is in their hearts and their minds, and they need to repent and turn to Me, the Lord Jesus Christ. Child, this room is very, very important, and I will bring you back to it later because there are more things I want to show you here."

While I was recording the revelations for this book, the Lord asked me, "Do you remember the demons that were standing in the circular area? I destroyed them because they were 'strong men,'[28] strongholds upon these things. Tell the people that the greatest weapons are My Word, Jesus Christ's mighty name, the Holy Spirit, the fire of God, the presence of God, and the anointing of God. Awake, church, awake. Awaken the giant that is asleep in the earth."

---

26. See Daniel 8:12.
27. See Daniel 8:15–27; 9:20–27.
28. See Matthew 12:29; Mark 3:27; Luke 11:21–22.

THROUGH DOOR 2

As I wrote earlier, there were fifteen open doors in the sides of the snake, and inside each door was something the devil had stolen from the earth. We were finished looking at the room connected with Door 1, and I walked with Jesus through the opening of Door 2. We entered a massive area, at least two hundred miles around. I don't understand it all, but it contained piles of all types of money, neatly stacked. I believe it represented money from the beginning of time until now. There were various currencies from all over the earth, and above the money from each nation something was written that I did not understand. I thought, *Oh, my God, this is the money Satan and his demons have stolen from the earth.* "Yes," said Jesus, "and they want to build their own kingdom. They are trying so hard through all kinds of deceitful tricks to rule the nations and take the money. But this day, I destroy it, child; I destroy their plans. I destroy these evil powers by My fire. This fire will not hurt humans, but it truly will break the chains off the humans. And this Holy Spirit fire, the fire of truth and righteousness, has so much power in it. It is alive, because remember that on the day of Pentecost, when the fire came, it sat on the heads of the disciples like cloven tongues. It was alive; you could touch it. Awake, church, and read about My fire; study about My consuming fire. Use My Word!"

> *Therefore, since we are receiving a kingdom which cannot be shaken, let us have grace, by which we may serve God acceptably with reverence and godly fear. For our God is a consuming fire.*
> —Hebrews 12:28–29

I watched, listened, and learned. "Exactly what does this money of every nation mean?" I asked. Jesus replied, "When My Father threw the enemy out of heaven, and all of his angels with him that are in everlasting chains and in the middle of hell here, he started thinking of ways to destroy God's people and get back at God. It is war, My daughter, war against good and evil. And I—Jesus Christ, the Son of God, Emmanuel, Yeshua, and other names I have—was the Key. I was the Key and the secret that God was using to bring back hope to the people, to bring back life to My Word."

Big tears flowed from Jesus' eyes, and He said, "Yes, My Word says I'll prosper My people. My Word says that I will give them nations to save. My Word says I will bless them like I did Abraham, like I did Jacob, like I did David. I hope the world understands what I am trying to say. It is a time to be holy. It is a time to get the junk out of your heart and your mind and your soul and your spirit. My Word says, 'Love the Lord thy God with all thy heart and thy mind and thy soul and thy strength.'[29]

"For some of this money, the devil tricked people deceitfully. They were My people, saved and serving Me, but he brought such seducing greed to them. He seduced them with greed to lie, to cheat, to steal with the gifts of God. This goes along with the book of Corinthians."

I stood in awe as I listened to my King explain Door 2. "Children have no food and are dying. Many older people and young people do not have enough money to pay their bills, their rent or anything, so they turn to evil. But I say that as they speak My Word, prosperity will return. Blessings upon blessings I want to give to My people. Tell the earth to repent, and awaken the giant. Tell the earth to repent, My daughter; you blow the trumpet in Zion. Tell My people of their transgressions. Tell My people of their sins."

As we were leaving the room where all the money was, Jesus said, "I want to restore that to My people."

---

29. See, for example, Deuteronomy 6:5 (KJV); Mark 12:30 (KJV).

> [Jesus said,] *"Therefore do not worry, saying, 'What shall we eat?' or 'What shall we drink?' or 'What shall we wear?' For after all these things the Gentiles seek. For your heavenly Father knows that you need all these things. But seek first the kingdom of God and His righteousness, and all these things shall be added to you."* —Matthew 6:31–33

WAKE UP AND SEEK GOD

We have to hear what Jesus is saying. We must believe Him and arise. There are times when I go through many battles, but I hang on to God's Word. I have seen His Word in action. Many times, when I am praying, I see angels open up a large book, the holy Word of God, and they slam it into the face of that serpent, that dragon, and into his demons, so that they fall and then run. The Word is a wall of protection. Additionally, Jesus gave us His blood and His name as our protection. He is Lord of All.

Let us wake up and seek God. Let us read and understand His Word. It's time for the army of God to arise. He is the living God. He is not made of stone or wood. (See, for example, Daniel 5:23.) Jesus Christ gave His life for you and me so that we could receive eternal life and be with Him forever. Hear ye the Word of the Lord, for Jesus Christ is Lord of All.

RECLAIMING THE KEYS AND GIFTS OF GOD:

God wants to restore financial provision and other blessings to His people, but we must make sure that our priorities are right and that we are obeying God's Word. Is there a specific sin or transgression that you need to repent of? If so, turn from it and ask God to forgive you. Are you using some of your current resources to help those less fortunate than you are? If not, begin to do what you can to help those in need.

11

BLOW THE TRUMPET IN ZION

THROUGH DOOR 3

Jesus and I had entered Doors 1 and 2 in the side of the serpent, and we next entered Door 3. Immediately, I smelled a very strong stench, and I began to grieve and cry. Tears ran from Jesus' eyes, too. Then He illuminated the place, and I saw stacks and stacks of little coffins. These were the caskets of babies that had died by the trickery of Satan. There also was a table of blood—an abortionist's table, Jesus told me.

I saw something like a timeline, with years and dates flashing in the air in a circle. The dates went back in time very quickly. I also heard the wailing of newborns, and I said, "Father, this is so horrifying." Jesus replied, "Yes, child, this is truly horrible. Satan has stolen many lives. These are his trophies. He keeps a record;

he tries to copy God. Satan had these thousands of little boxes and thousands of little coffins put in here as symbols of what he has done. But the babies themselves are not here in hell. Look at them closely; there is no vapor or smoke inside their little bodies." Sure enough, there were no souls inside the tiny skeletons that were in the boxes and coffins.

Jesus emphasized, "I want the world to know that there are absolutely no babies in hell. If someone has told you that there were, what they saw and wrote about was an illusion. It was not the truth."

I thought, *This room is like an illusion of these little babies stacked up here by the thousands and thousands without number.* And the number of caskets seemed to expand. I began to think these truly were Satan's trophies, for which he had seduced and deceived people. Jesus told me, "Yes, this room is an illusion of what Satan has done to the unborn and to the newborn. It is an illusion."

Then Jesus spoke, and everything within Door 3 disappeared for a moment before reappearing. He said, "I want the world to understand that Satan has done this thing. That is why I am showing you this room within this serpent. I am trying to tell the earth all these things and to warn them of Satan's seducing powers. Love Me, trust Me. I want to bring back hope to you. All through hell, people who did these wicked things are burning and screaming. Many people had abortions and never repented, and they are burning in hell here tonight. Please, earth, awake; awake."

I looked all around at the innumerable coffins. The Lord said, "This is a revelation of God to tell the world that from the time of conception, a baby has an eternal soul that is precious to God; that soul is alive. And if you deliberately, willfully abort that child, it is a great sin; it is the sin of murder. You must understand that this sin carries the judgment of God. The blood of aborted babies is crying out to Him from the ground."[30]

30. See Genesis 4:8–10.

For You formed my inward parts; You covered me in my mother's womb. I will praise You, for I am fearfully and wonderfully made; marvelous are Your works, and that my soul knows very well. My frame was not hidden from You, when I was made in secret, and skillfully wrought in the lowest parts of the earth. Your eyes saw my substance, being yet unformed. And in Your book they all were written, the days fashioned for me, when as yet there were none of them.

—Psalm 139:13–16

Jesus said, "If it is a matter of life or death for the mother, then that is her choice. Yet Satan has tricked many people into thinking that their best option is to get rid of their unborn baby because they won't be able to take care of the child, or they won't be able to give the child a good life, or the child will be an interruption to their own lives. They are being deceived.

"All these little children who were killed are in heaven. God has completed them, and now they are whole. They were meant to bring blessings to people, but instead the people killed them. Oh, the strong force of temptation, the strong force of delusion, when a woman is out there working and tired and single, and she falls in love with a man, and they have that relationship of what they call love. And she ends up pregnant, but he doesn't want the baby and neither does she, and so they go and have it aborted. Over and over, this happens throughout the whole earth. I want young girls to hear Me. Do not have an abortion. I will make a way for you and your baby. Hear what the Spirit of the Lord is saying to the world. Hear, hear, awake!

"If you have had an abortion, and you repent, God will forgive you. Call on Me and ask Me to wash you clean in My blood. I will do it."

We need to bring the teaching of God's Word to young women who are considering having an abortion. If this is your situation, Jesus wants to bring you hope. He does not want you to hurt yourself or your unborn child. Read the Word of God. God is holy. He is pure. He loves you, and He will make a way for you. He will forgive you if you have had an abortion. He is full of grace and mercy.

> *The Lord is gracious and full of compassion, slow to anger and great in mercy. The Lord is good to all, and His tender mercies are over all His works.* —Psalm 145:8–9

THROUGH DOOR 4

We left that place and went over to Door 4. I wondered what I would see within that opening because Jesus was crying again. The walls inside were like a large movie screen, depicting the evil things that Satan had done from the beginning of time up until the present. It was like a rotating mural. It showed, for example, demons tormenting people with alcohol and drugs. But then it portrayed the angels of God coming to set them free; many of the people were delivered, and demons were destroyed. Jesus said, "Satan tries to copy God, but he is evil. I come to give life and to give it to you more abundantly. Satan comes to steal, kill, and destroy."[31]

It seemed as if we stood for hours watching these images of the many evil things that had happened over the years, including the Holocaust and various wars. Jesus said, "My daughter, I came to bring peace on the earth, but in the last few years, they have watered down My gospel, so that people don't have the strength to fight or the strength to stand. Many people are being saved in this hour; yes, they are. But knowledge is increasing in the land."

---

31. See John 10:10.

> [The angel said to the prophet Daniel,] *"At that time Michael shall stand up, the great prince who stands watch over the sons of your people; and there shall be a time of trouble, such as never was since there was a nation, even to that time. And at that time your people shall be delivered, every one who is found written in the book. And many of those who sleep in the dust of the earth shall awake, some to everlasting life, some to shame and everlasting contempt. Those who are wise shall shine like the brightness of the firmament, and those who turn many to righteousness like the stars forever and ever. But you, Daniel, shut up the words, and seal the book until the time of the end; many shall run to and fro, and knowledge shall increase."*
>
> —Daniel 12:1–4

I watched many wicked events on the walls of that room. I saw Satan on his throne, laughing about how he had killed thousands of people with earthquakes. And Jesus said, "My covenant is standing for My people. Even if they fall, I send angels to draw them back, and I do it by My Spirit. I send them, My daughter, so that Satan must be bound. I send My powerful Word. Look, I can see many angels fighting for the saints of God and for children." It was so beautiful to watch the glory come in and the blood of Jesus appear. And Satan would be so angry.

The Holocaust was horrifying. As I witnessed those scenes, I screamed, "Oh, God." Tears were coming down Jesus' face, and He said, "My daughter, this also is a vision in hell for you to understand that there are murderers, rapists, and all kinds of evil people in this earth. I want My people to repent, and such things will fall away." Then I saw a scene in which shackles fell off of people. They had been bound, but the chains just melted off.

But I saw other unthinkable horrors, and I thought, *Oh, God, this is awful. I can't stand any more.* Jesus turned to me and said,

"You must. You must see these things to tell the people of the earth, to warn them that I love them, that I've sent My power and My presence, that I want them to give all to Me—not just part of themselves, but all to Me—so that they'll have the anointing and the power to set their families free." And then I saw a scene of a crying mother and her babies, and the power of God came and washed and cleansed them with the blood of Jesus. Life came upon them, and they began to receive provision and other good things.

I understood that we must give everything to Jesus. Yes, we are still going to have problems; we must recognize that. But Jesus is trying to tell us, "Return, return to God, you backslider; return to the King of Kings and Lord and Lords. Stop your greed and your unfaithfulness; stop the murderers and the rapists." I fell down and cried. Jesus gently picked me up and said, "Blow that trumpet, My daughter; blow it hard with My love."

WE HAVE AUTHORITY OVER SATAN IN JESUS' NAME

In chapter 14, we will return to the open doors on the sides of the serpent and see the trophies of Satan in the rooms connected with Doors 5, 6, and 7. The "trophies" behind all these doors in the sides of the serpent represent the wickedness that the devil has worked on the earth to stop Christians from arising as a great army to defeat him. Satan has abused us with powerful seductions, but we must understand that we have the authority in Jesus' name to rebuke him. Jesus is truly Lord of All. The Father has given Him all power in heaven, on earth, and below the earth. (See Matthew 28:18.)

RECLAIMING THE KEYS AND GIFTS OF GOD:

Jesus wants us to give everything to Him—our heart, our soul, our mind, our strength—every aspect of our lives. When we surrender all to Jesus and are continually seeking His purposes, we can live according to His power and anointing. Then we will be able to release our family members and others from Satan's grasp. Have you given all to Jesus? What might you be holding back from Him?

12

SATAN'S SEDUCEMENT OF THE CHURCH

"A PROTECTION TO MY PEOPLE"

In this chapter, I want to talk more about hell's punishment and how Satan has seduced people to fall away from God. One time, Jesus and I were walking in hell when the Lord raised His arm in the darkness, as He had so many times before, so that our surroundings could be clearly viewed. I stood in amazement as I looked around. We were in a place where there were thousands and thousands of skeletons stacked up from the ground. They were screaming, "Help us; help us." I looked at Jesus and said, "What is this?" He answered, "These are those who laid down and died for the devil. They gave their hearts and souls to the devil." I said, "Oh, my God. Oh, my Jesus."

I stared at those numberless souls. They were surrounded by laughing demons that were about three feet high. Jesus raised His arm, fire came out, and all those demons were reduced to ashes. The Lord said in regard to the skeletons, "Many people are in the occult and witchcraft and all types of worship of the devil. This is their end if they do not repent. I am calling them to repent today. Repent ye and turn to Me."

One of the corpses screamed, "I was a great voodoo man, and I deceived and killed many and worked many spells on people. But when I died and came here, Satan laughed and said, "This is your kingdom." And all of the skeletons said, "Oh, woe unto us. Why did we do the evil? We were so evil." Then I heard one of the skeletons swear and blaspheme.

I cried for a long time, although without tears. But tears were rolling down Jesus' face. He said, "Humanity, humanity repent. Repent ye, repent. Repent of your evil, your voodoo, your black magic against the innocent, for I will be a protection to My people and a glory in their midst. And My glory will return to the earth.[32] Turn from your evil, you wicked people doing witchcraft and voodoo. Repent, repent in My name, and I will save you. Whosoever calls upon the Lord, I will save them."[33]

> *If you confess with your mouth the Lord Jesus and believe in your heart that God has raised Him from the dead, you will be saved. For with the heart one believes unto righteousness, and with the mouth confession is made unto salvation. For the Scripture says, "Whoever believes on Him will not be put to shame." For there is no distinction between Jew and Greek, for the same Lord over all is rich to all who call upon Him. For*

32. See Zechariah 2:5.
33. See Joel 2:32; Acts 2:21; Romans 10:13.

"whoever calls on the name of the Lord shall be saved."
—Romans 10:9–13

After seeing those stacked skeletons and hearing what they were saying, I thought, *Oh, my God, this is horrible. I can't take it anymore.* So we left that place, and Jesus brought me back home.

A PANORAMIC VIEW OF JUDGMENT IN HELL

The next night, Jesus and I were again walking in hell past burning, screaming souls and laughing demons. We were passing by many things I had seen before, such as pits of raging, boiling fire, and an opening in the earth into which skeletons and black objects were falling. It seemed as if I was seeing a panoramic view of hell. Everywhere I looked, souls were being tormented. Many were clothed in fire. There would be flesh on their skeletons for a little while before it melted off like hot lava and slid down around their feet. Their bones would become dry, and worms would crawl out of them. They would scream, gnash their teeth, and cry because they desperately wanted to get out of hell. All around me, a multitude of voices could be heard cursing, blaspheming, and screaming words that I had heard so often during my sojourns in hell: "Why didn't somebody warn me? Why didn't somebody tell me about hell and give me a chance to repent?"

The voices of the dead seemed to get louder and louder, so I asked Jesus about it, and He said, "I wanted you to hear it. Every race and every nation is here. But," He reemphasized, "there are absolutely no babies or children in hell." Then He said, "Look, listen, and learn."

As I looked at that panoramic view of hell, which appeared to be hundreds of miles wide, I also seemed to be able to see right to where individual souls were being tormented, or right to where individual souls were having judgment brought to them. I thought,

Judgment is being carried out by demons in every imaginable, horrible way to torment these lost souls, because these people have the sensation that they have a physical body, and that God has cast both their body and soul into hell. (See Matthew 10:28.)

HELL HAS ENLARGED ITSELF

Jesus said, "We are going to a place where you will hear voices; the dead talk in hell." When we went to this place, I couldn't see the skeletons, but I could hear them. A man's voice said, "I was a serial killer on the earth." Then he screamed at another skeleton, "What did you do?" The second one said, "I killed babies. And I hear the voices of those babies tormenting me in hell." All at once, I heard screams, and I saw demons come up and transform themselves into the form of little babies that were wailing. Then these fabricated forms would burn up and disappear, and the demons would reappear.

I thought, *My Lord, this is an illusion, isn't it?* Jesus replied, "Yes. The devil wants people to abort their children, to kill people, to murder, to steal, to take drugs and alcohol. Listen to some of their conversations."

I heard another man say, "Well, I was an alcoholic, and my wife kept telling me to repent and go get help, but I wouldn't. I became meaner and meaner toward her and more and more of a drunk until my liver was destroyed. Then I died and came here. I never repented, but I did hear that Jesus was the truth, and I knew the way."

After this, I heard the voice of another man saying, "Yes, I was a drug dealer and an alcoholic. I sold drugs, and I began to take hard drugs and died from an overdose. And here I am today, burning and screaming until the day of the great white throne judgment of God. Oh, how I hurt, and oh, how I burn. And I still have the same thoughts and feelings for drugs that I had on earth.

I crave drugs, and the craving never leaves me." Then he screamed, "Help me, help me, God."

Then I heard a man moaning. This man had been a gang leader, and he had died a horrible death by gangs. I heard the voice of another soul screaming, "When will this end? Day and night, I suffer. There is no day here; there is no night here. But I know that there were day and night when I was on the earth. Oh, when will this end?"

A woman's voice said, "I was a prostitute. They paid me good money. When I died, I came here, and I suffer so. Can't somebody help me? Why didn't somebody on the earth tell me of this? I heard a little bit about God, but I was never interested. I am the wicked." I looked at Jesus and said, "These are the voices of the dead that are—the dead talk in hell." He said, "Yes, they do. And some of them are still trying to justify their wickedness. These are the souls of the wicked."

Another voice said, "I had sex with an animal, and I died in sin and came here." Another spoke the language of a different nation, but I understood that he was saying, "I was paid to kill people. I blew up trains and planes, and that is why I am here."

All these voices of the dead were talking about the evil they had committed on the earth. As I saw all that activity and heard all those voices, I thought, *Surely, the world needs to be aware of what is down here, because hell has enlarged itself to hold the souls of the wicked.* (See Isaiah 5:14.) I looked at Jesus, and He knew what I was thinking. The Lord said to me, "Child, blow your trumpet in Zion. Tell My people their transgression, and the house of Jacob their sins."

> *Cry aloud, spare not; lift up your voice like a trumpet; tell My people their transgression, and the house of Jacob their sins.*
>
> —Isaiah 58:1

DEMONIC POWERS INFILTRATING THE CHURCH

Then Jesus said, "Come on, I am going to show you something else," and we moved into the next area. Jesus caused light to shine, and He cremated demons by His fire. Any demon that the fire didn't touch screamed and ran away. We came to a large opening, which I think was still in the right arm of hell, and there was such an evil section in it—it was like a pool of quicksand and dung with fire. Demons were coming, and they were leading skeletons by the hundreds with black chains around them. The souls were screaming, "Oh, my God, I didn't know hell was real. I mocked. I was an atheist. I made fun. Oh, my God, this is real; this is real."

Then I saw a demon holding a plaque with names on it. This demon was very big and broad-shouldered, and he had fangs, long dirty nails, and big webbed feet. The demons were laughing and saying, "We seduced them. We seduced them." I was greatly grieved at this sight. The name of a soul was called, and demons unchained it, brought it over to the demon with the plaque, and said, "This is your torment; this is your servant. You served the devil well on earth, but in hell you shall be tormented. Satan shall win against God."

I screamed, "No, Lord, no. What have these done, Lord Jesus? What sin of the flesh have they committed?" Jesus said, "Child, listen to the voices of the dead." There were lines and lines of these skeletons bound together, one after another, in black chains. I heard them saying, "Oh, can we get out of here? Is there any hope? Oh, why did we not listen to the gospel of Jesus Christ? Why did we fight against the King who would have saved us from this place? Woe unto us, for our wound is grievous. Woe unto us." Thousands began to say those words and to cry, while others blasphemed God, even though they were in hell.

The demons told these souls, "No man cares for your soul. This is your torment; this is your judgment." I heard two demons scream, in succession, "O fire, burn brighter; fire burn brighter in this quicksand pit to hold more souls that have been seduced by our king, the devil; and we helped him to deceive these."

Jesus said, "I am going to show you a vision in this midst of this revelation." The vision was of one man who had been brought before the large demon. In the vision, the man was on the earth, and he was a preacher of God's Word. Jesus didn't say anything else; the vision said it all. I saw a fine church. I don't know the name of the preacher or the name of his church. I just saw the inside of a large, beautiful church. There was wonderful singing, and people were praising God.

The demon was enjoying looking at this vision; in fact, he was laughing. Then I saw beings in black robes infiltrate the church. They came in, sat down, and were transformed into what looked like church people; then their black robes came back on them. They were demons, but they seemed to be in the form of men and women. After this, I saw the church invite them to assist in the ministry—to work in the office, to help with the offering, and everything. The Christians were so deceived.

Then there was a time lapse of about five years. The church was almost empty, and there was darkness all over it. I looked outside the church building, and the parking lot was cracked and broken up, and the word *Ichabod* was written over the door. (See 1 Samuel 4:19–21.)

I said, "My God, what is this?" Jesus answered, "The Spirit of the Lord has departed from that church building. When those evil powers came in, in darkness, and the black cloaks turned into people, they came as seducing spirits to seduce that church, to check it out. My people are dying from lack of knowledge.[34] They need to understand that they know the Spirit of God. And when they feel this evil around people, they need to pray. They need to

34. See Hosea 4:6.

go to their pastor and ask him about it; they are not to be paranoid but to know and understand the Spirit of the living God." I thought back to a time when I had spoken at a particular church that was prospering. I had seen evil powers sitting in the audience, but I didn't understand what they were at that time. God hadn't yet given me the knowledge. But a few years later, that church was gone.

Jesus is telling us that if we don't pray for the protection of our fellow believers and travail for those who need to be saved, there will be few spiritual new births. Satan does not want us to intercede like that, because he desires to keep people from coming to a knowledge of the truth in Jesus Christ. Once I was participating in a church prayer meeting in which a woman was earnestly travailing for souls to be saved, and I saw another woman go over and lay a hand on the stomach of the first woman, while speaking in a strange language; this caused the woman's travail to abruptly end. The first woman got up and cried, saying, "You stopped my travail." I knew that the second woman was associated with the devil, and it turned out that she was a practicing witch. Some of Satan's workers are deliberately infiltrating our churches. The devil uses people like that to try to stop our travail to God. We must fight against the enemy so that our prayers can go forth to the Lord for ourselves and for the rest of His people.

> [The Lord said,] *"I sought for a man among them who would make a wall, and stand in the gap before Me on behalf of the land, that I should not destroy it; but I found no one."*
>
> —Ezekiel 22:30

I told Jesus, "Oh, my God, this is horrible." Then Christ said, speaking of the church (all believers throughout the world—men and women, boys and girls), "Arise, O bride; My bride, come out of this filth, come out of this. The bride of Christ, arise."

EXERCISE DISCERNMENT AND UNDERSTANDING

As I watched the vision of the church from which the Spirit of the Lord had departed, the dead in hell began to scream and talk again. I said, "Oh, God, you mean all these standing here in chains are going to be thrown into that quicksand because they were deceived and seduced by the devil and enjoyed it?" He said, "I am God. I will save My elect and My righteous from this place. I know how to give them the power to overcome temptation. You blow your trumpet on them and let them seek My Word. It is time to arise from a dead sleep and hear what the Spirit of the Lord is saying to the churches. Repent, repent."

Therefore let him who thinks he stands take heed lest he fall. No temptation has overtaken you except such as is common to man; but God is faithful, who will not allow you to be tempted beyond what you are able, but with the temptation will also make the way of escape, that you may be able to bear it.

—1 Corinthians 10:12–13

The Lord continued, "Watch over My flock, you leaders. I have given you the discernment and the understanding. Pray with your wife or your husband. You are not alone. Don't be so deceived, saith the Lord, when you know in your heart things aren't right and somebody is trying to destroy you. Satan is very cunning and very wise. He tricks many people. So understand that I came to give life and love and happiness and joy. Help the poor, feed the little children, do the work of an evangelist, preach My Word. For I have many great churches in the earth, and many great pastors and leaders. They take care of the homeless and the widows."

I said, "Jesus, I am so afraid that I will not relate this just like You want it." He replied, "Child, you have the Holy Spirit, and the Holy Spirit is your Leader and your Teacher, bringing all things to your remembrance."

I looked back at the demon that held the plaque of names and saw him take that skeleton whose church I had seen in the vision and throw him into the boiling hot, raging fire and quicksand. Then my eyes were opened to see further into this place, and there were at least twenty more of those quicksand pits, and twenty more demons and many more skeletons screaming and crying. I said, "Oh, my God." Jesus said, "Come and see."

We walked to another area of quicksand where demons were doing the same thing to a different group of skeletons in chains. These souls were some backslidden leaders who had left their cross behind instead of taking it up and continuing to follow Jesus. Some of them had received a great calling, but they had laid down that calling, saying it was too hard. (I know that fulfilling one's calling does get very hard at times.) And then there were others who had been given musical gifts. It seemed to me that their situation was related to some of the glass cages I had seen with the musical instruments and the music sheets. They had stopped using their gifts, and Satan had stolen those gifts and put bondage after bondage on the people, and they wouldn't trust the Lord.

Jesus said, "I have many who have obeyed Me and kept My charge on the earth. I want the world to know—those to whom I have given calls and blessings and great gifts—that your gifts are very important to the body of Christ. How will the bride arise if you don't use your gifts to set the captives free? I gave you the power in My name to set the captives free. That means to rebuke the devil, cast out evil spirits, heal the sick, raise the dead. Awake, awake, My bride. Katherine, awaken them."

Our time in hell was completed for that night. But as Christ was speaking, I was thinking that what He was saying summed up one of the primary purposes for my journey into hell, which is also the main purpose of this book. It was to show us that as time goes on, some people change; they fall and compromise God's Word, and they ultimately end up in hell. We are being warned not to be careless or unfaithful or hard-hearted so that we will not experience the same fate.

These revelations are for today. God is showing us how people end up in hell because they desire the works of the flesh more than obeying God's commandments.

RECLAIMING THE KEYS AND GIFTS OF GOD:

After reading the following passage of Scripture, answer these questions: In what ways does this passage describe genuine faith? What are some things that cause us to compromise the Word of God? How can we stay faithful to God's Word?

> *Therefore lay aside all filthiness and overflow of wickedness, and receive with meekness the implanted word, which is able to save your souls. But be doers of the word, and not hearers only, deceiving yourselves. For if anyone is a hearer of the word and not a doer, he is like a man observing his natural face in a mirror; for he observes himself, goes away, and immediately forgets what kind of man he was. But he who looks into the perfect law of liberty and continues in it, and is not a forgetful hearer but a doer of the work, this one will be blessed in what he does. If anyone among you thinks he is religious, and does not bridle his tongue but deceives his own heart, this one's religion is useless. Pure and undefiled religion before God and the Father is this: to visit orphans and widows in their trouble, and to keep oneself unspotted from the world.*
>
> (James 1:21–27)

13

AWAKE, MY BRIDE

The Lord Jesus again appeared to me at night, and we were immediately standing in hell. He was holding my spiritual hand, and my hand felt so warm. I looked up at my King, and He said, "Child, this new book that we are doing is given to you by the Holy Spirit, the Father, and Me. This is the one that will bring back and awaken My bride. This is the one that will bring in many souls all over the earth. My hand is upon you, upon this work, and upon your whole family. All things are going to come into order now." I noticed that Jesus was smiling for the first time in a long while.

He continued, "Child, I know it is very hard on you to walk among the dead and to relate these stories, but these are true revelations given from almighty God. And to those who would try to think it is witchcraft, or those who would try to think it is 'way out there,' I say, 'Study your Bible, understand the mysteries, the revelations, given by God Almighty to My prophets and My prophetesses and My apostles.' This is the hour like no other, and I say,

'Woe to you who touch My child, for she is Mine. And hear the Word of the Lord. This book will awaken thousands in the earth and give them the reality and the understanding of how Satan works to destroy them. But yet there is hope in Me; there are blessings in Me; there is truth in Me. And I will watch over you, your families, and all that belongs to you, and I will add blessings, if you will only believe and call out to Me. Now hear ye the Word of the Lord. It is now time for the earth to awaken. Awake, My bride.'" And with that, we began to walk.

GOD WILL POUR OUT HIS SPIRIT AND GRACE IN ABUNDANCE

This time, it seemed only a very short distance to where we were going. Around me were the cries of the dead, the skeletons reaching up and screaming, and the pits. As we walked, Jesus would speak and cause light to appear. At times, demons that came too near the light and the fire of God would be cremated.

The closer we got to the top of a hill, I wondered if it was the same hill I had been on before. Jesus knew my thoughts, and He said, "No. I want to show you something, child." When we reached the summit, we could see everything that was going on in a certain area in hell. I said, "Jesus, are we still in the right arm of hell?" He said, "Yes. The right hand or arm of My Father or of Me or of individuals means power. Now, as you look down below, I want to show you certain torments in this place and explain that Satan has devised and sent out many powerful spirits, seducing powers, against My elect and against the mighty, mighty, mighty power of God. We need people, Katherine, on the earth. We need people to listen to the Spirit of God and to hear His truth. We need the earth to awaken and know that there is a God Almighty over all gods, over every god; a God Almighty, the Lord. Hear what I am saying."

We sat down on a rock, and Jesus said, "Look, child, and behold. God did not make hell for people but for the devil and his angels,[35] but because sin has run rampant, hell has enlarged itself to hold more lost souls. Satan knows much about the kingdom of God, but he does not know all; neither do the angels. My Father is the One who can speak and cause things to happen. I can speak and cause things to happen. Child, there is much for you to report in this book. I am guarding over it with My mighty angels. My warfaring angels are around your home, watching over you and your families. Now, where sin does abound, My grace does much more abound.[36] My Spirit and My grace are going to be poured out in abundance, and thousands are going to come to Me. I have a network of people whom I am going to use to bring in a great revival."

> *And it shall come to pass afterward that I will pour out My Spirit on all flesh; your sons and your daughters shall prophesy, your old men shall dream dreams, your young men shall see visions. And also on My menservants and on My maidservants I will pour out My Spirit in those days.*
>
> —Joel 2:28–29

Jesus continued, "Now let us talk about what is around us here. Look over to your left." He was revealing to me things about the earth. I looked over to my left, all the way to the bottom of the mountain, which appeared to be miles below us. Naturally, there were no trees but only burned, dry, rotten stuff and burned black rocks. I saw a swiftly flowing river, but it was full of corruption, such as dung and slithering snakes. Skeletons were bobbing up and down in this river. I said, "Oh, my God, what is that?" Jesus said, "Child, that is the River of Death. Many times on the

35. See Matthew 25:41.
36. See Romans 5:20.

earth, I called those people whom you see screaming in the slime. I worked with them, I ministered to them, I sent others to prophesy to them, but they were stiff-necked and strong-willed and would not humble themselves before Me. When death came, they did not have time to repent. They were people whom My Father wanted to use to awaken My bride and put order in the earth. But the enemy used much seduction and many deceiving powers on them. And yes, they knew the way, they understood the way, but they did not want the narrow way. So, they chose the broad way."[37]

As I looked more closely, it was as if I was standing right by the river. Jesus was standing by the river, too. We had instantly moved from the mountaintop down to the river through Jesus' power. And the skeletons, with their bony hands, could see us.

I looked behind me and saw large, ugly demons. Some of them were twenty feet high, some thirty, and some fifty. They were growling, but they could not come near us because of Jesus' power. And then Jesus and I instantly returned to the top of the mountain. The Lord said, "Tell My people out there, Katherine; blow the trumpet in Zion. Tell them that if I have chosen them and called them to repent and turn unto Me, they are able to do the work for Me in the ministry to save the lost from eternal damnation."

Then He said, "Look over to your right." As I looked, I saw something down below the mountain that seemed to be an enormous tree, about a hundred feet high and a hundred feet wide, standing in the middle of an area surrounded by muck, dirt, rocks, and fire.

Very quickly, we were down the mountain again, and we were standing next to that huge tree, which was full of corruption and evil and had a horrible stench, like death. I said, "What is this, Lord Jesus?" He said, "This is Satan's tree of evil." Immediately, the

37. See Matthew 7:13–14.

tree changed so that it appeared healthy. It looked like it had good fruit on it. I said, "Oh, my Lord, what does this mean?" He said, "Keep watching." I looked again, and the tree had turned to gold; then it turned to silver, and then it turned back into the corrupt tree that it really was. Jesus said, "I have called My bride to be trees of righteousness.[38] Satan therefore has a tree of evil to corrupt My bride, enticing My people with gold, with silver, and with many corrupt ways."

As I watched the tree of evil, its fruit became full of worms and maggots and fell off the branches. Jesus said, "The fruit that people are bearing is like that. They are not using My Holy Scriptures to be humble, kind, and forgiving, and to keep from greed, lust, and the love of money. Their god is money." As Jesus said that, the tree again turned to gold; there were big gold coins all over it. I thought, *Oh, my God, it is all an illusion, isn't it, Jesus?* He said, "It's an illusion that the devil is using to deceive his bride. The true bride of Christ will awaken and praise Me and thank Me for everything, Katherine, good or bad. The true bride of Christ will surrender all to Me. I am their King. I am their powerful King. I can do anything for them."

> *Now to Him who is able to do exceedingly abundantly above all that we ask or think, according to the power that works in us, to Him be glory in the church by Christ Jesus to all generations, forever and ever.* —Ephesians 3:20–21

I looked at the tree again, and there were strange, wicked-looking objects on it. They were so wicked I can't even describe them. But the tree seemed to enjoy them; it sprang to life, and all at once its leaves were green. New leaves were growing on it, too, but inside them were demonic faces. I said, "Oh, my Lord, what

38. See Isaiah 61:3.

is this?" He said, "This is the occult, the black arts, the white arts of Satan working with him to corrupt My bride. My bride cannot lust after the world; My people must stop their lust and look to Me, for this is an hour like no other. And these things I am showing you in here will awaken My bride. I tell My people to repent. I tell others to repent."

From the top of the mountain, we walked over to another place where there was a huge bank vault sitting on top of a bunch of corruption and floating in debris. Then I saw demons come and open the vault. They put riches into it—gold, paper money, and coins—and they laughed and said, "We deceived people. We stole their money. We had them make bad investments. We had them lie. Oh, is Satan going to be proud of us!" They had a list of the works they had done on the earth. The vault closed, but many other demons also came and placed into it treasures they had stolen from people on the earth.

There was a bridge over the foul-smelling debris that the vault was floating in. I looked at the Lord and asked, "Jesus, what is this?" He said, "Awaken My bride, My people; tell them not to put their money into foolish things, into lies and debris. Tell My bride to seek first the kingdom of God, and all these things will be added unto them.[39] Tell My bride to awaken to truth and righteousness and to repent of their sins, to truly repent.

"This vault contains things stolen from My bride, things that I had planned for My bride. People say, 'Well, what about Abraham and Isaac and Jacob? They had abundance.' Yes, and you shall have what you need, and some of you shall have abundance to help and to filter back into the kingdom of God. But, My bride, you have greed in you. You have the spirit of greed and lust. Repent, My bride, of greed and lust."

---

39. See Matthew 6:33.

So are the ways of everyone who is greedy for gain; it takes away the life of its owners. —Proverbs 1:19

PRAY FOR THE WORLD AND SEEK GOD'S COUNSEL

We walked on to another area, and Jesus showed me a vision that amazed me. There was a huge bar, or tavern, that looked just like one on the earth. In it, some people were playing pool and others were sitting at the bar drinking, but they were so drunk; they were so evil. A man got up and stabbed another man. The man who had been stabbed pulled a gun, but then he dropped dead because somebody else had suddenly shot him. I screamed, "Oh no, Lord, You said this is going on in the earth today."

Then He showed me a flash of something that I didn't understand. There were scenes upon the earth of great corruption and violence. Jesus said, "Awaken My bride to pray." He showed me little children who were being used for sex objects. It was as if I was watching a movie of various corrupt things going on throughout the whole earth. He said, "Tell My bride to awaken and pray. Tell people to repent of their sins." I said, "Oh, Jesus; oh, Jesus."

He said, "Come, there is much more to show you." We went to an area where there were many huge cages. I wept when I saw them. I was standing beside the Lord, and He was crying, too. Jesus told me, "Child, look at the cages." In each cage was something that was part human and part beast. He said, "Man is trying to copy God and create a human with beasts. They are trying to raise an army. My Father is so grieved over this, and I am so grieved, that He is going to destroy the earth with great judgment if My bride does not awaken and begin to pray and seek His counsel and do what I say. There are secret laboratories all over the earth, including the jail system. Woe to you, earth, woe to those doing this, for they are using the jail inmates for scientific purposes, and you never hear from them again. Woe, saith Jesus, to these evil works in the earth and to those who are operating them."

I began to cry again. Jesus said, "Come and see this, child. Awaken My bride; blow the trumpet in Zion." We went to a different area, and I was shown another vision. Jesus said, "Look and behold." I saw a very large hospital on which the word "Death" was written. Many pregnant women were standing inside. They would go into the abortion room, at least five at a time, and different doctors would abort their babies. I saw the blood flow out of the women and onto the floor. Some of the women died, and the doctors actually killed some of the women and the babies. I said, "Oh, my God, how can this be?" He said, "Secret laboratories. Look at the baby." The baby was part beast and part human.

I remembered that many years ago, I had had a vision of the same thing. I had been deep in prayer when the Lord showed me this, and I've never revealed it until now. Jesus said, "It is time to warn the earth that this wickedness must stop; it is time for My people to arise and seek God for wisdom and knowledge."

THE CALL OF GOD

Jesus and were back at the top of the mountain, and He said, "There is a time to reap and a time to sow. This book is coming out just on time.

"I have many fine churches in the earth and many fine leaders. But yet I need more to arise and to answer My call and to be chosen by God. After you are called by God, you walk through testing times and times of trial. It's like an army. An army goes through a lot to be on the front lines. God calls you, and then, when you answer, Satan will put you through certain situations, but then God always delivers. He knows how to deliver the godly out of temptation.[40] But I need more people to stop being occupied

40. See 2 Peter 2:9.

with the cares of the world and to hear what I am saying. I have chosen you, Katherine, as a prophetess, a visionary, a writer, for you were born to see and to tell these things. And in the midst of it, I blessed you with children, a home, grandchildren, great-grandchildren. I blessed you. And I am going to continue to bless you, little one, for you are sincere and you are righteous in Me. You are a tree of righteousness, and you are bearing good fruit."

As we were sitting on that mountain in hell, I was thinking about how Jesus was talking to me and encouraging me. And all around, I saw thousands who hadn't obeyed Him. I saw thousands and thousands who hadn't understood that hell was real. I began to be grieved again. I held the Lord's hand, and we both wept. He said, "Child, I raised up others, too, to whom I showed hell. And some of them were made to tell about it. Some of them were afraid. Some of them just said, 'Absolutely no; I'll never tell it. They'll think I'm crazy.' Behold, I've told you secret things that you've never told anybody. Behold, there is much more that I am going to reveal to you. But if the people would hear and listen to the Holy Bible and to the voices of the apostles, prophets, evangelists, pastors, and teachers, they would understand that the call of God is so important. And then the enemy comes and sends everything in your way to get you caught up in the cares of the world."

The ones sown among thorns...are the ones who hear the word, and the cares of this world, the deceitfulness of riches, and the desires for other things entering in choke the word, and it becomes unfruitful. But these are the ones sown on good ground, those who hear the word, accept it, and bear fruit: some thirtyfold, some sixty, and some a hundred.

—Mark 4:18–20

Often, when I have been in prayer, the Holy Spirit has said, "I called, and I called, and I called. And I call those to repent and to come unto Me. And I call, and I call, and they do not come. They are too busy with the cares of this world to stop and hear what I have to say."

We must make time for God. Yes, we have to take time to address the concerns in our life. We have to take time for our children. We have to take time for other things. But if we put God first, it will all fall into place. Of course, we are going to make mistakes and fall short, but God understands that. He is not going to crush us or destroy us when we fail or make a mistake. He loves us so much. He is concerned about us, our children, our grandchildren, and our great-grandchildren. He cares about all our loved ones. He made a covenant with us when He went to the cross and shed His powerful blood for us. And we have a God who will keep His covenant with us even if we fall. He is there to pick us up, to give us hope, and to tell us how much He loves us and wants us to continue on.

I looked at Jesus my Savior, and His face began to light up. He touched me and gave me strength. Even now, He is touching me and giving me strength. I think back on the call of God for my life. Truly, to be chosen by God is the greatest honor in the world. But if all of you pastors, evangelists, and other fivefold ministry leaders wrote a book about your life, I know it would describe trials and heartaches similar to the ones I've had. It would reveal some of the difficulties that you've walked through but never before told anyone about. It would show how much you love God, and how you rejected the devil when he came and tempted you with fleshly desires, and how you've had to give up many things that the world refers to as pleasures—but that do not bring pleasure to God—because you are accountable to Him. The responsibility of God's leaders, and of all His children, is very serious. I know this book will bring much wisdom and knowledge from God for the body of

Christ and for those who need to repent of their sins and receive Jesus as their Lord and Savior.

Thank You, God. I love You and trust You. You are our Father, our Savior, our Healer, and our Deliverer.

RECLAIMING THE KEYS AND GIFTS OF GOD:

Have you been spending time with God regularly? If not, begin today to set aside time daily to worship God, to pray, to read His Word, and to seek His counsel. Ask Him to show you how to pray for the needs of your loved ones and for the state of the world.

14

BACK TO THE DOORS

The next night, when Jesus took me into hell, He said, "Come, child, we are going back to the doors of hell. I told you I would bring you back here." In chapters 10 and 11, I described how we had gone to the "Chamber of Death," where we began to enter the open doors in the sides of the large serpent. Each door represented the wickedness of the devil—something that Satan had taken from the body of Christ through his temptations and deceit and was holding captive, or something that Satan had inflicted on the people of the earth.

Door 1 contained many beautiful, valuable items, and Door 2 had piles of money from nations around the globe. These things had been stolen by Satan to rob God's people of His blessings and to deplete their means of spreading the gospel and helping the poor. Door 3 was the illusion of the coffins from the multitude of babies that had died as a result of Satan's trickery. Door 4 held the "movie theater" depicting many of Satan's evil acts throughout history.

Again, there were fifteen open doors and five closed ones in the snake. In this chapter, I will describe Doors 5 through 7. (An account of the other doors will be given in a later book.)

THROUGH DOOR 5

As Jesus and I walked through Door 5, I received a word in my mind from Jesus, saying, *The devil has stolen the communication between the people, the communication to Me, the prayers to Me, and the prayers for the people's family members and others. He has stolen the communication that I want from My people.*

Inside Door 5 was a very large room that looked like an office in a corporation or a bank. There were desks, computers, printers, sound devices, and paperwork. I said to Jesus, "What is this, Lord?" He replied, "The devil has stolen the communication between My people and Me, and also from My people's families. Whereas they should be communicating and talking and praying, they are fighting and arguing and doing the things of the world. The devil makes sure that there are times when people do not communicate. He works devices of evil to separate people and to separate things that should not be separated. For instance, when a ministry is going well, and the staff is all there and the leader gives people instructions, some of those people have not yet died to the flesh. They are with Me, but they are still in the world, too. They have not overcome, and I want them to overcome. I want them to stop complaining, murmuring, and grumbling and to seek My counsel and My face for the communication between them and God."

Therefore, my beloved, as you have always obeyed,…work out your own salvation with fear and trembling; for it is God who works in you both to will and to do for His good pleasure.

Do all things without complaining and disputing, that you may become blameless and harmless, children of God without fault in the midst of a crooked and perverse generation, among whom you shine as lights in the world, holding fast the word of life.

—Philippians 2:12–16

Jesus continued, "It is now time for the world to awaken and for people to recognize where they have hurt or wounded anybody deliberately. I am not saying innocently, but if you have done it deliberately and willfully and with manipulation, you need to repent. You need to come back to holiness, and you need to go make amends with your brother and your sister. Now, there are other times when what happens is justified. But always seek My face, seek My counsel, and obey Me; do what I tell you to do and read My holy Word."

I turned to the Lord and said, "You mean, Lord, even in our own lives, we don't communicate with certain people and clear up certain matters that are important to us because we fear that we are going to hurt or offend them?" And the Lord said, "That is true. I want My people to know that I love them and that there is My grace and My forgiveness. I want them to begin to communicate again and to love again and to share again. And I want to restore the hearts of the fathers to the children and the children's hearts unto the fathers—and that also means restoring people's hearts to God, My Father and your Father. I want to restore your relationships like the spirit of Elijah.[41] I want to restore the relationship between the people and My God; and in My name, you can restore that. You now have the power in My name to come to God anytime and ask for help from the sanctuary."[42]

I looked at Jesus, and strength came to His face. Of course, strength was already there, but I saw something else reflected, like

---

41. See Malachi 4:6; Luke 1:17.
42. See Psalm 20:2.

a new hope. I said, "Lord, it looks like there is hope all over You." And He said, "Yes, yes. These revelations of My Word will awaken My bride and bring back hope to the people, for I am a God who loves and forgives. Have them communicate with Me and talk to Me and tell Me their troubles and their sorrows. I will care because I love them unconditionally. I hate wickedness, I hate evil, but I love My people. And I love the sinners, though not the evil things they are doing. Many of My people used to do the things of the world, but they turned from those things. They made up their minds, and they turned from their wicked ways back unto God. And I helped them overcome. That's My Word. That's My promise. And the Holy Spirit is a Comforter. Come, child, we are going to Doors 6 and 7."

Let us awaken to what Jesus is saying to us! We must be restored to God and to other people whom we have hurt and offended! It is a sin to manipulate and abuse others; this is a manifestation of the lusts of the flesh, "*fulfilling the desires of the flesh and of the mind*" (Ephesians 2:3). Those who do not repent, receive Christ, and remain in the love of God will face consequences for their manipulation. For example, in another place in hell, I had seen an enormous pile of mud that had four sides and reminded me of a skyscraper. Out of the top of it, mud spewed out like an exploding volcano. The thick mass of "mud lava" flowed into the river. Stuck within that mud were souls who had manipulated people on earth. They were screaming to die because they were being carried by this stream of mud up through the mud tower and out the top of it and down to the river again in an endless cycle.

Let us therefore humble ourselves, go to the Lord, repent of all our sins, and learn to love Him and other people.

Humble yourselves under the mighty hand of God, that He may exalt you in due time, casting all your care upon Him, for He cares for you. —1 Peter 5:6–7

THROUGH DOOR 6

I asked, "Lord, what's in Door 6?" He said, "Awaken My people; let them hear the sound of the alarm." I thought, *What in the world is in Door 6?* Inside, there were puzzles and games everywhere. There were tables with checkerboards and other kinds of games that I had never seen before. Jesus said, "This is called the Game Door, where people play games with God, where people threaten God." I saw writings on the wall in which people were declaring things like, "God, if You don't do this, I'm not going to do that." I heard voices saying, "I blame You, God, for my child dying." Then I heard other voices demanding, "Who do You think You are, God? I am not going to do this." I heard all kinds of excuses, all kinds of judgment of God, in the voices of men and women. I even heard people tell God, "Well, I am going to turn to Satan because he can give me more. I am going to go follow another god. I don't believe You." Such words were coming and going in this room. I told Jesus, "Oh, my Lord, this is horrible, horrible, what the people are saying against God."

Nobody was at the tables with the games, but the puzzle parts would move on their own, as if a force was controlling them. However, nothing about the games would fit or work out. I began, "Lord Jesus—," and then I saw writing appear on tablets. I don't know who was doing the writing, but the words were blaspheming God, blaming God, and saying that they had turned from God to familiar spirits.

I fully understand that these evil works were the result of Satan's efforts to get people to backslide, but the other side of it is that the Holy Spirit would give people a word or a prophecy from God, and many of them would change and return to Him; they would regain their hope and read their Bible.

The lessons from Door 6 are very important. Awake, bride of Christ. You have to stop blaming and hating God when something goes wrong. To do so is a great error. God Almighty could smite and destroy you if He wanted to, but He loves you and cares for you. Stop blaming Him and turn back to Him. He is the One who can help you.

I was very upset when we left Door 6, and I said, "Jesus, what awful, awful things." I looked down the row of other doors that we had not yet gone into, and I thought, *I don't know if I can take this.* However, we continued on.

THROUGH DOOR 7

We walked through Door 7, and Jesus said, "This is a vision. I am showing a church service." Many people were praising God with their hands raised. Some people were barely raising their hands and praising God, which was okay. And Jesus said, "I read the hearts of people."[43] When the people lowered their hands, I could read their hearts, too. I saw that the hearts of many of them were not clean. Many of them were continuing in their sins. Some people's hearts had black in them and some had white in them.

Then the service was over, and the people left. Some of them got in their cars and began to curse and blaspheme God. I said, "Oh, my Lord, they were in there praising Him." One person went out after church and got stone drunk. Another went out and sat with drug dealers. Other people did other wrong things.

The Lord said, "Yes, many whom I call unto Me have a lot of sin in their hearts, Katherine. And I want them to know I love them, but I want to change them. The ones with a bright light on them that you saw praising Me were those who have overcome. I want My people to overcome the sins of their flesh. I want them to call upon Me and ask Me to help them and deliver them. It is good that they go to My house and learn, even if they have not overcome yet. That is why I am showing you this in hell. This deceitfulness,

43. See, for example, 1 Chronicles 28:9.

this covertness, this drawing back to the world is from hell. I come to give My people liberty. I come to give them freedom and love."

Now the Lord is the Spirit; and where the Spirit of the Lord is, there is liberty. But we all, with unveiled face, beholding as in a mirror the glory of the Lord, are being transformed into the same image from glory to glory, just as by the Spirit of the Lord.
—2 Corinthians 3:17–18

Then Jesus said, "Now I want to show you another church service." The first vision went away, and I thanked God for His grace that pulls us in even when we haven't yet overcome. In the next vision, there was a wonderful movement of the power of God. I don't know where the church service was, but the people were shouting and praising, and all their hearts, except perhaps those of a few in the back of the church, were aflame for God.

Jesus said, "Katherine, bring liberty to My people through this book. Bring liberty back to My people." Then He shouted, "Liberty. Where God is, there is liberty!"

Lord, that is awesome, wonderful, beautiful!

RECLAIMING THE KEYS AND GIFTS OF GOD:

When things go wrong in your life, how do you react? Do you tend to blame God for them? Or do you keep trusting Him and thanking Him in the midst of the situation? When we blame God, we open the door for Satan to draw us away from our heavenly Father and His truth. God loves us unconditionally and cares for us. If you have been blaming God for anything, tell Him how you feel about what has gone wrong. Ask Him to forgive you for holding this situation against Him. Then ask Him to use it for good in your life, as only He is able to do, so that He can restore your joy and spiritual strength.

And we know that all things work together for good to those who love God, to those who are the called according to His purpose. (Romans 8:28)

15

PREPARE THE WAY OF THE LORD

It's been almost forty years since God first gave me revelations of hell. As I related things in this book that I've never before told anyone or written down, it was as if I was reliving it. Sometimes it feels as if all these things that Jesus reveals to me are too much, but He does so for the sake of people in every nation of the world. He wants them to know God, to live a life of freedom in Him, and to be saved for eternity.

JESUS WILL SHOW HIMSELF STRONG

Jesus has revealed to me more sections of hell in the last few years. For example, He showed me where there was a big sign in hell that said "False Gods." In that place, millions of souls were burning; fire came over their heads and under their feet; the fire flowed, then came together in a narrow space and burst out and shot up, falling down a mountainside that was burned and dry. As the screams of souls filled the air, Satan laughed and roared in the background. I thought, *Oh my God, who's going to stop people from reaching these fires?*

I remember looking up and seeing a dark opening. Jesus caused light to shine, and I could see many more skeletons falling down into the fire. Then He said, "Come on, I want to show you another thing." I said, "What is it, Lord?" He replied, "I know the heart of every man and woman, and when they give their heart to me, I come to live inside of them and be with them; I teach them and guide them. But I also know that there are many people with wicked hearts who can't wait to hurt, kill, steal, or lie, and yet I send workers to them. I send My Word to them to repent; I give them a space to repent. I send out My great mercy and grace.

"As you notice, there are many worms teething on these bones of the skeletons, and they feel that, Katherine. It's excruciating pain, and there's no relief." I thought, *Oh, God, thank You for saving me; thank You for saving people whom I know. Thank You, Jesus, for coming to earth to be our Savior.* And Jesus said, "My daughter, as I told you before, I'm going to raise up others who have seen hell. But I'm going to raise up some new people to see hell as the movie about this book is being made. I'm going to prove to the world who I am. And I'm going to do things and show Myself strong in these last days."

EVIL WILL BE UNCOVERED

As we walked, multitudes and multitudes were burning. Thousands of voices were clanging, "Let us die; let us die." I knew that many of these souls had come there since Jesus had first shown me hell. I *knew* it. And Jesus said, "Yes, child, I'm revealing to you new things, things that are so sad and so powerful that some people will be saved from the very fires of hell because of what I'm showing you."

It is so, so sad to understand this wisdom of God. Oh, how horrible to be in hell.

Jesus continued, "There are many seducing spirits in the earth, and yes, I did open your mind, bring back your remembrance to know all these things you've been talking about. But these are some new things now that I'm showing you and telling you. In heaven, God has a justice scale, just like any courtroom on the earth. My Father is a righteous Judge, He's a holy Judge, and you're going to see a place here for lawyers, doctors, and thieves who lied in the courtrooms, even some judges who lied for that 'almighty dollar,' the money. There are some righteous lawyers, judges, and doctors who deal justly with people. I am not talking about them."

I looked into that place and saw thousands of men and women who were wearing beautiful suits or other professional clothes. And then I saw the earth shake underneath them, and fire burst up out of the earth and engulfed them. Their clothes burned off, and they melted down to skeletons who screamed, "Let us die!" Jesus said, "My Word says, 'Woe to the lawyers.'[44] They have put many innocent people in jail, My child. They've let the wicked go free. They have put men and women in prison who did not need to be there. They have done many wicked things. If you notice, there were jail keepers in there also. They did it for the 'almighty dollar' and 'almighty manna.' I've seen people being beaten and killed, and then buried or burned—destroyed—in these prisons and jails in the earth, as if nobody knew. But I know. My Father knows. And a lot of this is going to be uncovered. When God sends His Spirit to uncover it, watch out, world!"

Again, there are honest lawyers, judges, and prison guards who deal justly with people. But there are others who commit terrible things such as these.

44. See Luke 11:46, 52.

I cringed as we walked away from that sight. Once more, I heard Jesus say, "Woe to the lawyers." And I thought, *These Scriptures are being fulfilled.*

The Lord Jesus turned to me, looked into my eyes, and said, "Child, we're going to go now. And this is the end of the journey for a while. I love you so much, and I'll be with you in the days ahead. I'll help you. I'll be with your family. I love you, child."

Then I heard Him say, "I'm coming to talk to you tomorrow night." With that, I was back in my home.

SATAN'S VISION IS CORRUPT

The next night, Jesus came and took me into hell one more time. The Lord said, "We're going to go to the eyes of hell, child." We went in where there were hollowed-out holes; all around them, as well as down into the head of hell, there were things that looked like rocks. And I saw the jaws of hell open and demons laughing.

I asked, "Lord, what are we doing here?" He said, "Look, listen, and learn." I watched as the circle around the eyes began to fill with worms and maggots. Satan came, and he had some kind of bucket. He scooped burning stuff into it and gave it to the demons to pour on the burning skeletons. Again, the fire didn't burn the worms or the rest of the vile stuff—just the skeletons. And Satan was laughing.

I looked at Christ, and He was crying. He said to me, "Child, you're going to tell the world about this place. And a movie shall be made out of this book. The world shall know that I am God Almighty. Bible Scriptures will come alive to people. They will fear the judgment of thy Father and turn unto Him. My Father and your Father gave Me permission to bring you here and to show you these things to prepare the earth for My return. I don't know when I will return; only My Father knows, not even the angels.[45] But I say to you, "Prepare ye the way of the Lord."

---

45. See Matthew 24:36.

> *As it is written in the book of the words of Isaiah the prophet, saying: "The voice of one crying in the wilderness: 'Prepare the way of the* Lord*; make His paths straight. Every valley shall be filled and every mountain and hill brought low; the crooked places shall be made straight and the rough ways smooth; and all flesh shall see the salvation of God.'"* —Luke 3:4–6

Then Jesus said, "Let's go." We began to ascend out of that place and into the fresh air above. I was so grateful. Yet, as we left, I could still hear the cries of the multitudes, the gnashing of teeth, the regret, the sorrow. I felt so sad and helpless. After we arrived at my home, Jesus sat by my bed until daylight, saying to me, "Peace, be still."

BELIEVE IN JESUS CHRIST

Jesus is so tender, so precious. I am telling you these things that He has related to me because He has asked me to, and because He loves you. Jesus doesn't want you to go to hell. He wants you to repent while you still can. He doesn't want you to think you have lots of time left on earth and then suddenly die and be gone from this life, only to end up in hell. Repent and trust in the Lord. Live for Him. Start attending a good church. Tell the truth about heaven and hell to your family members and neighbors, and let the Spirit of God draw them to salvation. Love one another as Christ has loved you. (See, for example, John 13:34.)

Hell is a place we need to fear so that we will not become complacent about our lives. We need to fear the judgment of God. We should fear God not because He can destroy us but because we reverence and love Him. We need to keep His Word as best we can. And if we fall, we must repent right away. Let us repent of all our sins and recommit our lives to God.

I don't really care if critics or other people laugh at this account, because I know a God who is going to show you that He is real. You don't want to die and wake up in hell for eternity because you didn't believe in Him. You can be saved. God asks you to believe that His Son Jesus Christ came to earth to die on the cross for your sins. He asks you to repent of your sins and to receive Jesus' sacrifice on your behalf, so that you can be cleansed from those sins through Jesus' precious blood.

If you don't know Jesus as your Savior, I urge you to receive Him right now. You can do so by praying this prayer:

> Heavenly Father,
>
> I believe in You and in Your Son Jesus Christ, who came to earth to die on the cross for my sins. I believe that You raised Him from the dead and that He is alive forever, so that everyone who believes in Him can receive eternal life. Because of what Jesus did for me, I ask You to forgive all my sins and to come into my heart and save my soul. Fill me with Your Holy Spirit, and help me to live for You from this day forward. Thank You for saving me and giving me a new life. In Jesus' name, amen.

> *For whatever is born of God overcomes the world. And this is the victory that has overcome the world—our faith. Who is he who overcomes the world, but he who believes that Jesus is the Son of God?*
>
> —1 John 5:4–5

STAND IN FREEDOM

If you already know Jesus Christ, remember that He came to set us free. The Lord told me, "Bring liberty to My people through this book." And the Scriptures say, *"It is for freedom that Christ has set us free. Stand firm, then, and do not let yourselves be burdened again by a yoke of slavery"* (Galatians 5:1 NIV).

We can live in freedom when we love God and stay faithful to Him, and when we recognize and expose Satan's deceptions. The Lord is calling all Christians to repent, to give ourselves wholeheartedly to Him, to understand the reality of hell, and to fight spiritually for those who are lost, sick, and oppressed by the devil. We need to exercise the gifts of the Spirit that God has given to us. And we must study the keys to the kingdom and diligently use them to win back what Satan has stolen from us.

In this book, we have discussed many keys to the kingdom, such as:

- binding and loosing
- the name of Jesus
- obedience to God
- compassion
- love
- a humble spirit
- spiritual discernment
- praise
- prayer
- righteousness
- the true Word of God
- faith
- the fire of God
- the gifts of the Spirit
- the restoration of the fivefold ministry gifts

When we all repent of our sins, when we turn to Jesus wholeheartedly, when we reject worldliness, disobedience, laziness, and greed, and when we use the keys to the kingdom and the gifts that Jesus has given to us, we can defeat Satan and reclaim the blessings and provision of God that we allowed the enemy to take from us. Remember that Jesus said this is a time of judgment for many of Satan's demons, when they will be destroyed and turned to ashes. This is a time for binding and loosing. We can have victory over the devil, and we can bring many people into salvation, freedom, and prosperity in God. We can bring deliverance, turning people from the power of Satan unto God, in Jesus' name! (See Acts 26:18.)

I recommend that you read this work alongside your Bible and balance what is written here with the Holy Scriptures. Love Jesus with all your heart, and serve Him to the glory of God!

Remember, if you fail and feel like giving up, go back to Jesus. He will be there to lift you up. Turn to Him for help, for He has promised to take you back. (See, for example, John 6:37.)

RECEIVE EVERLASTING LIFE

Just as I was finishing *A Divine Revelation of Satan's Deceptions,* the Lord gave me a vision to share with you so that you would understand His intention for this book. I saw the hands of the Lord, and light was upon them. In His left hand, the Lord was holding an old-fashioned, long-necked, transparent bottle. With His right hand, He began to unscrew the lid. The water inside that bottle was alive!

And the Lord told me that you should read about His *"living water"* in John 4:10–14, 23 and John 7:38. The reason for this entire book is to pour out His living water on us. He also said to read about the *"bread of life"* in John 6:35–58. He wants to bring us into an understanding of who He is and of the bread of life He wants to give us, if we would only come to Him. This living water, this bread of life, is everlasting life. When we receive Christ, we have life eternal with Him, and we will never die.

> *For God so loved the world that He gave His only begotten Son, that whoever believes in Him should not perish but have everlasting life.* (John 3:16)

EPILOGUE:

WORDS OF LIBERTY FROM THE LORD

The spirit of prophecy (see Revelation 19:10) spoke to me and said, "Yea, saith the Spirit of the Lord, this is the end of this book, but there will be another book to reveal more to the body of Christ. This book will bring liberty, liberty, liberty to My people and to sinners. I will bless this book. It will go around the world in every language. This book, My daughter, will be blessed financially. This book is of God Almighty. It is dedicated to the Father, to the Son, and to the Holy Spirit. It is liberty I am bringing through these pages, My children. Arise, My bride. Awake, My bride. Awake, My preachers and My leaders. Come back to Me, for I love you. And I need you. I need you in the earth to spread My gospel; I need you for the work of God. The supernatural power of God will come and give you visions and dreams and revelations. So, this is the work of the Holy Spirit, My children. And yea, I say that liberty will come through the reading of this book and of the Holy Bible. Liberty, My children; this is to all, saith the Lord Jesus Christ."

SELECT SCRIPTURES ON SATAN, SPIRITUAL DECEPTION, AND TEMPTATION

SATAN'S CHARACTERISTICS

The devil...was a murderer from the beginning, and does not stand in the truth, because there is no truth in him. When he speaks a lie, he speaks from his own resources, for he is a liar and the father of it. (John 8:44)

The thief [the devil] *does not come except to steal, and to kill, and to destroy.* (John 10:10)

He who sins is of the devil, for the devil has sinned from the beginning. For this purpose the Son of God was manifested, that He might destroy the works of the devil. (1 John 3:8)

Be sober, be vigilant; because your adversary the devil walks about like a roaring lion, seeking whom he may devour. (1 Peter 5:8)

The great dragon was cast out, that serpent of old, called the Devil and Satan, who deceives the whole world; he was cast to the earth, and his angels were cast out with him. Then I heard a loud voice saying in heaven, "Now salvation, and strength, and the kingdom of our God, and the power of His Christ have come, for the accuser of our brethren, who accused them before our God day and night, has been cast down."

(Revelation 12:9–10)

SATAN'S DECEPTIONS

The L*ORD* *God said to the woman, "What is this you have done?" The woman said, "The serpent deceived me, and I ate."* (Genesis 3:13)

For false christs and false prophets will rise and show great signs and wonders to deceive, if possible, even the elect.

(Matthew 24:24)

If our gospel is veiled, it is veiled to those who are perishing, whose minds the god of this age has blinded, who do not believe, lest the light of the gospel of the glory of Christ, who is the image of God, should shine on them.

(2 Corinthians 4:3–4)

The coming of the lawless one is according to the working of Satan, with all power, signs, and lying wonders, and with all unrighteous deception among those who perish, because they did not receive the love of the truth, that they might be saved. And for this reason God will send them strong delusion, that they should believe the lie, that they all may be condemned who did not believe the truth but had pleasure in unrighteousness. (2 Thessalonians 2:9–12)

Then I saw an angel coming down from heaven, having the key to the bottomless pit and a great chain in his hand. He laid hold of the dragon, that serpent of old, who is the Devil and Satan, and bound him for a thousand years; and he cast him into the bottomless pit, and shut him up, and set a seal on him, so that he should deceive the nations no more till the thousand years were finished. But after these things he must be released for a little while. (Revelation 20:1–3)

SATAN'S TEMPTATIONS

Then Jesus was led up by the Spirit into the wilderness to be tempted by the devil. And when He had fasted forty days and forty nights, afterward He was hungry. Now when the tempter came to Him, he said, "If You are the Son of God, command that these stones become bread." But He answered and said, "It is written, 'Man shall not live by bread alone, but by every word that proceeds from the mouth of God.'" Then the devil took Him up into the holy city, set Him on the pinnacle of the temple, and said to Him, "If You are the Son of God, throw Yourself down. For it is written: 'He shall give His angels charge over you,' and, 'In their hands they shall bear you up, Lest you dash your foot against a stone.'" Jesus said to him, "It is written again, 'You shall not tempt the LORD your God.'" Again, the devil took Him up on an exceedingly high mountain, and showed Him all the kingdoms of the world and their glory. And he said to Him, "All these things I will give You if You will fall down and worship me." Then Jesus said to him, "Away with you, Satan! For it is written, 'You shall worship the LORD your God, and Him only you shall serve.'" Then the devil left Him, and behold, angels came and ministered to Him. (Matthew 4:1–11)

Watch and pray, lest you enter into temptation. The spirit indeed is willing, but the flesh is weak. (Matthew 26:41)

Therefore let him who thinks he stands take heed lest he fall. No temptation has overtaken you except such as is common to man; but God is faithful, who will not allow you to be tempted beyond what you are able, but with the temptation will also make the way of escape, that you may be able to bear it.
(1 Corinthians 10:12–13)

Let the husband render to his wife the affection due her, and likewise also the wife to her husband. The wife does not have authority over her own body, but the husband does. And likewise the husband does not have authority over his own body, but the wife does. Do not deprive one another except with consent for a time, that you may give yourselves to fasting and prayer; and come together again so that Satan does not tempt you because of your lack of self-control.
(1 Corinthians 7:3–5)

Blessed is the man who endures temptation; for when he has been approved, he will receive the crown of life which the Lord has promised to those who love Him. Let no one say when he is tempted, "I am tempted by God"; for God cannot be tempted by evil, nor does He Himself tempt anyone. But each one is tempted when he is drawn away by his own desires and enticed. Then, when desire has conceived, it gives birth to sin; and sin, when it is full-grown, brings forth death.
(James 1:12–15)

SATAN'S DISTORTION OF GOD'S WORD/FALSE DOCTRINE

Now the Spirit expressly says that in latter times some will depart from the faith, giving heed to deceiving spirits and doctrines of demons, speaking lies in hypocrisy, having their own conscience seared with a hot iron...."

(1 Timothy 4:1–2)

For such are false apostles, deceitful workers, transforming themselves into apostles of Christ. And no wonder! For Satan himself transforms himself into an angel of light. Therefore it is no great thing if his ministers also transform themselves into ministers of righteousness, whose end will be according to their works. (2 Corinthians 11:13–15)

A servant of the Lord must not quarrel but be gentle to all, able to teach, patient, in humility correcting those who are in opposition, if God perhaps will grant them repentance, so that they may know the truth, and that they may come to their senses and escape the snare of the devil, having been taken captive by him to do his will. (2 Timothy 2:24–26)

SATAN'S STEALING OF THE WORD/TRIALS/ THE CARES OF THE WORLD

The sower sows the word. And these are the ones by the wayside where the word is sown. When they hear, Satan comes immediately and takes away the word that was sown in their hearts. These likewise are the ones sown on stony ground who, when they hear the word, immediately receive it with gladness; and they have no root in themselves, and so endure only for a time. Afterward, when tribulation or persecution arises for the word's sake, immediately they stumble. Now these are the ones sown among thorns; they are the ones who hear the word, and the cares of this world, the deceitfulness of riches, and the desires for other things entering in choke the word, and it becomes unfruitful. But these are the ones sown on good ground, those who hear the word, accept it, and bear fruit:

some thirtyfold, some sixty, and some a hundred.
(Mark 4:14–20)

But Martha was distracted with much serving, and she approached [Jesus] *and said, "Lord, do You not care that my sister has left me to serve alone? Therefore tell her to help me." And Jesus answered and said to her, "Martha, Martha, you are worried and troubled about many things. But one thing is needed, and Mary has chosen that good part, which will not be taken away from her."* (Luke 10:40–42)

THE WORKS AND LUSTS OF THE FLESH

Now the works of the flesh are evident, which are: adultery, fornication, uncleanness, lewdness, idolatry, sorcery, hatred, contentions, jealousies, outbursts of wrath, selfish ambitions, dissensions, heresies, envy, murders, drunkenness, revelries, and the like; of which I tell you beforehand, just as I also told you in time past, that those who practice such things will not inherit the kingdom of God. (Galatians 5:19–21)

Do not love the world or the things in the world. If anyone loves the world, the love of the Father is not in him. For all that is in the world—the lust of the flesh, the lust of the eyes, and the pride of life—is not of the Father but is of the world. And the world is passing away, and the lust of it; but he who does the will of God abides forever. (1 John 2:15–17)

Do not be deceived, God is not mocked; for whatever a man sows, that he will also reap. For he who sows to his flesh will of the flesh reap corruption, but he who sows to the Spirit will of the Spirit reap everlasting life. (Galatians 6:7–8)

Come now, you who say, "Today or tomorrow we will go to such and such a city, spend a year there, buy and sell, and make a profit"; whereas you do not know what will happen tomorrow. For what is your life? It is even a vapor that appears for a little time and then vanishes away. Instead you ought to say, "If the Lord wills, we shall live and do this or that." But now you boast in your arrogance. All such boasting is evil.

(James 4:13–16)

Now godliness with contentment is great gain. For we brought nothing into this world, and it is certain we can carry nothing out. And having food and clothing, with these we shall be content. But those who desire to be rich fall into temptation and a snare, and into many foolish and harmful lusts which drown men in destruction and perdition. For the love of money is a root of all kinds of evil, for which some have strayed from the faith in their greediness, and pierced themselves through with many sorrows. (1 Timothy 6:6–10)

SELECT SCRIPTURES ON THE KEYS AND GIFTS OF GOD

SEEKING THE KINGDOM

But seek the kingdom of God, and all these things shall be added to you. Do not fear, little flock, for it is your Father's good pleasure to give you the kingdom. Sell what you have and give alms; provide yourselves money bags which do not grow old, a treasure in the heavens that does not fail, where no thief approaches nor moth destroys. For where your treasure is, there your heart will be also. (Luke 12:31–34)

BINDING AND LOOSING

Upon this rock I will build my church; and the gates of hell shall not prevail against it. And I will give unto thee the keys of the kingdom of heaven: and whatsoever thou shalt bind on earth shall be bound in heaven: and whatsoever thou shalt loose on earth shall be loosed in heaven.

(Matthew 16:18–19 KJV)

Assuredly, I say to you, whatever you bind on earth will be bound in heaven, and whatever you loose on earth will be loosed in heaven. Again I say to you that if two of you agree on earth concerning anything that they ask, it will be done for them by My Father in heaven. For where two or three are gathered together in My name, I am there in the midst of them. (Matthew 18:18–20)

JESUS' AUTHORITY

The Spirit of the Lord *is upon Me, because He has anointed Me to preach the gospel to the poor; He has sent Me to heal the brokenhearted, to proclaim liberty to the captives and recovery of sight to the blind, to set at liberty those who are oppressed.* (Luke 4:18)

God anointed Jesus of Nazareth with the Holy Spirit and with power, who went about doing good and healing all who were oppressed by the devil, for God was with Him. (Acts 10:38)

And when He had called His twelve disciples to Him, He gave them power over unclean spirits, to cast them out, and to heal all kinds of sickness and all kinds of disease. (Matthew 10:1)

Then [Jesus] *went down to Capernaum, a city of Galilee, and was teaching them on the Sabbaths. And they were astonished at His teaching, for His word was with authority. Now in the synagogue there was a man who had a spirit of an unclean demon. And he cried out with a loud voice, saying, "Let us alone! What have we to do with You, Jesus of Nazareth? Did You come to destroy us? I know who You are—the Holy One of God!" But Jesus rebuked him, saying, "Be quiet, and come out of him!" And when the demon had thrown him in their midst, it came out of him and did not hurt him. Then they were all amazed and spoke among themselves, saying, "What a word this is! For with authority and power He commands the unclean spirits, and they come out."* (Luke 4:31–36)

And Jesus came and spoke to [His disciples], *saying, "All authority has been given to Me in heaven and on earth. Go therefore and make disciples of all the nations, baptizing them in the name of the Father and of the Son and of the Holy Spirit, teaching them to observe all things that I have commanded you; and lo, I am with you always, even to the end of the age."* (Matthew 28:18–20)

Having disarmed principalities and powers, [Jesus] *made a public spectacle of them, triumphing over them in it.* (Colossians 2:15)

God also has highly exalted [Jesus] *and given Him the name which is above every name, that at the name of Jesus every knee should bow, of those in heaven, and of those on earth, and of those under the earth, and that every tongue should confess that Jesus Christ is Lord, to the glory of God the Father.* (Philippians 2:9–11)

Most assuredly, I say to you, the hour is coming, and now is, when the dead will hear the voice of the Son of God; and those who hear will live. For as the Father has life in Himself, so He has granted the Son to have life in Himself, and has given Him authority to execute judgment also, because He is the Son of Man. Do not marvel at this; for the hour is coming in which all who are in the graves will hear His voice and come forth—those who have done good, to the resurrection of life, and those who have done evil, to the resurrection of condemnation. (John 5:25–29)

THE NAME OF JESUS

Then the seventy [disciples] *returned with joy, saying, "Lord, even the demons are subject to us in Your name." And He said to them, "I saw Satan fall like lightning from heaven. Behold, I give you the authority to trample on serpents and scorpions, and over all the power of the enemy, and nothing shall by any means hurt you. Nevertheless do not rejoice in this, that the spirits are subject to you, but rather rejoice because your names are written in heaven."* (Luke 10:17–20)

Most assuredly, I say to you, he who believes in Me, the works that I do he will do also; and greater works than these he will do, because I go to My Father. And whatever you ask in My name, that I will do, that the Father may be glorified in the Son. If you ask anything in My name, I will do it.
(John 14:12–14)

And truly Jesus did many other signs in the presence of His disciples, which are not written in this book; but these are written that you may believe that Jesus is the Christ, the Son of God, and that believing you may have life in His name.
(John 20:30–31)

Then Peter, filled with the Holy Spirit, said to them, "Rulers of the people and elders of Israel: If we this day are judged for a good deed done to a helpless man, by what means he has been made well, let it be known to you all, and to all the people of Israel, that by the name of Jesus Christ of Nazareth, whom you crucified, whom God raised from the dead, by Him this man stands here before you whole. This is the 'stone which was rejected by you builders, which has become the chief cornerstone.' Nor is there salvation in any other, for there is no other

name under heaven given among men by which we must be saved."
(Acts 4:8–12)

Now it happened, as we went to prayer, that a certain slave girl possessed with a spirit of divination met us, who brought her masters much profit by fortune-telling. This girl followed Paul and us, and cried out, saying, "These men are the servants of the Most High God, who proclaim to us the way of salvation." And this she did for many days. But Paul, greatly annoyed, turned and said to the spirit, "I command you in the name of Jesus Christ to come out of her." And he came out that very hour.
(Acts 16:16–18)

You did not choose Me, but I chose you and appointed you that you should go and bear fruit, and that your fruit should remain, that whatever you ask the Father in My name He may give you.
(John 15:16)

And these signs will follow those who believe: In My name they will cast out demons; they will speak with new tongues; they will take up serpents; and if they drink anything deadly, it will by no means hurt them; they will lay hands on the sick, and they will recover.
(Mark 16:17–18)

[Jesus'] *name, through faith in His name, has made this man strong, whom you see and know. Yes, the faith which comes through Him has given him this perfect soundness in the presence of you all.*
(Acts 3:16)

OBEDIENCE TO GOD

Has the Lord *as great delight in burnt offerings and sacrifices, as in obeying the voice of the* Lord*? Behold, to obey is*

better than sacrifice, and to heed than the fat of rams.
(1 Samuel 15:22)

Though [Jesus] *was a Son, yet He learned obedience by the things which He suffered. And having been perfected, He became the author of eternal salvation to all who obey Him.*
(Hebrews 5:8–9)

If you love Me, keep My commandments. (John 14:15)

Through [Jesus] *we have received grace and apostleship for obedience to the faith among all nations for His name.*
(Romans 1:5)

Do you not know that to whom you present yourselves slaves to obey, you are that one's slaves whom you obey, whether of sin leading to death, or of obedience leading to righteousness?
(Romans 6:16)

For the weapons of our warfare are not carnal but mighty in God for pulling down strongholds, casting down arguments and every high thing that exalts itself against the knowledge of God, bringing every thought into captivity to the obedience of Christ, and being ready to punish all disobedience when your obedience is fulfilled. (2 Corinthians 10:4–6)

COMPASSION

Then Jesus went about all the cities and villages, teaching in their synagogues, preaching the gospel of the kingdom, and healing every sickness and every disease among the people. But when He saw the multitudes, He was moved with compassion for them, because they were weary and scattered, like sheep having no shepherd. Then He said to His disciples, "The harvest truly is plentiful, but the laborers are few."

(Matthew 9:35–37)

Repay no one evil for evil. Have regard for good things in the sight of all men. If it is possible, as much as depends on you, live peaceably with all men. Beloved, do not avenge yourselves, but rather give place to wrath; for it is written, "Vengeance is Mine, I will repay," says the Lord. Therefore "if your enemy is hungry, feed him; if he is thirsty, give him a drink; for in so doing you will heap coals of fire on his head." Do not be overcome by evil, but overcome evil with good. (Romans 12:17–21)

Brethren, if a man is overtaken in any trespass, you who are spiritual restore such a one in a spirit of gentleness, considering yourself lest you also be tempted. Bear one another's burdens, and so fulfill the law of Christ. (Galatians 6:1–2)

Finally, all of you be of one mind, having compassion for one another; love as brothers, be tenderhearted, be courteous; not returning evil for evil or reviling for reviling, but on the contrary blessing, knowing that you were called to this, that you may inherit a blessing. (1 Peter 3:8–9)

LOVE

"...And you shall love the LORD *your God with all your heart, with all your soul, with all your mind, and with all your strength." This is the first commandment. And the second, like it, is this: "You shall love your neighbor as yourself." There is no other commandment greater than these.*

(Mark 12:30–31)

But I say to you, love your enemies, bless those who curse you, do good to those who hate you, and pray for those who

spitefully use you and persecute you, that you may be sons of your Father in heaven; for He makes His sun rise on the evil and on the good, and sends rain on the just and on the unjust. For if you love those who love you, what reward have you?
(Matthew 5:44–46)

Walk worthy of the calling with which you were called, with all lowliness and gentleness, with longsuffering, bearing with one another in love, endeavoring to keep the unity of the Spirit in the bond of peace. (Ephesians 4:1–3)

Therefore be imitators of God as dear children. And walk in love, as Christ also has loved us and given Himself for us, an offering and a sacrifice to God for a sweet-smelling aroma.
(Ephesians 5:1–2)

Let us consider how we may spur one another on toward love and good deeds. (Hebrews 10:24 NIV)

A HUMBLE SPIRIT

Let nothing be done through selfish ambition or conceit, but in lowliness of mind let each esteem others better than himself. Let each of you look out not only for his own interests, but also for the interests of others. (Philippians 2:3–4)

[Jesus] *made Himself of no reputation, taking the form of a bondservant, and coming in the likeness of men. And being found in appearance as a man, He humbled Himself and became obedient to the point of death, even the death of the cross. Therefore God also has highly exalted Him....*
(Philippians 2:7–9)

Assuredly, I say to you, unless you are converted and become as little children, you will by no means enter the kingdom of heaven. Therefore whoever humbles himself as this little child is the greatest in the kingdom of heaven. Whoever receives one little child like this in My name receives Me.

(Matthew 18:3–5)

Likewise you younger people, submit yourselves to your elders. Yes, all of you be submissive to one another, and be clothed with humility, for "God resists the proud, but gives grace to the humble." Humble yourselves under the mighty hand of God, that He may exalt you in due time, casting all your care upon Him, for He cares for you. (1 Peter 5:5–7)

But He gives more grace. Therefore He says: "God resists the proud, but gives grace to the humble." Therefore submit to God. Resist the devil and he will flee from you. Draw near to God and He will draw near to you. Cleanse your hands, you sinners; and purify your hearts, you double-minded. Lament and mourn and weep! Let your laughter be turned to mourning and your joy to gloom. Humble yourselves in the sight of the Lord, and He will lift you up. (James 4:6–10)

SPIRITUAL DISCERNMENT

Beloved, do not believe every spirit, but test the spirits, whether they are of God; because many false prophets have gone out into the world. By this you know the Spirit of God: Every spirit that confesses that Jesus Christ has come in the flesh is of God, and every spirit that does not confess that Jesus Christ has come in the flesh is not of God. And this is the spirit of the Antichrist, which you have heard was coming, and is now already in the world. (1 John 4:1–3)

If anyone says to you, "Look, here is the Christ!" or, "Look, He is there!" do not believe it. For false christs and false prophets will rise and show signs and wonders to deceive, if possible, even the elect. (Mark 13:21–22)

And do not be conformed to this world, but be transformed by the renewing of your mind, that you may prove what is that good and acceptable and perfect will of God. (Romans 12:2)

May [God the Father] *give to you the spirit of wisdom and revelation in the knowledge of Him, the eyes of your understanding being enlightened; that you may know what is the hope of His calling, what are the riches of the glory of His inheritance in the saints, and what is the exceeding greatness of His power toward us who believe, according to the working of His mighty power.* (Ephesians 1:17–19)

And it shall come to pass in the last days, says God, that I will pour out of My Spirit on all flesh; your sons and your daughters shall prophesy, your young men shall see visions, your old men shall dream dreams. And on My menservants and on My maidservants I will pour out My Spirit in those days; and they shall prophesy. (Acts 2:17–18)

For everyone who partakes only of milk is unskilled in the word of righteousness, for he is a babe. But solid food belongs to those who are of full age, that is, those who by reason of use have their senses exercised to discern both good and evil. (Hebrews 5:13–14)

PRAISE

The oil of joy for mourning, the garment of praise for the spirit of heaviness. (Isaiah 61:3)

Therefore by Him let us continually offer the sacrifice of praise to God, that is, the fruit of our lips, giving thanks to His name. (Hebrews 13:15)

You are a chosen generation, a royal priesthood, a holy nation, His own special people, that you may proclaim the praises of Him who called you out of darkness into His marvelous light. (1 Peter 2:9)

But at midnight Paul and Silas were praying and singing hymns to God, and the prisoners were listening to them. Suddenly there was a great earthquake, so that the foundations of the prison were shaken; and immediately all the doors were opened and everyone's chains were loosed. And the keeper of the prison, awaking from sleep and seeing the prison doors open, supposing the prisoners had fled, drew his sword and was about to kill himself. But Paul called with a loud voice, saying, "Do yourself no harm, for we are all here." Then he called for a light, ran in, and fell down trembling before Paul and Silas. And he brought them out and said, "Sirs, what must I do to be saved?" So they said, "Believe on the Lord Jesus Christ, and you will be saved, you and your household."

(Acts 16:25–31)

Whatever things are true, whatever things are noble, whatever things are just, whatever things are pure, whatever things are lovely, whatever things are of good report, if there is any virtue and if there is anything praiseworthy—meditate on these things. (Philippians 4:8)

PRAYER

Therefore I say to you, whatever things you ask when you pray, believe that you receive them, and you will have them. And whenever you stand praying, if you have anything against anyone, forgive him, that your Father in heaven may also forgive you your trespasses. (Mark 11:24–25)

Our Father in heaven, hallowed be Your name. Your kingdom come. Your will be done on earth as it is in heaven. Give us day by day our daily bread. And forgive us our sins, for we also forgive everyone who is indebted to us. And do not lead us into temptation, but deliver us from the evil one.
(Luke 11:2–4)

Watch and pray, lest you enter into temptation. The spirit indeed is willing, but the flesh is weak. (Mark 14:38)

When Jesus saw that the people came running together, He rebuked the unclean spirit, saying to it: "Deaf and dumb spirit, I command you, come out of him and enter him no more!" Then the spirit cried out, convulsed him greatly, and came out of him. And he became as one dead, so that many said, "He is dead." But Jesus took him by the hand and lifted him up, and he arose. And when He had come into the house, His disciples asked Him privately, "Why could we not cast it out?" So He said to them, "This kind can come out by nothing but prayer and fasting." (Mark 9:25–29)

Confess your trespasses to one another, and pray for one another, that you may be healed. The effective, fervent prayer of a righteous man avails much. (James 5:16)

Rejoice always, pray without ceasing, in everything give thanks; for this is the will of God in Christ Jesus for you.
(1 Thessalonians 5:16–18)

The Spirit also helps in our weaknesses. For we do not know what we should pray for as we ought, but the Spirit Himself makes intercession for us with groanings which cannot be uttered. Now He who searches the hearts knows what the mind of the Spirit is, because He makes intercession for the saints according to the will of God. (Romans 8:26–27)

Praying always with all prayer and supplication in the Spirit, being watchful to this end with all perseverance and supplication for all the saints. (Ephesians 6:18)

The end of all things is at hand; therefore be serious and watchful in your prayers. (1 Peter 4:7)

Be anxious for nothing, but in everything by prayer and supplication, with thanksgiving, let your requests be made known to God; and the peace of God, which surpasses all understanding, will guard your hearts and minds through Christ Jesus. (Philippians 4:6–7)

Therefore I exhort first of all that supplications, prayers, intercessions, and giving of thanks be made for all men, for kings and all who are in authority, that we may lead a quiet and peaceable life in all godliness and reverence. (1 Timothy 2:1–2)

Men always ought to pray and not lose heart. (Luke 18:1)

RIGHTEOUSNESS

For I am the Lord *your God. You shall therefore consecrate yourselves, and you shall be holy; for I am holy.* (Leviticus 11:44)

For [God] *made* [Jesus] *who knew no sin to be sin for us, that we might become the righteousness of God in Him.*
(2 Corinthians 5:21)

For if by the one man's offense death reigned through the one, much more those who receive abundance of grace and of the gift of righteousness will reign in life through the One, Jesus Christ. (Romans 5:17)

If anyone among you thinks he is religious, and does not bridle his tongue but deceives his own heart, this one's religion is useless. Pure and undefiled religion before God and the Father is this: to visit orphans and widows in their trouble, and to keep oneself unspotted from the world. (James 1:26–27)

We know that whoever is born of God does not sin; but he who has been born of God keeps himself, and the wicked one does not touch him. We know that we are of God, and the whole world lies under the sway of the wicked one. And we know that the Son of God has come and has given us an understanding, that we may know Him who is true; and we are in Him who is true, in His Son Jesus Christ. This is the true God and eternal life.
(1 John 5:18–20)

Put off, concerning your former conduct, the old man which grows corrupt according to the deceitful lusts, and be renewed in the spirit of your mind, and…put on the new man which was created according to God, in true righteousness and holiness. Therefore, putting away lying, "Let each one of you speak truth with his neighbor," for we are members of one another. "Be angry, and do not sin": do not let the sun go down on your wrath, nor give place to the devil. (Ephesians 4:22–27)

We have had human fathers who corrected us, and we paid them respect. Shall we not much more readily be in subjection to the Father of spirits and live? For they indeed for a few days chastened us as seemed best to them, but He for our profit, that we may be partakers of His holiness. Now no chastening seems to be joyful for the present, but painful; nevertheless, afterward it yields the peaceable fruit of righteousness to those who have been trained by it. (Hebrews 12:9–11)

Do not let sin reign in your mortal body, that you should obey it in its lusts. And do not present your members as instruments of unrighteousness to sin, but present yourselves to God as being alive from the dead, and your members as instruments of righteousness to God. For sin shall not have dominion over you, for you are not under law but under grace.
(Romans 6:12–14)

THE WORD OF GOD

This Book of the Law shall not depart from your mouth, but you shall meditate in it day and night, that you may observe to do according to all that is written in it. For then you will make your way prosperous, and then you will have good success.
(Joshua 1:8)

My people are destroyed for lack of knowledge. (Hosea 4:6)

All Scripture is given by inspiration of God, and is profitable for doctrine, for reproof, for correction, for instruction in righteousness, that the man of God may be complete, thoroughly equipped for every good work. (2 Timothy 3:16–17)

Therefore lay aside all filthiness and overflow of wickedness, and receive with meekness the implanted word, which is able to save your souls. But be doers of the word, and not hearers only, deceiving yourselves. For if anyone is a hearer of the word and not a doer, he is like a man observing his natural face in a mirror; for he observes himself, goes away, and immediately forgets what kind of man he was. But he who looks into the perfect law of liberty and continues in it, and is not a forgetful hearer but a doer of the work, this one will be blessed in what he does. (James 1:21–25)

For this reason we also thank God without ceasing, because when you received the word of God which you heard from us, you welcomed it not as the word of men, but as it is in truth, the word of God, which also effectively works in you who believe. (1 Thessalonians 2:13)

FAITH

Now faith is the substance of things hoped for, the evidence of things not seen. (Hebrews 11:1)

For whatever is born of God overcomes the world. And this is the victory that has overcome the world—our faith. Who is he who overcomes the world, but he who believes that Jesus is the Son of God? (1 John 5:4–5)

Resist [your adversary, the devil], *steadfast in the faith, knowing that the same sufferings are experienced by your brotherhood in the world. But may the God of all grace, who called us to His eternal glory by Christ Jesus, after you have suffered a while, perfect, establish, strengthen, and settle you. To Him be the glory and the dominion forever and ever. Amen.*

(1 Peter 5:9–11)

But without faith it is impossible to please [God], *for he who comes to God must believe that He is, and that He is a rewarder of those who diligently seek Him.* (Hebrews 11:6)

Faith comes by hearing, and hearing by the word of God. (Romans 10:17)

For indeed the gospel was preached to us as well as to them; but the word which they heard did not profit them, not being mixed with faith in those who heard it. (Hebrews 4:2)

THE FIRE OF GOD

For [God] *is like a refiner's fire and like launderer's soap. He will sit as a refiner and a purifier of silver; He will purify the sons of Levi, and purge them as gold and silver, that they may offer to the* LORD *an offering in righteousness.* (Malachi 3:2–3)

"You shall trample the wicked, for they shall be ashes under the soles of your feet on the day that I do this," says the LORD *of hosts.* (Malachi 4:3)

[God] *makes His angels spirits, His ministers a flame of fire.* (Psalm 104:4)

John [the Baptist] *answered, saying to all, "I indeed baptize you with water; but One mightier than I is coming, whose sandal strap I am not worthy to loose. He* [Jesus] *will baptize you with the Holy Spirit and fire."* (Luke 3:16)

When the Day of Pentecost had fully come, they were all with one accord in one place. And suddenly there came a sound from heaven, as of a rushing mighty wind, and it filled the whole house where they were sitting. Then there appeared to them divided tongues, as of fire, and one sat upon each of them. And they were all filled with the Holy Spirit and began to speak with other tongues, as the Spirit gave them utterance.

(Acts 2:1–4)

Now when the thousand years have expired, Satan will be released from his prison and will go out to deceive the nations which are in the four corners of the earth, Gog and Magog, to gather them together to battle, whose number is as the sand of the sea. They went up on the breadth of the earth and surrounded the camp of the saints and the beloved city. And fire came down from God out of heaven and devoured them. The devil, who deceived them, was cast into the lake of fire and brimstone where the beast and the false prophet are. And they will be tormented day and night forever and ever.

(Revelation 20:7–10)

THE GIFTS OF THE SPIRIT

"Not by might nor by power, but by My Spirit," says the Lord *of hosts.*

(Zechariah 4:6)

And it shall come to pass afterward that I will pour out My Spirit on all flesh; your sons and your daughters shall prophesy, your old men shall dream dreams, your young men shall see visions. And also on My menservants and on My maidservants I will pour out My Spirit in those days.

(Joel 2:28–29)

Having then gifts differing according to the grace that is given to us, let us use them: if prophecy, let us prophesy in proportion to our faith; or ministry, let us use it in our ministering; he who teaches, in teaching; he who exhorts, in exhortation; he who gives, with liberality; he who leads, with diligence; he who shows mercy, with cheerfulness. (Romans 12:6–8)

There are diversities of gifts, but the same Spirit. There are differences of ministries, but the same Lord. And there are diversities of activities, but it is the same God who works all in all. But the manifestation of the Spirit is given to each one for the profit of all: for to one is given the word of wisdom through the Spirit, to another the word of knowledge through the same Spirit, to another faith by the same Spirit, to another gifts of healings by the same Spirit, to another the working of miracles, to another prophecy, to another discerning of spirits, to another different kinds of tongues, to another the interpretation of tongues. But one and the same Spirit works all these things, distributing to each one individually as He wills.

(1 Corinthians 12:4–11)

And He Himself gave some to be apostles, some prophets, some evangelists, and some pastors and teachers, for the equipping of the saints for the work of ministry, for the edifying of the body of Christ. (Ephesians 4:11–12)

Do not neglect the gift that is in you, which was given to you by prophecy with the laying on of the hands of the eldership.

(1 Timothy 4:14)

RELATED SCRIPTURES:

THE WHOLE ARMOR OF GOD

Finally, my brethren, be strong in the Lord and in the power of His might. Put on the whole armor of God, that you may be able to stand against the wiles of the devil. For we do not wrestle against flesh and blood, but against principalities, against powers, against the rulers of the darkness of this age, against spiritual hosts of wickedness in the heavenly places. Therefore take up the whole armor of God, that you may be able to withstand in the evil day, and having done all, to stand. Stand therefore, having girded your waist with truth, having put on the breastplate of righteousness, and having shod your feet with the preparation of the gospel of peace; above all, taking the shield of faith with which you will be able to quench all the fiery darts of the wicked one. And take the helmet of salvation, and the sword of the Spirit, which is the word of God; praying always with all prayer and supplication in the Spirit, being watchful to this end with all perseverance and supplication for all the saints. (Ephesians 6:10–18)

But let us who are of the day be sober, putting on the breastplate of faith and love, and as a helmet the hope of salvation. (1 Thessalonians 5:8)

THE FRUIT OF THE SPIRIT

But the fruit of the Spirit is love, joy, peace, longsuffering, kindness, goodness, faithfulness, gentleness, self-control. Against such there is no law. (Galatians 5:22–23)

Do men gather grapes from thornbushes or figs from thistles? Even so, every good tree bears good fruit, but a bad tree bears bad fruit. A good tree cannot bear bad fruit, nor can a bad tree bear good fruit. Every tree that does not bear good fruit is cut down and thrown into the fire. Therefore by their fruits you will know them. (Matthew 7:16–20)

For you were once darkness, but now you are light in the Lord. Walk as children of light (for the fruit of the Spirit is in all goodness, righteousness, and truth), finding out what is acceptable to the Lord. And have no fellowship with the unfruitful works of darkness, but rather expose them.

(Ephesians 5:8–11)

And this I pray, that your love may abound still more and more in knowledge and all discernment, that you may approve the things that are excellent, that you may be sincere and without offense till the day of Christ, being filled with the fruits of righteousness which are by Jesus Christ, to the glory and praise of God. (Philippians 1:9–11)

THE BLOOD OF JESUS

Then [Jesus] *took the cup, and gave thanks, and gave it to them, saying, "Drink from it, all of you. For this is My blood of the new covenant, which is shed for many for the remission of sins.* (Matthew 26:27–28)

[Jesus] *has delivered us from the power of darkness and conveyed us into the kingdom of the Son of His love, in whom we have redemption through His blood, the forgiveness of sins.*

(Colossians 1:13–14)

The blood of Christ, who through the eternal Spirit offered Himself without spot to God, [shall] *cleanse your conscience from dead works to serve the living God.* (Hebrews 9:14)

And they overcame him by the blood of the Lamb and by the word of their testimony, and they did not love their lives to the death. (Revelation 12:11)

Now I saw heaven opened, and behold, a white horse. And He who sat on him was called Faithful and True, and in righteousness He judges and makes war. His eyes were like a flame of fire, and on His head were many crowns. He had a name written that no one knew except Himself. He was clothed with a robe dipped in blood, and His name is called The Word of God. And the armies in heaven, clothed in fine linen, white and clean, followed Him on white horses.

(Revelation 19:11–14)

SELECT SCRIPTURES ON SALVATION AND JESUS' POWER TO KEEP US IN HIM

SALVATION

Multitudes, multitudes in the valley of decision! For the day of the LORD is near in the valley of decision. (Joel 3:14)

Seek the LORD while He may be found, call upon Him while He is near. Let the wicked forsake his way, and the unrighteous man his thoughts; let him return to the LORD, and He will have mercy on him; and to our God, for He will abundantly pardon. (Isaiah 55:6–7)

God so loved the world that He gave His only begotten Son, that whoever believes in Him should not perish but have everlasting life. For God did not send His Son into the world to condemn the world, but that the world through Him might be saved. He who believes in Him is not condemned; but he who does not believe is condemned already, because he has not

believed in the name of the only begotten Son of God.
(John 3:16–18)

The Lord is…longsuffering toward us, not willing that any should perish but that all should come to repentance.
(2 Peter 3:9)

If you confess with your mouth the Lord Jesus and believe in your heart that God has raised Him from the dead, you will be saved. For with the heart one believes unto righteousness, and with the mouth confession is made unto salvation.
(Romans 10:9–10)

If we say that we have no sin, we deceive ourselves, and the truth is not in us. If we confess our sins, He is faithful and just to forgive us our sins and to cleanse us from all unrighteousness. (1 John 1:8–9)

And you He made alive, who were dead in trespasses and sins, in which you once walked according to the course of this world, according to the prince of the power of the air, the spirit who now works in the sons of disobedience, among whom also we all once conducted ourselves in the lusts of our flesh, fulfilling the desires of the flesh and of the mind, and were by nature children of wrath, just as the others. But God, who is rich in mercy, because of His great love with which He loved us, even when we were dead in trespasses, made us alive together with Christ (by grace you have been saved), and raised us up together, and made us sit together in the heavenly places in Christ Jesus, that in the ages to come He might show the exceeding riches of His grace in His kindness toward us in Christ Jesus. For by grace you have been saved through faith, and that not of yourselves; it is the gift of God, not of works, lest anyone should boast. For we are His workmanship, created in Christ

Jesus for good works, which God prepared beforehand that we should walk in them. (Ephesians 2:1–10)

JESUS' POWER TO KEEP US IN HIM

Lo, I am with you always, even to the end of the age.
(Matthew 28:20)

Peace I leave with you, My peace I give to you; not as the world gives do I give to you. Let not your heart be troubled, neither let it be afraid. (John 14:27)

My little children, these things I write to you, so that you may not sin. And if anyone sins, we have an Advocate with the Father, Jesus Christ the righteous. And He Himself is the propitiation for our sins, and not for ours only but also for the whole world. (1 John 2:1–2)

Now may the God of peace Himself sanctify you completely; and may your whole spirit, soul, and body be preserved blameless at the coming of our Lord Jesus Christ. He who calls you is faithful, who also will do it.
(1 Thessalonians 5:23–24)

For in that He Himself has suffered, being tempted, He is able to aid those who are tempted. (Hebrews 2:18)

Who shall separate us from the love of Christ? Shall tribulation, or distress, or persecution, or famine, or nakedness, or peril, or sword? As it is written: "For Your sake we are killed all day long; we are accounted as sheep for the slaughter." Yet in all these things we are more than conquerors through Him who loved us. For I am persuaded that neither death nor life, nor angels nor principalities nor powers, nor things present nor things to come, nor height nor depth, nor any other created thing, shall be able to separate us from the love of God which is in Christ Jesus our Lord. (Romans 8:35–39)

The Lord is faithful, who will establish you and guard you from the evil one. (2 Thessalonians 3:3)

Seeing then that we have a great High Priest who has passed through the heavens, Jesus the Son of God, let us hold fast our confession. For we do not have a High Priest who cannot sympathize with our weaknesses, but was in all points tempted as we are, yet without sin. Let us therefore come boldly to the throne of grace, that we may obtain mercy and find grace to help in time of need. (Hebrew 4:14–16)

You are of God, little children, and have overcome them, because He who is in you is greater than he who is in the world. (1 John 4:4)

Now to Him who is able to keep you from stumbling, and to present you faultless before the presence of His glory with exceeding joy. (Jude 1:24)

A DIVINE REVELATION OF SPIRITUAL WARFARE

CONTENTS

APPENDICES

PREFACE AND ACKNOWLEDGMENTS

by Mary K. Baxter

I am a veteran of spiritual warfare. I have engaged the enemy on many battlefields of the world, the flesh, and the devil. This book tells how God revealed to me the secrets of defeating Satan and his legions of evil spirits. It is about the existence of evil in the invisible realm—the effects of which we confront in our daily lives—and of overcoming that evil. God has promised,

> *Because you have made the* Lord, *who is my refuge, even the Most High, your dwelling place, no evil shall befall you, nor shall any plague come near your dwelling; for He shall give His angels charge over you, to keep you in all your ways.*
>
> —Psalm 91:9–11

I want to thank my coauthor, the Reverend T. L. Lowery, for his invaluable assistance. He has been a mentor and spiritual advisor to me, and I thank God for him. Without his assistance, prayers, and help, this book would not and could not have been written. I honor him and his beautiful wife, Mildred, for their support and encouragement to me in this ministry.

I gratefully recognize and credit those at Whitaker House who have been so instrumental in making these messages from God available to the reading public.

Most of all, I am grateful to God, who has called me to share these messages. I give all praise and honor and glory to God the Father, God the Son, and God the Holy Spirit.

INTRODUCTION

by T. L. Lowery

In the spiritual realm, pitched battles are occurring day and night—battles that affect the human situation on a very real level. Although these battles are unobserved by human eyes and unreported on the daily newscasts, believing men and women are grappling with sinister forces as they *"fight the good fight of faith"* (1 Timothy 6:12).

I believe Jesus was referring to spiritual warfare when He said, *"Do not think that I came to bring peace on earth. I did not come to bring peace but a sword"* (Matthew 10:34). As long as there are evils to overcome and injustices to fight, as long as the ungodly rage and the undisciplined ignore the laws of God, spiritual warfare will continue to be a chilling reality.

The cosmic battles between the righteous forces of God and the demonic forces of evil play out continually in a thousand different ways. Some of these battles are small—local conflicts, by comparison—while others are gigantic, affecting nations and impacting movements of history.

God is leading us toward the climax of human history and the return of Jesus Christ, while Satan, our enemy, is trying to prevent God's purposes from being fulfilled. Spiritual warfare is therefore an essential aspect of our Christian walk, yet many Christians are uncertain about how they can and should participate in spiritual battles. They need to know what the Bible says about the nature of this warfare and how we are to wage it.

Mary K. Baxter and I have collaborated in the writing of this book, which we pray will demonstrate and teach these vital biblical principles. We have diligently searched the Scriptures, and we present this material with the assurance that its teaching is backed up by the Word of God. In addition to Mary's descriptions of what God has revealed to her biblically about the spiritual realm, we have included her testimonies as well as the testimonies of others who have fought spiritual battles with the forces of evil and have come out victorious.

In this book, we have endeavored to describe the equipment needed for victory in this war, making it clear that God and righteousness will emerge as the ultimate winners.

The other books that Mary and I have written have already blessed millions of people in many countries. The wide acceptance of these writings and the enthusiastic feedback from people whose lives have been changed by reading them is gratifying, indeed.

My prayer for you is that God will bless you and keep you. May He cause His face to shine on you, and may He bless you in everything you do. I pray that God will give you a fresh anointing and abundant fruitfulness.

Part One:

THE EXISTENCE OF EVIL

1

HISTORY'S MOST CRUCIAL CONFLICT

For we do not wrestle against flesh and blood, but against principalities, against powers, against the rulers of the darkness of this age, against spiritual hosts of wickedness in the heavenly places.
—Ephesians 6:12

Every human being is involved in a war that will ultimately end all wars. It is *spiritual* warfare, and it is much more critical than a battle between powerful countries with nuclear armaments. It is more evil than a terrorist plot and more dangerous than a ticking time bomb. In fact, the war being waged in the spiritual realm is more devastating than all the battles of all the nations throughout history.

Our enemy seeks to conquer and destroy the *souls, spirits,* and *bodies* of human beings.

This spiritual war is not like earthly warfare, although earthly wars may be part of it. Our warfare is in the realm of the supernatural. Although they are invisible to human eyes, our enemy and his opposition are real. The conflict is taking place between the forces and powers of God and the lesser forces and powers of Satan. These are battles between good and evil, right and wrong, between the power that builds up and the power that destroys.

Human beings are right in the middle of this conflict. We are the treasure that is being fought over because we are the crown of God the Father's creation, made in His own image. Yet we are also foot soldiers in the fight. We must understand the nature of this war and learn how to fight effectively because many lives—including our own—are at stake.

Considering the cataclysmic conflict we are involved in, it is not surprising that the Bible metaphorically compares the Christian life to warfare. For example, Timothy was encouraged by his mentor, the apostle Paul, to *"fight the good fight of faith, lay hold on eternal life"* (1 Timothy 6:12), and to *"endure hardship as a good soldier of Jesus Christ"* (2 Timothy 2:3). Paul also exhorted other believers to *"put on the armor of light"* (Romans 13:12), and to *"put on the whole armor of God"* (Ephesians 6:11).

THREE COSTLY ERRORS

Although a war is being fought against them in the spiritual realm, most people are not really aware of their covert enemy, Satan. A recent survey revealed that nearly seventy percent of the American public believes Satan is real. However, this statistic doesn't reflect the average person's appalling lack of knowledge about his true nature or activities. Many in our society have some idea of Satan, or the devil, but their understanding of him is confused and distorted because they have bought into popular images of the devil. For example, they may see him as a jokester who goes around tempting people to do mischievous things. They don't see the devil for the malicious being he really is.

The widespread ignorance and confusion regarding Satan reflects three major—and costly—errors in most people's approach to the spiritual realm and spiritual warfare.

DENYING THE EXISTENCE OF EVIL FORCES

The first error people make is to deny the existence of evil spirits and the spiritual world in general. Some people think that Satan and his demons are like Santa Claus and his elves—mere figments of childish imaginations. They do not understand that much evil in our world is the work of Satan; instead, they choose to believe that bad things happen only by accidents of nature, or that people do evil things because of poor socialization.

The Bible tell us beyond a shadow of a doubt, however, that the spiritual world is real, and that there are evil as well as good spiritual forces. The apostle Paul identified these evil forces as *"principalities," "powers," "rulers of the darkness of this age,"* and *"spiritual hosts of wickedness in the heavenly places"* (Ephesians 6:12).

The existence of our spiritual enemy, Satan, is an undeniable fact. Jesus Himself called Satan the *"ruler of this world"* (John 12:31). He referred to the devil as the enemy, as in Matthew 13:39: *"The enemy who sowed* [tares, or weeds] *is the devil."* In 1 Peter 5:8, the Bible calls Satan *"your adversary the devil."*

The wickedness of the visible world is influenced, fueled, and powered by the spiritual underworld, which is populated by Satan and other fallen spirit beings. As we grapple with the reality of evil, we must be aware of the fact that evil spirits influence things that happen in our everyday lives. Everything that is good and righteous is being attacked by the devil and his forces.

Spiritual struggle, or the conflict of the human spirit with evil spirits, is not a myth but a sobering and sometimes frightening reality. In my travels, I have seen many wounded souls walking around, not realizing that intense spiritual warfare is being waged against them. You know you are in a physical battle when you get shot or you see someone else bleeding from being shot. I have been "shot at" and I have been "wounded." I know the reality of spiritual warfare.

Satan's job is to get us to ignore the spiritual realm or give it low priority. If he can distract us from the reality of the supernatural realm, he can divert us from finding spiritual solutions for critical issues in the world and in our own lives.

ATTRIBUTING TO SATAN EVERYTHING THAT GOES WRONG

A second error is attributing to the devil *every* negative action or situation that takes place in the world. We must be cautious not to give Satan undue attention by excessive thinking and studying about him. This approach often leads to a fascination, fearfulness, and overestimation of his power. It can even lead people to inadvertently engage in a form of satanic worship by attributing to him qualities that belong only to God, such as omniscience (being all knowing), omnipresence (being everywhere at once), and omnipotence (being all powerful). People end up living in fear of Satan rather than with trust in God.

It is true that the devil does everything he can to destroy and deceive. He is not some impersonal benign influence; he is a real spirit being, and he is at war with us. However, not all bad things come directly from him.

Sickness, for example, may sometimes be caused by an evil spirit, but not always. While satanic attack is a possible cause of sickness, as the book of Job indicates, sickness does not necessarily come from the devil. Jesus clearly distinguished between the healing of sickness and the casting out of demons. When sickness is caused by willful sin or natural causes, then attempting to cast out demons will not bring about healing.

Being exposed to a virus is not the same thing as being demon-possessed. If you break your arm in an accidental fall, you don't necessarily have a demon in your arm. Some things come our way simply because we live in a fallen world. Tragic things happen to both the righteous and the unrighteous. It will continue to be this way until Jesus returns, when *"there shall be no more death, nor sorrow, nor crying. There shall be no more pain, for the former things* [will] *have passed away"* (Revelation 21:4).

BELIEVING THAT CHRISTIANS ARE IMMUNE FROM SATANIC ATTACK

Third, some Christians think that believers are immune to demonic assault. Many Scriptures prove that this is not so. For example, consider the experience of Jesus' temptation by the devil (see Matthew 4:1–10; Luke 4:1–13), and of Paul's harassment by a *"spirit of divination,"* which possessed a servant girl (see Acts 16:16–18). The clear warning of 1 Peter 5:8 is that we need to be on guard because the devil is on the prowl, seeking those whom he can devour.

Taking the position that believers cannot be attacked by the devil leaves Christians ignorant of their enemy's tactics and gives them a false sense of security. God's people must be aware of Satan and his schemes so they can stand against him, for their own protection as well as the protection of others. Sometimes believers tend to joke about the devil, but the demonic underworld is not something to be careless about. Jude said that even the archangel Michael *"dared not bring against* [Satan] *a reviling accusation, but said, 'The Lord rebuke you!'"* (Jude 9).

However, many Christians seem to think that they can just go to church, mind their own business, and not cause any trouble to the devil or anyone else. They have no desire to "do battle" with Satan or evil. Yet when their sons become strung out on drugs or their unmarried daughters become pregnant and want abortions, they learn about spiritual warfare because of personal necessity.

Satan opposes the people of God in every way he can and seeks to destroy human life. It is unrealistic to think we can ignore our enemy.

BECOMING EQUIPPED FOR SPIRITUAL WARFARE

Therefore, while a great spiritual struggle is taking place, most people do not even believe in the reality of what is happening. When they are aware, many in the church do not fully understand how to appropriate the protection and spiritual weapons that are rightfully theirs in Jesus Christ. They may have been told about victory in Jesus and even sung about it, yet, for the most part, they have not been *shown how to walk in that victory*. In other words, many Christians do not know how to claim and use Christ's victory for themselves.

Because so many believers are unequipped spiritually, they are susceptible to the attacks of the devil. And if these Christians are easy prey for the enemy, consider how vulnerable nonbelievers are to him!

We must wake up to the truth of God's Word about the spiritual struggle we are engaged in. My spiritual calling is in visions and revelations. God has given me special insight into spiritual warfare. He has opened up many Scriptures to my mind, and He has instructed me in how to tell other Christians about spiritual battle and how they can overcome the enemy of our souls.

I have seen visions of hell and the judgment of God on sin, as well as visions of heaven. I know that God desires men and women to come to Him and to learn to defeat the devil through spiritual warfare. The purpose of this book is to make the truth about spiritual warfare clearer to understand so that it will be easier for you to grasp and use the spiritual weaponry available to you.

If you haven't guessed already, I'm angry at the devil! He is sneaky, low-down, deceitful, abhorrent, and anything else negative you can say about him. There never has been a greater affront to God and a bigger threat to His people than Satan. But I want to reassure you that there never has been and never will be a more thorough defeat than Satan will experience in the final outcome of world history. I want to show you how you can be part of that victory over the enemy even now.

2

THE NATURE OF OUR ENEMY

Be sober, be vigilant; because your adversary
the devil walks about like a roaring lion,
seeking whom he may devour.
—1 Peter 5:8

THE ORIGIN OF EVIL

SATAN'S FALL

In order to understand the nature of spiritual warfare, we must comprehend how evil and sin began. Satan was once an angel in heaven named Lucifer. However, he became arrogant and tried to exalt himself over God. The Bible says this about his beginning and his fall:

This is what the Sovereign Lord *says: "You were the model of perfection, full of wisdom and perfect in beauty. You were in Eden, the garden of God; every precious stone adorned you....*

> *You were anointed as a guardian cherub, for so I ordained you. You were on the holy mount of God; you walked among the fiery stones. You were blameless in your ways from the day you were created till wickedness was found in you....You were filled with violence, and you sinned. So I drove you in disgrace from the mount of God, and I expelled you, O guardian cherub, from among the fiery stones. Your heart became proud on account of your beauty, and you corrupted your wisdom because of your splendor. So I threw you to the earth; I made a spectacle of you before kings."* —Ezekiel 28:12–17 NIV

Although Lucifer was a magnificent angel in heaven, he was not content. He gloried in his beauty and brightness, but it wasn't enough for him. He aspired to supremacy. He coveted *the* honor and glory that belongs to God alone. So Lucifer began to sow a spirit of deception and discontent among the angels that were under his command. Before long, this discontent blossomed into open revolt.

> *And war broke out in heaven: Michael and his angels fought with the dragon; and the dragon and his angels fought, but they did not prevail, nor was a place found for them in heaven any longer. So the great dragon was cast out, that serpent of old, called the Devil and Satan, who deceives the whole world; he was cast to the earth, and his angels were cast out with him.* —Revelation 12:7–9

Satan was kicked out of heaven because of his rebellion. He was no longer Lucifer, which means "the morning star,"[1] or "a shining one."[2] Instead, he became Satan, which means "the accuser"[3] or

1. *Strong's Exhaustive Concordance*, #H1966.
2. *New American Standard Exhaustive Concordance of the Bible*, (NASC), #H1966, © 1981 by The Lockman Foundation. All rights reserved.
3. *Strong's*, #G4567.

"the adversary."[4] The Bible gives us a number of designations and names for the fallen Lucifer, such as the following:

- *"the prince of the power of the air"* (Ephesians 2:2)
- *"the ruler of the demons"* (Matthew 12:24)
- *"king"* over the demons in *"the bottomless pit"* (Revelation 9:11)
- *"the ruler of this world"* who is already judged (John 16:11)
- *"the god of this age"* (2 Corinthians 4:4)
- *"the serpent"* (2 Corinthians 11:3)
- *"a great...dragon"* (Revelation 12:3)
- *"the enemy"* (Matthew 13:39)
- *"the tempter"* (Matthew 4:3)
- a false *"angel of light"* (2 Corinthians 11:14)
- *"the accuser of our brethren"* (Revelation 12:10)
- *"the Devil and Satan"* (Revelation 12:9)

SATAN'S COHORTS

The angels who rebelled with Satan were thrown out of heaven, too, and they became demons, or evil spirits. The Bible indicates that one third of the angels may have rebelled. (See Revelation 12:4.) Any spiritual being who did not obey the Lord received swift judgment. *"God did not spare the angels who sinned, but cast them down to hell and delivered them into chains of darkness, to be reserved for judgment"* (2 Peter 2:4). The term *"unclean spirit[s]"* occurs in the Bible twenty-two times to describe Satan's cohorts. (See, for example, Matthew 10:1; Acts 8:7.) *"Foul spirit"* (Revelation 18:2) is also used. Paul referred to demons that operate through people to deceive others as *"deceiving ["seducing"* KJV*] spirits"* (1 Timothy 4:1).

4. *NASC*, #G4567.

SATAN'S DECEPTION OF HUMANKIND

Remaining rebellious against God after his fall, Satan turned his attention to destroying humankind. He likely used the same tactics on human beings that he had used with the angels who rebelled in heaven. In the Garden of Eden, the devil deceived our first parents into thinking they could be equal with God. Then he enticed them to rebel against Him, too. (See Genesis 3:1–19.)

When humanity succumbed to the adversary's temptation, disobeyed God, and fell, Satan enlisted the human race in his war against God. The spirit of rebellion still dwells in all unbelievers—those whom the Bible calls *"the sons of disobedience"* (Ephesians 2:2). Even believers have to fight this spirit of rebellion, which tries to rear its head even after we have received salvation through Christ. The Bible calls this spirit of rebellion or disobedience the *"old man,"* or the *"flesh"* that serves the *"law of sin"*:

> *Put off, concerning your former conduct, the **old man** which grows corrupt according to the deceitful lusts, and be renewed in the spirit of your mind, and…put on the new man which was created according to God, in true righteousness and holiness.* —Ephesians 4:22–24, emphasis added

> *But I see another law in my members, warring against the law of my mind, and bringing me into captivity to the **law of sin** which is in my members. O wretched man that I am! Who will deliver me from this body of death? I thank God; through Jesus Christ our Lord! So then, **with the mind I myself serve the law of God, but with the flesh the law of sin.***
> —Romans 7:23–25, emphasis added

The sinful nature revolts against God's Word. It opposes all the things of God; it fights against His will. Unless the hearts of the disobedient are turned toward God, they are naturally evil, living as children of their "father," the devil. Jesus said to some with unchanged hearts,

> *You are of your father the devil, and the desires of your father you want to do. He was a murderer from the beginning, and does not stand in the truth, because there is no truth in him. When he speaks a lie, he speaks from his own resources, for he is a liar and the father of it.* —John 8:44

Those who follow the devil willfully (or even ignorantly) are called the "*sons of the wicked one*" (Matthew 13:38). The apostle John said they are the "*children of the devil*" (1 John 3:10). Paul called false apostles "*ministers*" of Satan (2 Corinthians 11:15). They belong to the devil's "church": In Revelation 2:9, the Holy Spirit said that some who only pretended to be God's people were from the "*synagogue of Satan.*"

SATAN'S ARMY

How does Satan carry out his warfare in his attempt to undermine God's ways and purposes? In the book of Ephesians, the devil is pictured as heading a well-organized army of evil spiritual agents. The terms "*principalities,*" "*powers,*" "*rulers of the darkness of this age*" and "*spiritual hosts of wickedness in the heavenly places*" (Ephesians 6:12) are believed by some biblical teachers to denote the ranks in his army.

The power of Satan's influence is multiplied through his vast army of evil spirits, which implement his will—gathering information, carrying out orders, and affecting human affairs. The Old Testament reveals that Satan influenced the rulers of Persia and exercised authority over them through a demon called the "*prince of the kingdom of Persia.*" (See Daniel 10:12–13.) The angel who spoke to Daniel identified another evil spirit, who influenced a different kingdom, as the "*prince of Greece*" (verse 20).

Satan and his evil spirits can assume visible form, as the devil did when he appeared as a serpent in the Garden of Eden, or they can cause a visible reaction, or manifestation, on people:

- Demons can cause blindness and muteness. (See Matthew 12:22.)
- Demons can cause convulsions and seizures. (See, for example, Mark 9:17–20.)
- Demons can cause a person to act in a self-destructive way or with bizarre behavior. (See, for example, Luke 8:27–29.)
- Demons have been known to compel animals to destroy themselves. (See, for example, Luke 8:30–33.)
- Demons can create powerful illusions and mimic the power of God. (See, for example, Exodus 7:11–12.)
- The devil and his followers can perform signs and wonders. (See Matthew 24:24.)

Just as a strong general can impose a high degree of control over his army, and through his troops carry out his program over a vast area, so the devil rules much of his worldwide kingdom of darkness through his subordinates.

SATAN IS DEFEATED

Yet the power that Satan has is limited. Remember that Lucifer is a created being whose powers are vastly inferior to the Creator's.

In addition, in His sovereignty and mercy, God the Father did not want humanity to remain in its fallen state and be captive to the wiles of the enemy. Because of His incomparable love for all people, and His desire to redeem them from sin and death, God sent His Son Jesus to the earth to engage Satan in open warfare and defeat him. *"For this purpose the Son of God was manifested, that He might destroy the works of the devil"* (1 John 3:8).

Jesus attacked Satan and his strongholds directly by casting evil spirits out of people, opening blind eyes, straightening crooked limbs, unstopping deaf ears, raising the dead, and releasing people from spiritual bondage. For example, Jesus healed and delivered...

- the man who was blind and mute because of demon-possession. (See Matthew 12:22.)
- the boy who had epileptic-like seizures and was deaf and mute because of an unclean spirit. (See, for example, Mark 9:17–29.)
- the man who became a maniac and isolated himself from society because he was demon-possessed. (See, for example, Luke 8:27–33.)
- the woman who was afflicted and bent over for eighteen years because she had a *"spirit of infirmity"* from Satan. (See Luke 13:10–16.)
- the little girl who was ill and was said to have been *"severely demon-possessed."* (See, for example, Matthew 15:22–28.)
- the man in the synagogue who was thrown to the floor by a *"spirit of an unclean demon."* (See Luke 4:33–36.)

The climax of Jesus' ministry on earth was His death on the cross for the sins of the world and His triumphant resurrection from the grave. He freed us from the snare of the enemy so that we could be reconciled to God the Father and start living in His kingdom of love and truth. Through His death and resurrection, Jesus struck the enemy with a mortal wound that will ultimately lead to the total demise of the devil.

In His victory, Jesus assures us that we, the born-again children of God, can also have victory in every battle against Satan.

"But thanks be to God! He gives us the victory through our Lord Jesus Christ" (1 Corinthians 15:57 NIV).

Christians are the redeemed who have turned from sin and Satan back to God and have joined His fight against the forces of darkness. The final outcome of our spiritual warfare with the enemy was actually determined by God from the beginning. Right after the devil led mankind into disobedience, the Lord told Satan, *"And I will put enmity between you and the woman, and between your seed and her Seed* [Jesus]; *He shall bruise your head, and you shall bruise His heel"* (Genesis 3:15). As the Second Adam, Jesus resisted evil and obeyed God even to the point of death on the cross.

When Christ overcame sin and death, Satan lost his claim over humanity. The Bible says that Jesus released us forever from the satanic bondage of fear:

> *Since then the children share in flesh and blood, He Himself likewise also partook of the same, that through death He might render powerless him who had the power of death, that is, the devil; and might deliver those who through fear of death were subject to slavery all their lives. For assuredly He does not give help to angels, but He gives help to the descendant of Abraham. Therefore, He had to be made like His brethren in all things, that He might become a merciful and faithful high priest in things pertaining to God, to make propitiation for the sins of the people.* —Hebrews 2:14–17 NASB

In Revelation, John described Satan's final, cosmic defeat in the drama of the ages: *"The devil, who deceived..., was cast into the lake of fire and brimstone where the beast and the false prophet are. And they will be tormented day and night forever and ever"* (Revelation 20:10). Centuries earlier, the prophet Isaiah had also seen Satan's demise through the telescope of prophecy:

> *How you are fallen from heaven, O Lucifer, son of the morning! How you are cut down to the ground, you who weakened the nations! For you have said in your heart: "I will ascend into heaven, I will exalt my throne above the stars of God; I will also sit on the mount of the congregation on the farthest sides of the north; I will ascend above the heights of the clouds, I will be like the Most High." Yet you shall be brought down to Sheol, to the lowest depths of the Pit. Those who see you will gaze at you,...saying: "Is this the man who made the earth tremble, who shook kingdoms, who made the world as a wilderness and destroyed its cities, who did not open the house of his prisoners?"*
>
> —Isaiah 14:12–17

Satan takes people prisoner, but Jesus frees them. At the beginning of His ministry, Jesus announced,

> *The Spirit of the LORD is upon Me, because He has anointed Me to preach the gospel to the poor; He has sent Me to heal the brokenhearted, to proclaim liberty to the captives and recovery of sight to the blind, to set at liberty those who are oppressed.*
>
> —Luke 4:18

SPIRITUAL WARFARE CONTINUES

Since Christ has defeated Satan, why is the devil still our enemy? You might think that he would have no more strength to use against us. But this is not the case, because we have not yet reached the end of the age, and God's purposes for the world are not yet complete. God's people are still locked in a tremendous conflict with satanic forces. Satan has not ceased fighting God and God's people. Evil spirits are still active and dangerous. As Paul told us, "*We do not wrestle against flesh and blood, but against principalities, against powers, against the rulers of the darkness of this age, against spiritual hosts of wickedness in the heavenly places"* (Ephesians 6:12). Our greatest struggles in life are against the powers of this dark world.

Why are so many people in the world today caught up in indescribable anguish and suffering? Some of this pain, as I wrote earlier, has to do with the fact that we live in a fallen world. Yet other suffering is due to the devil's increasing attacks. At the end of time, when Satan is defeated, he will no longer be able to exert any power or influence over the world. Satan knows his time is short, and he wants to destroy as many people as he can in the time he has left.

The fallen angels who followed Satan in rebellion also know their time is limited. In fact, they fear a "premature" final judgment. In Matthew 8:29, a legion of demons asked Jesus why He had come to punish them "before their time." *"Suddenly* [the demons] *cried out, saying, 'What have we to do with You, Jesus, You Son of God? Have You come here to torment us before the time?'"* They were startled because they knew they would lose a final confrontation with Jesus, but they didn't expect Him to appear at that time and exercise authority over them. In Luke's account of this incident, the unclean spirits begged Jesus not to send them to the abyss. (See Luke 8:27–35.)

Satan and the angels who fell with him know there is an appointed day for their final judgment, and they also know they are always subject to Jesus' commands. In the Bible, Satan is never referred to as having power beyond the ability to deceive those who are willing to believe his lies and trust in the limited power granted to him. Yet, although he is limited in what he can do, he uses everything in his power and at his disposal to deceive and destroy.

Therefore, until the day when Christ returns and the enemy is ultimately defeated, spiritual warfare will continue. Even though we know that Christ will eliminate the forces of evil in the end, this knowledge does not lessen the fierceness of the struggle or its importance. The enemy that prompted rebellion in heaven still inspires rebellion on earth. Remember that the Bible refers to Satan as the *"god of this age"* (2 Corinthians 4:4). The antagonism between the Spirit of Christ and the spirit of Satan is evident in every arena of life.

We should not be surprised at these battles. Peter wrote, *"Do not think it strange concerning the fiery trial which is to try you, as though some strange thing happened to you"* (1 Peter 4:12). Jesus said, *"In the world you will have tribulation; but be of good cheer, I have overcome the world"* (John 16:33).

We now have the means of victory! Instead of being at the enemy's mercy, we can defeat him through Christ and the power of His resurrection. The victory is ours to receive and apply. We are to battle against injustice, evil, and all the works of Satan.

SUCCESSFULLY BATTLING THE FORCES OF DARKNESS

How can we successfully do battle with the forces of darkness? It is through the anointing of the Holy Spirit and the ministry of the Word of God that we can learn to appropriate what Jesus won for us at Calvary and defeat the work of the enemy. To begin, we must do the following.

BE REDEEMED FROM THE POWER OF SATAN

In order to understand and engage in spiritual warfare, you first have to be redeemed from the power of the enemy. Have you asked God to forgive your sins, and have you received Jesus as the Lord and Savior of your life? You need to do this right now, so that you can comprehend and put into practice scriptural truths concerning this spiritual war.

When Saul was converted and became the apostle Paul, Jesus told him that he was to *"turn* [people] *from darkness to light, and from the power of Satan to God, that they may receive forgiveness of sins and an inheritance among those who are sanctified by faith in Me"* (Acts 26:18). God redeems all those who put their faith in Jesus. He transfers them out of the "*dominion of darkness,*" or the realm of Satan, and brings them into Christ's realm, which is the kingdom of God. (See Colossians 1:13 NIV.)

If you do not know which kingdom you truly belong to, why not pause in your reading right now, and pray this prayer?

> Dear God, I confess that I have lived in rebellion against You and tried to live my life in my own way. I haven't acknowledged You as My Creator and Lord. There are conflicts and problems in my life that I cannot cope with alone. I cannot counteract the assaults of the enemy against me. I need Your help. I confess to You all my sins and shortcomings. I ask You to forgive me and come into my heart. I ask You to free me from my guilt. Lift the heavy burden of condemnation from my soul through the blood of Jesus. Fill me with Your Holy Spirit and help me to live by Your Spirit from now on. Grant me the joy and peace that can come only from You. In Jesus' name, I pray. Amen.

At the very instant of your conversion, you become a child of God, fully justified, fully forgiven, and sharing in the inheritance with Christ. Your life can begin to be conformed to that of Jesus Christ as you bring your thoughts and actions in line with God's Word and respond daily to the leading of the Holy Spirit.

LEARN SATAN'S TACTICS AND HOW TO COUNTERACT THEM

Second, to effectively engage your spiritual enemy, you must know his tactics and how to counteract them. You cannot leave yourself open to all manner of satanic assaults and constantly be crippled or defeated by the enemy. Our example is Jesus and how He confronted the devil. He demonstrated mastery over all the powers and forces of evil. During the ministry of the Master, He challenged Satan whenever He had an opportunity, whether it was in the synagogue or in a cemetery. (See, for example, Luke 4:33–35; Mark 5:2–15.)

The devil is deceitful, presumptuous, cruel, fierce, wicked, subtle, and powerful. Yet he also is cowardly and, again, has limitations. He flees at the name of Jesus or when a believer pleads the blood of the Son of God over a person or situation. Through Christ's victory, we can tread on the head of Satan; we can keep him under our feet. Through the precious blood of Jesus, we *can* overcome the devil.

In New Testament days, the Romans enjoyed throwing Christians to the lions in a mainly futile attempt to have them renounce their faith in Christ. The Romans gathered in the Coliseum, where they would throw fifty or more Christians into the arena and wait to see who would deny Christ first. Those who didn't deny the Lord were literally eaten alive.

Satan is more like the lions than the Romans. *"Be sober, be vigilant; because your adversary the devil walks about like a roaring lion, seeking whom he may devour"* (1 Peter 5:8). He is not interested in entertainment; he wants to annihilate the work of the church. He wants to destroy people and usher them into hell. Again, Satan knows his fate—eternity in the lake of fire—is sealed, and he will do whatever it takes to carry as many souls with him as he can. He is willing to use any tactic or device to make people listen to him and follow him. We must be equipped for spiritual combat. We need to learn to resist the rebellion that caused the fall of Lucifer and to do spiritual battle on behalf of those who are vulnerable to the enemy. This book is designed to show you the spiritual armor God has given you and how to use it.

Satan is the foe of every human being, and especially of believers who trust in the Lord Jesus Christ. In spiritual warfare, we must clearly understand that we are not at war with other people.

We do not fight against unbelievers, "sinners," and reprobates; we are at war with Satan, who holds people captive to his will:

> *A servant of the Lord must not quarrel but be gentle to all, able to teach, patient, in humility correcting those who are in opposition, if God perhaps will grant them repentance, so that they may know the truth, and that they may come to their senses and escape the snare of the devil, having been taken captive by him to do his will.* —2 Timothy 2:24–26

We often try to change people who are not doing what is right. But their behavior has its roots in something much larger. This does not excuse the wrong things they do or relieve them of their responsibility, but it helps us to focus on the real enemy. As bad as some people may seem, they are merely conduits for spiritual battle. Satan has been successful in getting us to fight people rather than battling what is really causing people to be the way they are.

THE FRONT LINES OF SPIRITUAL WARFARE

We are on the front lines of spiritual warfare every day. God's people are experiencing attack as perhaps never before. Trouble is all around us. The natural consequences of our fallen world are depicted in our daily newscasts and newspapers with sad accounts of violence, suffering, and disaster. We can sense a spirit of rebellion in the attitudes of the world. We confront the world's temptation and the devil's deceit in our everyday lives as we struggle with unseen, sinister forces that want to pull us down and destroy us. Sin is rampant in the earth as we draw closer to the final confrontation between God and Satan. The devil is frantically working to try to wreck the plans and programs of God.

Paul wrote in 2 Corinthians 2:11 that we are not to let Satan "*take advantage of us; for we are not ignorant of his devices.*" Many times, he gets the advantage over people who are not aware of how he works. It is time for God's people to know the tactics of the devil. It is high time for the army of God to rise up and say, "Enough is enough!"

The Lord has promised in His Word that we can be wiser than our enemies. The psalmist said to God, *"You, through Your commandments, make me wiser than my enemies; for they are ever with me"* (Psalm 119:98). Satan is our greatest enemy, and yet we can be wiser and stronger than he is through the power and guidance of the Holy Spirit.

I have been engaged in spiritual warfare for a number of years. I know from personal experience what it is like to be opposed by unseen, diabolical spiritual enemies that have great strength and power. I have been attacked by the devil and his coalition of evil forces, but the almighty God has always given me the victory.

In the same way, certain victory is assured to you through Christ. When we are in Christ and have appropriated the grace and protection of His sacrificial death on Calvary, we have nothing to fear. The message of deliverance and empowerment by the Holy Spirit that Jesus came to earth to proclaim is His message for us today.

Hallelujah! Jesus provides the promise of glorious victory. In Him, we *have* won and *will* win over the enemy.

3

THE ENEMY'S STRATEGIES

Lest Satan should take advantage of us;
for we are not ignorant of his devices.
—2 Corinthians 2:11

The apostle Paul talked about the "*wiles*" (or "*schemes*" NIV, NASB) of the devil in Ephesians 6:11. Notice that these words are in the plural. Satan uses many different methods and devices to cause people to stumble. Wiles involve deceit and trickery. Deception, seduction, and lies are powerful tools of the enemy.

TACTICAL MANEUVERS EMPLOYED BY THE ENEMY

As we discussed earlier, the devil is a created being; therefore, he is not omnipresent (everywhere at once), omnipotent (all powerful), or omniscient (all knowing). He is subject to the limits God has placed on him. In order to carry out his program, he has to work through subordinates—both demonic and human. The following are some of his major strategies.

KEEPING PEOPLE IN SPIRITUAL DARKNESS

It is Satan's goal to keep people in ignorance and apathy toward salvation through Jesus Christ. I have had many visions in which I saw people walking in darkness, which I understood to be spiritual darkness. Their eyes and ears would be covered with what looked like some kind of skin. God revealed to me that spiritual blindness and deafness is the condition of many people today.

The Bible speaks about this condition in a number of Scriptures, such as the following:

> *Hear this now, O foolish people, without understanding, who have eyes and see not, and who have ears and hear not.*
>
> —Jeremiah 5:21

> *Son of man, you dwell in the midst of a rebellious house, which has eyes to see but does not see, and ears to hear but does not hear; for they are a rebellious house.* —Ezekiel 12:2

> *The hearts of this people have grown dull. Their ears are hard of hearing, and their eyes they have closed, lest they should see with their eyes and hear with their ears, lest they should understand with their hearts and turn, so that I should heal them.* —Acts 28:27

The "*god of this age*" has blinded the minds of unbelievers to keep them from believing the gospel. (See 2 Corinthians 4:3–4.) The devil's primary strategy is to keep each person from hearing the gospel, recognizing the truth, and accepting Jesus Christ as Savior, thus ensuring his or her continual spiritual bondage and condemnation.

STEALING THE WORD FROM PEOPLE'S HEARTS

Yet the old deceiver doesn't stop at that. In Luke 8:5–15, in the parable of the sower, Jesus taught that when some people do hear the gospel, *"the devil comes and takes away the word out of their hearts, lest they should believe and be saved"* (Luke 8:12).

The Bible says that Satan works *"with all power, signs, and lying wonders, and with all unrighteous deception among those who perish, because they did not receive the love of the truth, that they might be saved"* (2 Thessalonians 2:9–10). When people hear God's truth, they must receive it and hold on to it because the enemy will try to snatch it from them.

TEMPTING PEOPLE AWAY FROM THE TRUTH

When people do receive the truth, Satan tries to draw them away from it through temptation. Jesus talked about those who, *"when they hear, receive the word with joy; and these have no root, who believe for a while and in time of temptation fall away"* (Luke 8:13). The temptation to doubt, fear, or turn back to the ways of the world is very real.

How can we develop deep spiritual roots? By staying close to Christ and holding on to faith in Him: *"That Christ may dwell in your hearts through faith; that you, being rooted and grounded in love..."* (Ephesians 3:17). *"As you have therefore received Christ Jesus the Lord, so walk in Him, rooted and built up in Him and established in the faith, as you have been taught, abounding in it with thanksgiving"* (Colossians 2:6–7). It is crucial that we become established in God's Word in order to remain steadfast in the Lord.

ENTICING PEOPLE WITH THE CARES AND RICHES OF THE WORLD

Jesus continued the parable of the sower by talking about *"those who, when they have heard, go out and are choked with cares, riches, and pleasures of life, and bring no fruit to maturity"* (Luke 8:14). Satan is at work constantly to delude people into submitting to him. The Bible says that, in his efforts to deceive, "*Satan…transforms himself into an angel of light*" (2 Corinthians 11:14). He "chokes" people spiritually by enticing them to feed on their own selfish desires rather than on the Word of God.

In another teaching, Jesus said that we are to seek God and His kingdom first in our lives. (See Matthew 6:33.) When our priorities become skewed so that we pursue our own comforts and ignore God's concerns, then we are falling into this deception of the enemy. Satan wants to keep us from bearing fruit for God and being effective for His kingdom.

> *Do you not know that friendship with the world is enmity with God? Whoever therefore wants to be a friend of the world makes himself an enemy of God.* —James 4:4

In order to bear spiritual fruit, we must remain in Christ and pursue God's thoughts and ways. Jesus said, "*The ones that fell on the good ground are those who, having heard the word with a noble and good heart, keep it and bear fruit with patience*" (Luke 8:15). We must let the Word of God be planted and bring forth fruit in our lives.

Jesus taught that if we remain in Him, we will bear fruit. If we do not, we will become like a withered branch that has no useful purpose:

> *Abide in Me, and I in you. As the branch cannot bear fruit of itself, unless it abides in the vine, neither can you, unless you abide in Me. I am the vine, you are the branches. He who abides in Me, and I in him, bears much fruit; for without Me you can do nothing. If anyone does not abide in Me, he is cast*

> *out as a branch and is withered; and they gather them and throw them into the fire, and they are burned.*
>
> —John 15:4–6

Psalm 1 emphasizes the same idea: When a person delights in God and His Word, *"he shall be like a tree planted by the rivers of water, that brings forth its fruit in its season, whose leaf also shall not wither; and whatever he does shall prosper"* (Psalm 1:3).

PLANTING COUNTERFEIT BELIEVERS AMONG US

As our sworn enemy, Satan hates God and His people, the church. Remember that he would like to destroy us. He wants to neutralize the body of Christ through doubts and questions. He wants to cause dissent and destruction by bringing jealousy and confusion among God's people. He wants to deceive believers and draw them away from the truth.

In Matthew 13:24–30, in the parable of the wheat and the tares, Jesus told of a man who sowed his field, and while he slept, an enemy came and sowed weeds among the wheat. Then, Jesus explained the symbolism of this parable to His disciples:

> *He who sows the good seed is the Son of Man. The field is the world, the good seeds are the sons of the kingdom, but the tares are the sons of the wicked one. The enemy who sowed them is the devil, the harvest is the end of the age.*
>
> —Matthew 13:37–39

Jesus said that only at the harvest (when He returns) can the tares be separated from the wheat.

In his evil mind, Satan has devised the cunning strategy of infiltrating the ranks of the righteous people of God by planting counterfeit Christians among them. Paul spoke of the dangers of *"false brethren"* (2 Corinthians 11:26). These pseudo-believers try to entrap followers of Christ and discredit those who speak the truth. Their deceptions can be very subtle. Such imposters teach *"a different gospel, which is not another; but there are some who trouble you and want to pervert the gospel of Christ"* (Galatians 1:6–7). Paul used strong words to warn believers against this false gospel: *"But even if we, or an angel from heaven, preach any other gospel to you than what we have preached to you, let him be accursed"* (verse 8).

Teachers who claim to teach the Bible, but are teaching doctrines from hell, are undermining the body of Christ in many places today. For example, through religious cults, and even within the church itself, counterfeit believers will try to substitute man's "righteousness" for God's righteousness. *"Being ignorant of God's righteousness, and seeking to establish their own righteousness, have not submitted to the righteousness of God"* (Romans 10:3). They teach a counterfeit doctrine that is not in agreement with the Word of God.

John wrote,

> *And we know that the Son of God has come and has given us an understanding, that we may know Him who is true; and we are in Him who is true, in His Son Jesus Christ. This is the true God and eternal life. Little children, keep yourselves from idols.*
> —1 John 5:20–21

Paul warned against the devil's strategy in 2 Corinthians 11:3: *"I fear, lest somehow, as the serpent deceived Eve by his craftiness, so your minds may be corrupted from the simplicity that is in Christ"* (2 Corinthians 11:3). Satan's battle strategy in spiritual warfare is to deceive us into believing his lies. He has been working this plan for years, and he's very good at it. Don't accept the devil's facsimiles, his substitutes, his look-alikes! Accept only the genuine that comes from God.

Anyone can quote from the Bible. Christians today need to be like the Bereans in the early church. They investigated what Paul and Silas were teaching them to see whether the apostles' teachings agreed with the Scriptures. (See Acts 17:11.)

It is clear that there is no place to hide or escape from the effects of spiritual warfare. Even in church, we must fight the devil at times. It is the responsibility of faithful pastors and elders to remove impostors and false teachers from local congregations through proper church discipline. Yet all Christians must learn to be discerning.

Again, in the parable of the wheat and the tares, Jesus indicated that we won't always be able to completely separate the false from the true until the truth is revealed at the end of the age. It is therefore impossible to completely cleanse the church of enemy agents. For this reason, we must be constantly on guard. We must measure all things by the Word of God, testing not only the words of fellow believers, but also their "fruit"—their behavior and attitudes. If you encounter a spirit of pride and willfulness, be careful. Apply the Word of God and church discipline with both conviction and humility. *"Correct, rebuke and encourage—with great patience and careful instruction"* (2 Timothy 4:2 NIV).

USING POPULAR CULTURE

Spiritual warfare has an impact on countries and their cultures. According to Daniel 10, entire nations are influenced by the invisible battle in the angelic realm. Working through the popular culture is a favorite tactic of Satan because it multiplies his effectiveness. As the enemy and his demons can each be in only one place at a time, and cannot personally work in every human heart, he influences multitudes through a system of thought the Bible calls *"the world."*

John wrote,

> *Do not love the world or the things in the world. If anyone loves the world, the love of the Father is not in him. For all that is in the world; the lust of the flesh, the lust of the eyes, and the pride of life; is not of the Father but is of the world.*
>
> —1 John 2:15–16

The Bible uses the term "*world,*" in this context, to describe fallen humanity's mind-set and desires, which dominate the lives of most people today. In general, the "world" controls the culture. Your worldview is vital because it affects your approach to spiritual warfare. It colors the way you see the nonmaterial world, and it determines whether you even believe in a spiritual realm. Worldly philosophies oppose the truth of the gospel, including all efforts to bring men and women to Christ. In Western society, the world system emphasizes the temporal rather than the eternal. It focuses on comfort and self-indulgence rather than responsibility and sacrifice for others. The devil influences multitudes of people into living for the moment. They follow him heedlessly as they buy into the popular thinking of the day.

Individual expressions of this thought-system may vary from one culture to another. For example, one culture may emphasize legalism rather than license. However, the end result is the same for people everywhere—deception and destruction.

PREYING ON THE SINFUL NATURE OF MAN

In the depths of depravity found in the human heart, our adversary has fertile soil. As is stated so clearly in the second chapter of Ephesians, before we came to Christ, we...

- "*were dead in trespasses and sins*" (verse 1).
- "*walked according to the course of this world, according to the prince of the power of the air*" (verse 2).

- *"all once conducted ourselves in the lusts of our flesh, fulfilling the desires of the flesh and of the mind, and were by nature children of wrath"* (verse 3).

The devil's power over fallen humanity is destructive and fearful. Multitudes of people help Satan function in his role as the god of this world by allowing him to exacerbate the lusts of their flesh, or their sinful natures.

When we are born again through Jesus, however, we become new creatures in Christ. *"Therefore, if anyone is in Christ, he is a new creation; old things have passed away; behold, all things have become new"* (2 Corinthians 5:17). We no longer need to obey sin or Satan. We have a new Master, the Lord Jesus Christ, and we serve Him and follow His commands.

We will discuss the conflict between the flesh and the spirit, as well as how to be victorious in this warfare, more fully in a later chapter.

USING DECEIT

Jesus often talked about the deceitful nature of the devil. One day, Jesus had a confrontation with the Pharisees. He told them in unmistakable terms that their inability to recognize the truth was due to the fact they were the "children of the devil," who is the *"father of lies"* (John 8:44 NIV):

Jesus said to them, "If God were your Father, you would love Me, for I proceeded forth and came from God; nor have I come of Myself, but He sent Me. Why do you not understand My speech? Because you are not able to listen to My word. You are of your father the devil, and the desires of your father you want to do. He was a murderer from the beginning, and does not stand in the truth, because there is no truth in him.

When he speaks a lie, he speaks from his own resources, for he is a liar and the father of it." —John 8:42–44

The devil is the creator of falsehoods. He is the fountainhead of all lies. He is forever trying to deceive. Sometimes, he plagiarizes and quotes reliable sources, but even then, he puts the truth in an altogether different context so that it creates an illusion. In fact, the devil began his career as Satan by deluding *himself* into believing that he could claim a position of equality with the Most High God. He is extremely self-centered and has an unrealistic view of his abilities: "*You have said in your heart: '...I will exalt my throne above the stars of God;...I will be like the Most High'*" (Isaiah 14:13–14).

Satan's self-deception caused him to fall from his position of high honor, and it is still his nature to lie and distort the truth. Not only does he deceive others in the manner of one who knows the truth and seeks to mislead, but he also lies because his own intelligence has been darkened by his perverted will. He is the father of lies because he deluded himself and willfully persists in this self-delusion.

We must be careful not to fall prey to his deceitful strategy—and his nature. We need to stick closely to God's truth and ask the Holy Spirit to direct us. Jesus promised us, "*When He, the Spirit of truth, has come, He will guide you into all truth*" (John 16:13).

USING ACCUSATION

Satan uses accusations, false indictments, and trumped-up charges to try to tear down the people of God. Revelation 12:10 calls the devil the "*accuser of our brethren, who accused them before our God day and night.*" In fact, the Greek word that we translate as *devil* is *diabolos*, which means "false accuser" or "slanderer."[5]

5. *Strong's*, #G1228.

Satan accused Jesus, and we can be assured that he will also accuse all who follow the Lord. He puts the worst possible interpretation on any act of faith and obedience, and he duplicates his accusing spirit in the fleshly nature of unbelievers. Some people are so warped and twisted that they perceive even the best actions of God's people to be evil. Believers are bombarded with all kinds of accusations from both inside and outside the church. As Christians, we have to guard against having a complaining and accusing attitude toward our fellow believers. We must recognize that such an attitude comes from our sinful nature—and that our enemy may be inciting it in us!

A classic example of Satan as accuser is in the book of Job:

Now there was a day when the sons of God came to present themselves before the Lord, and Satan also came among them....So Satan answered the LORD and said, "Does Job fear God for nothing? Have You not made a hedge around him, around his household, and around all that he has on every side? You have blessed the work of his hands, and his possessions have increased in the land. But now, stretch out Your hand and touch all that he has, and he will surely curse You to Your face!" And the LORD said to Satan, "Behold, all that he has is in your power; only do not lay a hand on his person." So Satan went out from the presence of the Lord.

—Job 1:6, 9–12

Satan claimed that Job served God only because he was prosperous and because God had put a wall around him, protecting him from misfortune. He contended (mistakenly) that Job would serve God only as long as God blessed him. God then granted Satan the authority to afflict Job, but within strict limits.

Through the book of Job, God permits us to grasp the issues of spiritual warfare in a more complete way by revealing what was going on beyond the earthly drama and giving us an insightful glimpse into His eternal purposes. While Job's sufferings appeared to be from natural causes, they were, in truth, of satanic origin. However, God always exercised sovereign control over the events of His servant's life and brought about justice and restoration.

In another example, the prophet Zechariah was given this vision of the spiritual realm: *"Then he showed me Joshua the high priest standing before the Angel of the LORD, and Satan standing at his right hand to oppose him"* (Zechariah 3:1). Apparently, God permitted Satan this privilege so that He could demonstrate His grace and forgiveness toward sinners. The passage continues,

---

> *And the LORD said to Satan, "The LORD rebuke you, Satan! The LORD who has chosen Jerusalem rebuke you! Is this not a brand plucked from the fire?" Now Joshua was clothed with filthy garments, and was standing before the Angel. Then He answered and spoke to those who stood before Him, saying, "Take away the filthy garments from him." And to him He said, "See, I have removed your iniquity from you, and I will clothe you with rich robes."* —Zechariah 3:2–4

Likewise, when we come before God in prayer, Satan may be there to accuse us. The devil may make a point of calling attention to our shortcomings and our sin or *"filthy garments,"* but there is an answer for his accusations.

In the case of Joshua the high priest, God said, *"The LORD rebuke you, Satan! The LORD who has chosen Jerusalem rebuke you!"* He let the devil know that He had chosen Joshua to be His servant. God instructed the angels standing nearby, "'*Take away the filthy garments from him.' And to* [Joshua] *He said, 'See, I have removed your iniquity from you, and I will clothe you with rich robes.'"*

Thank God, He removes our sins, and He clothes us in His righteousness when we are washed by the blood of Jesus! One of the greatest weapons we have in spiritual warfare is the knowledge that God dismisses Satan's accusations against us, showing him that we are now covered by the righteousness of Christ. God always responds to us in mercy and love. We must recognize that, because of Jesus, we are truly righteous in God's eyes.

> *If God is for us, who can be against us? He who did not spare His own Son, but delivered Him up for us all, how shall He not with Him also freely give us all things? Who shall bring a charge against God's elect? It is God who justifies. Who is he who condemns?*
> —Romans 8:31–34

COUNTERACTING SATAN'S STRATEGIES

In our own strength, we are helpless to resist the devil's temptations and accusations. God's children are often confused, paralyzed, and even driven to despair when they are exposed to the merciless attacks of the accuser. However, you don't have to be a victim; you can be a victor! Knowledge of the Word will help you to wage spiritual warfare against the devil and the forces of evil in his kingdom.

Since we war against unseen forces, we must wage our battles by faith and not by sight. (See 2 Corinthians 5:7.) We cannot fight back in our own strength; we must remember to rely on the power of the Holy Spirit, and not our own resources, in our battles with the enemy. The apostle Peter learned this lesson the hard way. Self-confidence prompted him to declare his willingness to die for Christ, but the Lord warned him,

> *Simon, Simon! Indeed, Satan has asked for you, that he may sift you as wheat. But I have prayed for you, that your faith should not fail; and when you have returned to Me, strengthen your brethren.*
> —Luke 22:31–32

Peter's rash boasting in his own abilities to remain faithful to Christ opened the door for the devil to cause him to fall. Jesus told Peter the devil's plan ahead of time and promised to intercede for him. Peter's failures, and the subsequent accusations of the devil, would sift Peter like wheat, confusing him, demoralizing him, and making him vulnerable to losing his faith. But Jesus' prayers sustained him.

Although Peter denied his Lord in fear three times, he repented, and His relationship with Christ was restored. Because of Jesus' intercession, Peter's faith did not fail. Likewise, our sins and failings make us vulnerable to Satan's accusations, but we have the prayers of Christ on our behalf. "*Christ…is even at the right hand of God, who also makes intercession for us*" (Romans 8:34). "*We have a great High Priest…, Jesus the Son of God….*[He can] *sympathize with our weaknesses,* [and] *was in all points tempted as we are, yet without sin*" (Hebrews 4:14–15). "*He always lives to make intercession for* [us]" (Hebrews 7:25). Jesus is the only One in history who could say, "*The ruler of this world is coming, and he has nothing in Me*" (John 14:30). Jesus' motives are always beyond question, His actions are always above reproach, and He is praying and working on our behalf.

I believe that, years after this interchange with Jesus, when Peter was writing to a group of Christians who were being persecuted, he remembered the attack of Satan. Wanting to encourage them to hold on to their faith, he called the devil an enemy who prowls around like a lion, looking for someone to devour, and he warned the believers to be alert to him. (See 1 Peter 5:8.) Peter knew by personal experience what it meant to be shaken in the grip of Satan.

Self-confidence is a noble trait only if we realize that our strength is in Christ. We must stand before God on the basis of the righteousness of Christ, not our own righteousness. *"For we... who worship God in the Spirit, rejoice in Christ Jesus, and have no confidence in the flesh"* (Philippians 3:3).

Satan hasn't been granted the power to devour the children of God, but he can influence us to the point of making us serve his ends if we don't watch and pray. He is a ruthless, merciless fiend whose goal is to defeat and destroy us. He should never be taken lightly.

If you yield to Satan, his evil influence can affect your health, moods, thoughts, and imagination. Why did Judas Iscariot betray Jesus and finally commit suicide instead of repenting? He allowed himself to listen to the temptations and lies of the enemy. The Bible tells us that *"Satan entered Judas...who was numbered among the twelve. So he went his way and conferred with the chief priests and captains, how he might betray Him to them"* (Luke 22:3–4). Then, after his betrayal, when the impact of what he had done hit him, Judas took his own life instead of repenting. Judas's response is in clear contrast with Peter's, who repented and was restored.

We cannot make the mistake of minimizing Satan's power or denying the reality of his kingdom of evil. But we must also avoid the error of falling into the devil's condemnation and losing our faith and trust in our heavenly Father. Remember that the enemy cannot go beyond the limits set by God. If we do fall into his deceitful traps and sin, we can repent and receive forgiveness through the blood of Christ. The born-again believer who submits to God and resists the devil will cause him to flee. (See James 4:7.)

4

THE ENEMY'S STRONGHOLDS

The weapons of our warfare are not carnal but mighty in God for pulling down strongholds, casting down arguments and every high thing that exalts itself against the knowledge of God, bringing every thought into captivity to the obedience of Christ.
—2 Corinthians 10:4–5

TYPES OF SPIRITUAL STRONGHOLDS

We have looked at the major strategies the enemy uses to draw people away from God and to serve his evil ends. In this chapter, I want to discuss various spiritual strongholds through which the enemy dominates and oppresses people. We must learn to recognize them for what they are so that we can effectively combat them.

EMOTIONAL PROBLEMS

In my experience, one type of spiritual stronghold is manifested through severe emotional problems. Not all emotional problems are strongholds, but they may be when emotional disturbances recur over and over and there seems to be no permanent cure or relief from them. In other words, when they persist in the life and personality of an individual. Some of the most common symptoms of this stronghold are anger, depression, fear, feelings of inferiority, feelings of insecurity, feelings of rejection (feeling unwanted and unloved), hatred, jealousy, resentment, self-pity, and worry.

MENTAL PROBLEMS

Another spiritual stronghold is the stifling grip of mental problems. These problems occur through disturbances in the mind or in the thought life. Caused by distorted thinking, this stronghold of evil brings about mental torment. It manifests itself in unrealistic and unexplained procrastination, incomprehensible indecision, wavering, compromise, confusion, delusions, doubt, rationalization, and even the loss of memory.

DISRUPTIVE SPEECH

Satan also builds spiritual strongholds in the lives of individuals through disruptive speech. This stronghold may be revealed in uncontrolled outbursts that occur suddenly and without warning. Yet it often manifests itself through lying, profanity, blasphemy, criticism, mockery, railing, and gossip.

SEXUAL PROBLEMS

Another form of spiritual oppression often seen today is the stronghold of sexual problems. This includes, but is not limited to, recurring unclean thoughts and impure sexual acts. It may include fantasy sexual experiences, masturbation, lust, provocative and lewd behavior, homosexuality, fornication, adultery, incest, and other perversions.

ADDICTIONS

The enemy wants to destroy as many souls as he can, and he has found that addictions are an effective weapon to use. Satan loves to oppress people through dependence on such things as nicotine, alcohol, illegal drugs, prescription and over-the-counter medications, gambling, television, the Internet, caffeine, and even food, including salt and sugar. Therefore, what some psychologists and psychiatrists call an "addictive personality" may actually be the result of a spiritual stronghold.

PHYSICAL INFIRMITIES

While not all physical infirmities are strongholds, God revealed to me that a number of diseases and physical afflictions are due to spirits of infirmity. When a demon of infirmity is cast out, there is often the need to pray for a healing of whatever damage has resulted. A close and necessary relationship exists between deliverance and healing.

HOW STRONGHOLDS DEVELOP

THROUGH OCCULT ACTIVITY

Becoming involved with the occult or spiritism in any form can open the door to spiritual strongholds. This includes séances, witchcraft, black magic, Wicca, ouija boards, levitation, palmistry, handwriting analysis, automatic handwriting, ESP, hypnosis, horoscopes, astrology, fortune-telling, seeking after spirits of the dead, new age meditation, yoga, divination, mantras, and any form of devil worship.

Many people today talk about spirituality, but they are plugged in to the wrong spirit. Unfortunately, psychics and mediums are popular today, as they were in certain Bible times, and many people are falling into this grievous stronghold.

Any method of seeking supernatural knowledge, wisdom, guidance, and power apart from God is forbidden in the Bible. (See, for example, Deuteronomy 18:9–14.) Believers are commanded to avoid every form of participation in demonic practices. We are not to watch movies or television programs that have demonic content, read demonic books, participate in demonic games, or listen to songs that have demonic lyrics.

Many times, I have seen demons attracted to certain homes because members of these households have taken objects or literature of occult or religious error into the homes. Occult items attract evil spirits.

THROUGH FALSE RELIGION AND DOCTRINE

Believing and adopting a false religion or doctrine can also allow Satan to build a stronghold in a person's mind. If you have ever tried to talk to someone who has accepted a pagan religion, philosophy, cult, or mind science, you know how entrenched these strongholds can be.

Paul warned us this way:

> *Beware lest anyone cheat you through philosophy and empty deceit, according to the tradition of men, according to the basic principles of the world, and not according to Christ.*
>
> —Colossians 2:8

We are warned in 1 Timothy 4:1 that, in the last days, there will be a great increase of doctrinal error promoted by "*deceiving*" or "*seducing*" (KJV) spirits and "*doctrines of demons,*" which will infiltrate the church. Any doctrine that attacks the humanity and deity of Jesus Christ or denies the inspiration of Scripture is a false doctrine. Moreover, those who promote disunity in the body of Christ or cause confusion in the church through their obsession with or insistence on false doctrines have fallen victim to a spiritual stronghold. In addition, teaching that distracts Christians from the authentic move of God's Spirit can lead to a stronghold.

THROUGH SPIRITUAL PRIDE OR VANITY

Being puffed up with a sense of superiority can be a manifestation of a religious stronghold. This is something we especially have to guard against. The apostle Paul was given a *"thorn in the flesh"* to keep him from being conceited by his many revelations. (See 2 Corinthians 12:7–10.) The stronghold of spiritual conceit or vanity fosters an emphasis on fleshly activities as a supposed gateway to the spiritual.

Vanity is a reflection of a prideful spirit, which was Satan's original sin. The Bible warns that if we are *"puffed up with pride,"* we may *"fall into the same condemnation as the devil"* (1 Timothy 3:6).

Vanity can make the person who is in error unteachable, and it is the ultimate expression of self-sufficiency. It says, "I can handle life by myself. I can save myself. I don't need God." In this way, vanity leads to personal idolatry (making a god of yourself and your capabilities) and can even lead to the worship of demons. The forces of evil try to persuade men and women to worship idols rather than God.

THROUGH FEAR

Satan wants us to be filled with fear and to doubt God's promises and provision. Fear is deadly; it cripples, stifles, and binds. Worry can be a terrible strain on the body. The enemy uses fear to oppress us so that we are paralyzed and ineffective in serving God. When we continually give in to fear, it can become a stronghold. We read in Revelation,

---

> *He who overcomes shall inherit all things, and I will be his God and he shall be My son. But the* ***cowardly****, unbelieving,*

> *abominable, murderers, sexually immoral, sorcerers, idolaters, and all liars shall have their part in the lake which burns with fire and brimstone, which is the second death.*
>
> —Revelation 21:7–8, emphasis added

In this passage, the word *"cowardly"* seems to imply fear that causes a person to be faithless,[6] perhaps to the point of denying or rejecting Christ. The Bible tells us that *"whatever is not from faith is sin"* (Romans 14:23). The oppression of fear, as well as its remedy, can be seen in John's statement, *"There is no fear in love; but* ***perfect love casts out fear****, because* ***fear involves torment****. But he who fears has not been made perfect in love"* (1 John 4:18, emphasis added).

We must not give in to fear that would keep us from loving and serving God. Remember that Jesus came to *"release those who through fear of death were all their lifetime subject to bondage"* (Hebrew 2:15). Paul emphasized,

---

> *For you did not receive the spirit of bondage again to fear, but you received the Spirit of adoption by whom we cry out, "Abba, Father." The Spirit Himself bears witness with our spirit that we are children of God, and if children, then heirs; heirs of God and joint heirs with Christ, if indeed we suffer with Him, that we may also be glorified together.*
>
> —Romans 8:15–17

Paul also wrote, *"God has not given us a spirit of fear, but of power and of love and of a sound mind"* (2 Timothy 1:7).

In combating fear, we must trust fully in our relationship with God the Father. As His children, we can rest in the knowledge of His perfect love toward us. We must not allow the enemy to cause us to doubt His guidance, protection, and provision.

6. See *Strong's*, #G1169.

THROUGH OTHER SIN

Willful participation in sin is another way the enemy can gain a foothold in our lives. If unchecked, a foothold can become a stronghold. The book of Ephesians explains how we are to replace the sin in our lives with new attitudes and actions that build up others and ourselves:

You were taught, with regard to your former way of life, to put off your old self, which is being corrupted by its deceitful desires; to be made new in the attitude of your minds; and to put on the new self, created to be like God in true righteousness and holiness. Therefore each of you must put off falsehood and speak truthfully to his neighbor, for we are all members of one body. "In your anger do not sin": Do not let the sun go down while you are still angry, and ***do not give the devil a foothold.*** *He who has been stealing must steal no longer, but must work, doing something useful with his own hands, that he may have something to share with those in need. Do not let any unwholesome talk come out of your mouths, but only what is helpful for building others up according to their needs, that it may benefit those who listen. And do not grieve the Holy Spirit of God, with whom you were sealed for the day of redemption. Get rid of all bitterness, rage and anger, brawling and slander, along with every form of malice. Be kind and compassionate to one another, forgiving each other, just as in Christ God forgave you.* —Ephesians 4:22–32 NIV, emphasis added

---

DEFEATING SATAN'S STRONGHOLDS

Ignorance, idolatry, and lust are Satan's strongholds in the lives of some people, while vain imaginations, proud conceits, and fear are his strongholds in others. With every stronghold, the devil attempts to keep men and women from faith and obedience to the gospel. He wants their hearts as his own property.

The Bible tells us that the weapons with which we are to fight the enemy are not the weapons of this world, which have no power over him. Instead, the spiritual weapons God gives us have divine power to demolish satanic strongholds. These strategic assets can take into captivity *every* thought to the obedience of Christ. We are to cast down *"arguments"* or *"imaginations"* (KJV), those carnal reasonings of the sinful nature that are opposed to God's purpose:

> *The weapons of our warfare are not carnal but mighty in God for pulling down strongholds, casting down arguments and every high thing that exalts itself against the knowledge of God, bringing every thought into captivity to the obedience of Christ.* —2 Corinthians 10:4–5

Three functions of spiritual weapons in pulling down strongholds are indicated in the above verses. Spiritual warfare...

1. demolishes everything that is opposed to Christ,
2. enables us to take control of our mind-set and thoughts,
3. transforms all that is alien and contrary to God into obedience to Christ.

The war we wage against evil must be fought with spiritual weapons. Through God's Word, we can cast down lies and everything that exalts itself against the knowledge of God. *"The word of God is living and powerful"* (Hebrews 4:12). It will defeat any argument of the devil.

The Lord has shown me that part of Satan's methodology is to keep God's people ignorant of His Word. For example, one day, I was sharing with a group of believers about the victory we have in

Christ Jesus. I talked about the joy of salvation and the power we have to live the Christian life. Afterward, several people came to me individually and said, "Mary, I know I have power in God, but I just don't know how to appropriate that power." Unfortunately, these believers were typical of many in the church today. However, I rejoiced that I had the answer for them because I had gone through the same experience years ago. I turned to Hosea 4:6 and read to them, *"My people are destroyed for lack of knowledge."*

We can defeat the strongholds of Satan by bringing all our thoughts in line with the mind of Christ. Those who give control of their thought life over to Satan and his lies will harm themselves. Yet, by submitting to God and His Word, we can capture our whole understanding and dedicate it to obeying Christ. A victorious believer takes as willing captives his thoughts, motives, and intentions. He voluntarily pledges their obedience to Christ. True fulfillment and power to live a victorious Christian life can come only when we are totally submitted to Him.

Satan's power over the believer is limited. The devil is a caged lion that seeks to devour, but he and his demonic forces have only the power God allows them or the authority a man or woman voluntarily gives over to them. We limit Satan's damage by serving God and living righteously before Him.

In contrast, Satan often has overwhelming power and influence over unbelievers. I have observed many people who said, "I will never do this," or "I will never do that." Then they contradicted themselves and did exactly what they promised they wouldn't. This is because they are susceptible to the enemy's deceit and temptations. They don't have the power and protection that believers have through God's Spirit.

Anthony Gomez from Brooklyn, New York, shared with me his awesome experience in spiritual warfare. It shows the devil's power over unbelievers and how only God can break the enemy's hold on someone:

I was with the Latin Kings [a well-known gang] on the mean streets of New York for several years. I have been very wicked and evil. I took pleasure in hurting people. I have been involved with Santeria, black magic, devil worshiping—I think I've done just about everything.

I've come a long way to where I am now. I can't believe I'm still alive. Once I was kidnapped. When I tried to run I couldn't because I had been beaten so badly. The last time I tried to run, I felt a hand picking me up and throwing me on the highway. Fortunately, a car stopped and the people called the police.

I have read two of your books, and they scared me to death before I turned to God. I've seen demons like the ones you describe—big, hairy bodies, brownish skin, eyes way back, long faces, and so on. I get a lot of dreams and visions. Once I saw little small demons put chains on me.

Then two beings held me and forced me to look at a scene I did not want to see. I felt hands holding me, forcing me to see these things; and I couldn't move. I cried for hours. I was so angry that they held me like that. I wound up in prison in Pennsylvania.

At Greensburg, I got one of your books, and it really put me straight. I thank God for Dr. T. L. Lowery and Mary K. Baxter, and for the work you are doing. You don't know how much you have helped me in this new way of life.

Believers may be tempted, deceived, and accused by Satan. They do not have to yield to these attacks, but if they continue to listen to Satan and turn from God's truth, they can be left with merely human resources, as in the case of unbelievers.

When a believer does not resist Satan, he may become entangled so deeply in wrong behavior that he cannot escape it without special prayer and counsel from other believers. It sometimes even alters his personality. A person can be dominated by a demon in the same way some wives are dominated by abusive husbands. It comes to the point where they lose their sense of personal worth and control.

RENOUNCING THE WORKS OF THE DEVIL

Through strongholds, the devil harasses and oppresses people. In order to defeat the enemy's schemes against us, we must reject Satan and all his works. His works are sin, not righteousness. The fruit of his actions produce poverty and lack, not fulfillment and peace. He deals in disease, affliction, and suffering, not healing, health, and wholeness. In Jesus' name, we must renounce all the enemy's empty promises. After prayerfully discerning that a problem is not the result of natural causes, or when the flesh will not respond to spiritual discipline, then you should consciously renounce the strongholds in Jesus' name. Do it specifically. Declare what you are renouncing.

- **Renounce the Occult**: Reject anything that has to do with zodiac signs, clairvoyance, horoscopes, reincarnation, fortune-telling, hypnosis, yoga, transcendental meditation, mind-control, ouija boards, or any other occult practices or superstitions.
- **Renounce False Religion and Doctrine**: Reject false beliefs and doctrine that do not line up with the Word of God and do not recognize the deity and humanity of Christ.
- **Renounce Spiritual Pride and Vanity**: Reject any thought of saving or sustaining yourself through your own abilities or of taking credit for what God has done in your life.
- **Renounce the Spirit of Bondage**: Reject mental and emotional bondage, addictions, compulsions, and sexual perversions. God will help you break the bonds of pornography,

adultery, or homosexuality. Renounce the spirits of lying and confusion. Rebuke all fear, worry, anxiety, and timidity, including the paralyzing fear of death. Memorize and repeat often to yourself this verse: "*For God has not given us a spirit of fear, but of power and of love and of a sound mind*" (2 Timothy 1:7).

- **Renounce the Spirit of Infirmity:** Rebuke, in Jesus' name, any sickness and pain the devil may be causing in your body. Renounce the spirits of depression, despair, and suicide. It does not matter how long you have been suffering with these things. Remember the woman who had a spirit of infirmity for eighteen years but was delivered. (See Luke 13:11.)
- **Renounce the Sins of the Heart:** In Jesus' name, rebuke any works of unforgiveness, jealousy, anger, resentment, bitterness, vengeance, and violence, which the Bible clearly teaches against. They are self-destructive habits that will wreck your life. You can rebuke a spirit of listlessness. You can overcome apathy. Before you can do battle against the enemy, you must release all these works of Satan. We will discuss this point in more detail in a coming chapter.

We must be continually on the alert, for our enemy is persistent. The devil tempted Jesus, but our Lord defeated him with the Word of God. When Satan realized he had lost that round, he went away, but only to regroup and plot his next move: "*Now when the devil had ended every temptation, he departed from* [Jesus] *until an opportune time*" (Luke 4:13). Yet remember that, whenever the devil returned to tempt Jesus, the Lord overcame Him.

Jesus is the only One who is fully willing and able to deliver us from sin and Satan, and to give us peace. We can rely completely on our Savior. Let us cheerfully and devotedly obey Him from the heart. Let us willingly submit to all His commands and promises. He alone can demolish every stronghold Satan plots to bring against us.

5

TAKING BACK WHAT SATAN HAS STOLEN

[Jesus] *said, "The thief does not come except*
to steal, and to kill, and to destroy.
I have come that they may have life, and that they may have
it more abundantly."
—John 10:10

Perhaps you are still wondering if the enemy can be defeated or whether you are meant to engage him in battle. There is a portion of Scripture that has been a special blessing in my life in regard to understanding and practicing spiritual warfare. First Samuel 30 gives an account of David taking back what his enemy had stolen from him and the people who were under his leadership. He and his four-hundred-man platoon of guerilla "mighty men" returned to their hometown of Ziklag one day and discovered that the Amalekites had raided and sacked it. These enemies had also kidnapped their families and were holding them captive. Grieving over the devastation they found in Ziklag, David and his men wept until they couldn't weep any longer. Then the men's grief turned to anger against David as their leader, until they were ready to stone him:

> *Now it happened, when David and his men came to Ziklag, on the third day, that the Amalekites had invaded the South and...attacked Ziklag and burned it with fire, and had taken captive the women and those who were there, from small to great; they did not kill anyone, but carried them away and went their way. So David and his men came to the city, and there it was, burned with fire; and their wives, their sons, and their daughters had been taken captive. Then David and the people who were with him lifted up their voices and wept, until they had no more power to weep....Now David was greatly distressed, for the people spoke of stoning him, because the soul of all the people was grieved, every man for his sons and his daughters. But David strengthened himself in the* Lord *his God.*
>
> —1 Samuel 30:1–4, 6

THE ENEMY IS TO BE COMPLETELY DEFEATED

How did David react to this overwhelming situation? First, he strengthened and encouraged himself in the Lord. Then he prayed and asked God whether he should fight back. (See verse 8.) The Lord responded, *"Pursue, for you shall surely overtake them and without fail recover all....So David recovered all that the Amalekites had carried away....And nothing of theirs was lacking...; David recovered all"* (verses 8, 18–19).

We should note that these events took place near the end of David's wilderness years. He had been running from Saul for about ten years, living in exile under stressful and trying circumstances. We all have wilderness experiences in which we encounter difficulties and trials. These are times that test our faithfulness to God, but they can also be times of spiritual education, if we will allow God to teach us. In addition, they can be times that strengthen the nature of our relationships with God, just as David turned to the Lord for strength and encouragement in his difficulties.

Was David successful in getting back what the enemy had stolen? *"David recovered* ***all*** *that the Amalekites had carried away"* (verse 18). Not only did he defeat his enemy, but he also got back *everything* that had been stolen.

Likewise, our spiritual enemy is out to steal from us and ruin us. Jesus called Satan a thief as He warned us, *"The thief does not come except to steal, and to kill, and to destroy"* (John 10:10). The devil does everything he can to rob whatever he can from us—spiritual blessings, physical health, financial resources, effectiveness for the kingdom, peace, and even mental soundness.

Satan has stolen too many things from God's people. We do not need to let this thief come into our lives and the lives of our family members. We must keep the enemy from stealing the resources of our churches, our ministries, and our jobs. It is time for us to show righteous anger and decide we are going to take back what this thief has stolen from us!

JESUS GIVES US HIS AUTHORITY AND POWER

We have already seen how the Old Testament gives us insight into Satan and his activities, through such passages as Satan's arrogance and fall (Isaiah 14:12–17), the temptation and fall of humanity (Genesis 3), and Satan's attack on Job (Job 1–2). Yet the gospel era seems to have been a unique time when spiritual warfare took a decided turn in intensity. Demonic manifestations became more pronounced when Jesus began His ministry. When the Son of God came to the earth, Satan finally realized his ultimate defeat was a certainty. He knew his time to do his evil works was limited. Therefore, demons openly displayed their presence within people and often challenged the authority of the Lord, as well as that of His disciples.

We know, of course, that Satan can do nothing without God's permission. God allowed these things to happen so that, as the Messiah of Israel, Jesus could demonstrate His power and authority over the devil and his demons. Through His mighty works, including subduing and casting out evil spirits, Jesus was declaring that the King had come. God's kingdom of freedom and life was now present on earth because He was present. Jesus' authority over sin, sickness, and Satan was a fulfillment of Scripture. For example, we read,

---

> *When evening had come, they brought to* [Jesus] *many who were demon-possessed. And He cast out the spirits with a word, and healed all who were sick, that it might be fulfilled which was spoken by Isaiah the prophet, saying: "He Himself took our infirmities and bore our sicknesses."*
>
> —Matthew 8:16–17

Jesus knew the importance of His coming for spiritual warfare and defeating the enemy:

- He said in John 12:31, "*Now is the judgment of this world; now the ruler of this world will be cast out.*"
- He said in John 16:11, "*The ruler of this world is judged.*"
- Colossians 2:15 says that Jesus "*disarmed principalities and powers,* [and] *made a public spectacle of them, triumphing over them in it.*"
- Hebrews 2:14–15 says that Jesus became flesh and blood so "*that through death He might destroy him who had the power*

of death, that is, the devil, and release those who through fear of death were all their lifetime subject to bondage."

Jesus said He had *"all authority."* Note that He also gave that same authority to us in His name:

All authority has been given to Me in heaven and on earth. Go therefore and make disciples of all the nations, baptizing them in the name of the Father and of the Son and of the Holy Spirit, teaching them to observe all things that I have commanded you; and lo, I am with you always, even to the end of the age.

—Matthew 28:18–20

Go into all the world and preach the gospel to every creature. He who believes and is baptized will be saved; but he who does not believe will be condemned. And these signs will follow those who believe: In My name they will cast out demons; they will speak with new tongues; they will take up serpents; and if they drink anything deadly, it will by no means hurt them; they will lay hands on the sick, and they will recover.

—Mark 16:15–18

Then the seventy returned with joy, saying, "Lord, even the demons are subject to us in Your name." And He said to them, "I saw Satan fall like lightning from heaven. Behold, I give you the authority to trample on serpents and scorpions, and over all the power of the enemy, and nothing shall by any means hurt you."

—Luke 10:17–19

The Bible clearly sets forth Christ's power over the enemy and our victory in Him. We must remember that *all* created beings—whether they are holy or fallen—were created through and for Christ. Therefore, they are naturally under His authority:

For by Him all things were created that are in heaven and that are on earth, visible and invisible, whether thrones or dominions or principalities or powers. All things were created through Him and for Him. —Colossians 1:16

Remember that the powers of evil are twice under Jesus' authority because He totally and publicly defeated them.

Having disarmed principalities and powers, He made a public spectacle of them, triumphing over them in it.
—Colossians 2:15

We must come to fully understand that, when Jesus triumphed over the devil, He released us from our enemy's grip. God wants us to take full advantage of the fact that we are already conquerors over our enemy. Paul wrote, "*We are more than conquerors through Him who loved us*" (Romans 8:37).

If we are already "*more than conquerors,*" why does Satan so often continue to get the upper hand with God's people? One way he gets away with stealing from us is that he lies and deceives in order to convince us that he has more power than he actually possesses. He does not want us to understand that Jesus Christ has stripped him of his power over us—and we believe him rather than God! Unfortunately, Satan has taken control of many individuals, groups, cities, and even countries. But as a Christian, you can exercise the authority of the believer over the devil and his works. Some people think that demons are running around wildly, wreaking havoc wherever they go, with nothing to stop them. As spiritual beings, however, they must obey the sovereign God, and He has given His people authority over them in Jesus' name.

In the revelations God has graciously permitted me to have, I have often seen that old serpent, the devil, forced to retreat. I have seen an angel with an open book, brandishing the Word of God like a sword and making the devil bow down and stop whatever evil he was doing. Many times, I have seen him slink away in defeat from certain people and places.

The Holy Spirit directs strong believers toward the most strategic battles that will help advance God's kingdom and righteousness. Certain battles are not worth fighting, and the Holy Spirit has the ability to guide us to those confrontations that are most strategic.

God will give His people great boldness, courage, and supernatural strength in fighting the good fight of faith. Paul wrote, *"I have strength for all things in Christ Who empowers me [I am ready for anything and equal to anything through Him Who infuses inner strength into me; I am self-sufficient in Christ's sufficiency]"* (Philippians 4:13 AMP).

God's people need to invade the enemy's camp with all diligence, confidence, and assurance. We can take back everything Satan has stolen from us and our households. It doesn't belong to the devil. He is a thief, and we demand that he give it all back *now*!

Part Two:

THE WEAPONS OF OUR WARFARE

6

OFFENSIVE AND DEFENSIVE ARMOR

Therefore take up the whole armor of God, that you may be able to withstand in the evil day, and having done all, to stand. Stand therefore, having girded your waist with truth, having put on the breastplate of righteousness, and having shod your feet with the preparation of the gospel of peace; above all, taking the shield of faith with which you will be able to quench all the fiery darts of the wicked one. And take the helmet of salvation, and the sword of the Spirit, which is the word of God.

—Ephesians 6:13–17

In the first chapter of Ephesians, Paul taught that, when we come to Christ and trust in Him as our Savior, we are blessed "*with every spiritual blessing in the heavenly places in Christ*" (verse 3). Later in this chapter, he talked about Christ's power and glory, and the tremendous victory Jesus gave us over sin and Satan.

> [Christ is] *far above all principality and power and might and dominion, and every name that is named, not only in this age but also in that which is to come. And He put all things under His feet, and gave Him to be head over all things to the church, which is His body, the fullness of Him who fills all in all. And you He made alive, who were dead in trespasses and sins, in which you once walked according to the course of this world, according to the prince of the power of the air, the spirit who now works in the sons of disobedience.*
>
> —Ephesians 1:21–2:2

As we have been learning, when we come to Christ, it is not just a time of unbelievable blessedness, but it is also a declaration of war. It is the beginning of a struggle with Satan and his forces. The kingdom of heaven within us begins to war against the kingdom of hell. To be effective in this war, we must *"be strong in the Lord and in the power of his might"* (Ephesians 6:10), *"put on the whole armor of God"* (verse 11), and go forth to engage and defeat the enemy.

Yet numerous Christians do not know how to specifically engage in spiritual warfare. For this reason, many try to fight the enemy with inadequate weapons. Bible teacher Diane Dew had a dream or vision about the weapons Christians are meant to use in spiritual warfare:

> *It was just a dream,* I kept telling myself. But I awoke from my sleep alarmed and concerned for the condition of the church. Seldom do I remember a dream so vividly. The impression it made upon me remains to this day.
>
> I stood in the entrance of a very old and musty fortress. It could have been an ancient castle. The air was damp, like a basement kept closed for many years. To the right, a

staircase wound around the wall, leading downstairs. No one was in sight, so I proceeded about halfway down the steps. The wall was cold, clammy.

In the lower level was a huge pile of swords of all shapes and sizes. All were rusty from the dampness. None had been used in some time.

Where is everyone? I wondered, aloud.

"Away at war," the answer came. My heart skipped a beat.

They can't be doing very well, I thought. *They left without their weapons!*[7]

We are engaged in a real, though unseen, war! It is disastrous for us to go into spiritual battle without our spiritual weapons. We see an illustration of this truth from human warfare during World War II. As Hitler gained total control over Germany, his thirst for power and conquest grew. His army began to march across Europe, taking over more and more territory. As he conquered nation after nation, in some cases, the fight could hardly be called a battle. Some countries' armies made futile efforts with inadequate weapons to try to resist Hitler's technologically equipped troops. They were woefully unprepared for the strength of their enemy's warfare.

Similarly, tragic consequences can occur when we take a complacent attitude toward spiritual warfare and fail to guard against Satan's armory of fierce weapons. Just as a nation must prepare and build up its resources in order to wage a physical war, believers must arm themselves against the onslaught of Satan and his demons. Sometimes, Christians forget they have an enemy. But Satan, ever watchful for an opening, waits to attack not only you, but your family as well. You must protect yourself and your home from his destructive powers.

7. <http://dianedew.com/castle2.htm> (October 18, 2005)

In warfare, going into the enemy's territory is dangerous and risky. However, God does not send us into the devil's territory unequipped and on our own. Instead, He gives us the necessary armor and equipment to protect ourselves against the attacks that are sure to come.

In his book, *The Weapons of Your Warfare*, Larry Lea provided us with a weapons manifest, or list, of some spiritual arms available to the believer for spiritual warfare. He emphasized that God's storehouse of spiritual weapons includes the following:

1. The blood of Jesus
2. Prayer
3. The whole armor of God
4. Praise
5. Speaking the Word
6. The name of Jesus
7. Perseverance[8]

Our authority over Satan can be expressed by "pleading the blood" of Jesus, praising the Lord, reading the Bible aloud, breaking the enemy's power in Jesus' name, and many other ways. Although the above list is very helpful, keep in mind that it is not an exhaustive one. As you pray, read the Word of God, and rely on the Lord, He will bring to your mind other spiritual weapons. These are just some of the things Satan cannot stand against.

When we see how varied the weapons are, we begin to realize that they must be used properly. Some should be used only during hand-to-hand combat. Others can be used in sophisticated offensive maneuvers, but only when the Commander in Chief

8. See Larry Lea, *The Weapons of Your Warfare* (Orlando, FL: Strang Communications, 1989).

gives explicit orders to do so. Timing is everything when you are engaged in warfare.

It takes a thoroughly trained, experienced, and purposefully armored soldier to see a spiritual battle all the way through to victory. I wonder how many combat veterans would be able to tell you stories of fallen soldiers who became complacent after they had been around the battlefield for a while, and who let down their guards. In a similar way, in the realm of the spiritual, many have been "wounded" or "killed" because they thought that, since they had made it so far, the rest of the way would be easy. The Christian cannot survive unless he puts on the whole armor of God. When we follow God's directives for spiritual warfare, we will not put ourselves at unnecessary risk.

When we go into spiritual battle, we fight with weapons that are not of this world. The following are biblical instructions for spiritual warfare, using the analogy of physical armor that was familiar to the first-century world. May God grant us the wisdom and ability to apply them in our spiritual battles.

THE WHOLE ARMOR OF GOD

Paul wrote in Ephesians 6:10–11:

Finally, my brethren, be strong in the Lord and in the power of His might. Put on the whole armor of God, that you may be able to stand against the wiles of the devil.

You may think that armor is an ancient term that was relevant only for ancient people. The uniforms of soldiers may now be different from what they were in biblical times, and the equipment they use may be different. Still, a soldier going into battle must be properly equipped, and the principles of protection and weaponry that the "*armor of God*" represents still apply to us today.

Spiritual armor protects and reinforces the Christian as he or she engages in spiritual warfare. The pieces of equipment are of both an offensive and defensive nature. Note that Paul said we are to put on the *"whole"* armor. We must pay attention to *all* the pieces of spiritual equipment available to us so that (1) we will be able to effectively wage an offensive campaign against the forces of evil, and (2) we will not have any weak places in our lives through which the enemy can attack us. Although I have categorized the weaponry into offensive and defensive armor, you will notice that there is some overlap between the two.

OFFENSIVE ARMOR

THE BELT OF TRUTH

God once showed me a revelation of a man putting on spiritual armor. The first piece of armor I saw was a wide belt that glowed with a brilliant light and seemed to be as tough as steel. I immediately remembered that the apostle Paul said, *"Stand therefore, having girded your waist with truth"* (Ephesians 6:14). An ancient soldier's first step in putting on his armor was to secure a wide belt around his waist, which served as a place to hang the scabbard or sheath that held his sword.

The belt could also be used to tuck in loose clothing that might otherwise hinder or trip the soldier. For example, with the loose clothing tied up, the enemy did not have something that would be easy to grab. Such a belt was used not only by the military of the day, but also by people who were working or getting ready for extensive travel. They would gather up their long robes and tuck them in a belt or waist sash. This freed their legs for unhindered movement.

One of the spiritual applications is that, before we can put on the full armor of God, we must bind up the things that hinder us. We must maintain a life of integrity so that we will have a basis from which we can effectively use the sword of the Spirit—the Word of God. A commitment to truth removes spiritual hindrances from our lives and gives us the freedom of movement in the kingdom of God that we need for battle.

In our age of relativism, we may forget how much God values, honors, and requires truth. Psalm 51:6 says, "*You* [God] *desire truth in the inward parts.*" Jesus said, "*I tell you the truth,*" seventy-nine times in the four Gospels (NIV). Other translations use this phrase or similar phrases. Our Lord also said, "*I am the way, the truth, and the life. No one comes to the Father except through Me*" (John 14:6).

Jesus demonstrated that He was the truth in two ways: by what He said and by what He did. Read the words He spoke. Even His enemies recognized the veracity of His statements, such as when the Roman soldiers declared, "*No man ever spoke like this Man!*" (John 7:46). No one has spoken words of truth, wisdom, and life as Jesus has—not the ancient philosophers, such as Socrates, Plato, and Virgil, and not even religious leaders, such as Buddha or Muhammad. Pilate confessed, "*I find no fault in Him at all*" (John 18:38).

Jesus spoke gracious utterances that offered humanity full pardon, peace, and reconciliation through the sacrifice of His blood. He offered eternal life as God's free gift to those who received Him and His words. Jesus' sweet words of truth continue to lift and liberate lost sinners.

Jesus also demonstrated the truth by what He did. The New Testament is an amazing account of the mighty deeds and historic events of Jesus' life. What He said was reliable and accurate. His predictions about Himself were fulfilled just as He said. His actions were always in accordance with the nature and Word of God. He said He came to free the captives, and He invaded the realm of the satanic underworld, delivering men and women from bondage. He stalked into the lair of Satan himself and defeated death.

As followers of Jesus, we also must live lives of integrity. We have been given the truth in Jesus; and when we wear it as the foundation of our armor, God will use it to cause us to make a difference in our world. People often have to see the truth in us before they will believe what we say about God's Word. A lack of integrity will hinder your spiritual movement at every turn.

God's instructions for the Israelites' first Passover meal were the following:

> *They shall take some of the blood* [of the sacrificial lamb] *and put it on the two doorposts and on the lintel of the houses where they eat it. Then they shall eat the flesh on that night; roasted in fire, with unleavened bread and with bitter herbs they shall eat it....You shall eat it: with a belt on your waist, your sandals on your feet, and your staff in your hand. So you shall eat it in haste. It is the Lord's Passover.*
>
> —Exodus 12:7–8, 11

Here is how I apply this passage to spiritual armor, particularly the belt of truth: When we come to God in faith, He applies the blood of the Lamb of God to our hearts, and His blood cleanses us from sin. He then expects us to immediately be prepared to move out of the old way of doing things and into new life in Jesus Christ.

When we put on the belt of truth, we are saying to God and to the world that we have no time for anything that would delay, hinder, or get in the way of the life God wants us to lead. "*Therefore gird up the loins of your mind, be sober, and rest your hope fully upon the grace that is to be brought to you at the revelation of Jesus Christ*" (1 Peter 1:13). We need to gather up the loose ends of our lives and the things that cause us to stumble and place them under the control of God's Spirit, in accordance with God's Word. As we read earlier, we are to "[cast] *down arguments and every high thing that exalts itself against the knowledge of God, bringing every thought into captivity to the obedience of Christ"* (2 Corinthians 10:5).

THE SWORD OF THE SPIRIT

Although not next in order in the list of spiritual armor in Ephesians, let us now look at the sword of the Spirit, since the sword is attached to the belt in our armor analogy.

"Take the...sword of the Spirit, which is the word of God" (Ephesians 6:17). A soldier is not completely armed unless he has a weapon with which to defend himself. Yet the Lord impressed on my heart that there can be no effective defense without a good offense. The sword was not just used as a defensive weapon with which to protect oneself; it was also an offensive weapon with which to destroy an opponent or enemy. In Paul's time, the sword was the main weapon of warfare. Similarly, the Word of God is the primary weapon of offense we use in spiritual warfare today.

The Roman short sword had a double-edged blade and was designed for close-quarter, one-on-one fighting. A soldier had to spend many years learning to use it effectively. The well-trained soldiers of Rome were able to conquer most of the known world using these unique weapons.

If we are going to destroy the works of Satan, we must learn to use our unique sword—the Word of God. *"For the word of God is living and powerful, and sharper than any two-edged sword, piercing even to the division of soul and spirit, and of joints and marrow, and is a discerner of the thoughts and intents of the heart"* (Hebrews 4:12). Note, too, that the Bible refers to Jesus, the Living Word, as having a double-edged sword: *"He had in His right hand seven stars, out of His mouth went a sharp two-edged sword, and His countenance was like the sun shining in its strength"* (Revelation 1:16).

To use God's Word in spiritual warfare, we must study it diligently. No good soldier would ever go into battle without having learned how to use his weapons. As we are trained through our study of the Bible, we learn to use the power of the Word, through the Holy Spirit, to demolish the strongholds that have existed in our lives. The Word enables us to take captive every thought we have and make it obedient to His truth.

The Word came through the Holy Spirit and is brought to our minds by the Holy Spirit:

> *All Scripture is God-breathed and is useful for teaching, rebuking, correcting and training in righteousness, so that the man of God may be thoroughly equipped for every good work.*
> —2 Timothy 3:16–17 NIV

> [Jesus said,] "*When He, the Spirit of truth, has come, He will guide you into all truth; for He will not speak on His own authority, but whatever He hears He will speak; and He will tell you things to come. He will glorify Me, for He will take of what is Mine and declare it to you.*" —John 16:13–14

The Greek term for "*word*" in Ephesians 6:17 is not the more familiar *logos*, but *rhema*.[9] This seems to indicate specific application of the Word. The "sword," the Word of God, is attached to the "belt," or the truth of God. We might consider the sword to be the immediate word of God and the belt to be the "stored" or written Word. The specific word is drawn from the stored Word. We must study and know the written Word of God so that we will be ready when the Holy Spirit desires to give us a specific word that we are to apply to our present circumstances. Thus, we must take the sword of the Spirit firmly in hand in both offensive and defensive warfare.

9. *Strong's*, #G4487.

THE PREPARATION OF THE GOSPEL OF PEACE

Let's look next at our spiritual "shoes." Paul wrote, *"Having shod your feet with the preparation of the gospel of peace"* (Ephesians 6:15). Our walk with God requires us to have proper footwear, which, like the sword, can be considered both offensive and defensive in nature. Through our spiritual shoes, we prepare to do battle and are protected from the sharp attacks with which the enemy tries to make us stumble.

The only way to be prepared to walk through the wilderness of this world as we progress in our life's journey, the only way to be ready to wage spiritual warfare, is to be equipped with the gospel of Jesus Christ. Our preparation will determine the ability and the stability of our walk with Christ.

> *Always be prepared to give an answer to everyone who asks you to give the reason for the hope that you have. But do this with gentleness and respect.* —1 Peter 3:15 NIV

The shoes of the gospel of peace will never wear thin, just as the Israelites' shoes never wore out during forty years in the desert because God kept them whole. Putting on the proper footwear in spiritual warfare is an act of security for the future; it is trusting God's promise of deliverance and eternal life. His gospel is a gospel of peace, and we know that we are involved in a war whose victory is assured, and whose peace will be won forever.

This footwear also indicates that, as soldiers, we are part of the peace delegation that is being sent to those who are currently fighting on the side of Satan. Remember that, even though other people can seem like soldiers of the enemy, they are also being held captive by him to do his will. (See 2 Timothy 2:24–26.) We can proclaim the message that we serve a gracious King who desires that they live in His kingdom and receive all the benefits and blessings of

His children. Isaiah 52:7 says, *"How beautiful upon the mountains are the feet of him who brings good news, who proclaims peace, who brings glad tidings of good things, who proclaims salvation,"* and Paul wrote, *"Now then, we are ambassadors for Christ, as though God were pleading through us: we implore you on Christ's behalf, be reconciled to God"* (2 Corinthians 5:20).

THE BREASTPLATE OF RIGHTEOUSNESS

Another piece of equipment I saw in the revelation of God's armor looked like a bulletproof vest. This is what Paul referred to as the *"breastplate of righteousness"* (Ephesians 6:14). The Roman breastplate was a sleeveless, vest-like piece of flexible metal plate that stretched from the shoulder to the hip. It was backed with a piece of tough cowhide. This piece of armor protected the vital organs of the chest—notably the lungs and heart.

Physically, our lungs enable us to breathe in oxygen and exhale carbon dioxide so that we will have purer air to live on. Similarly, we are to protect our spiritual lungs so that we can freely take in a pure flow of the life of the Holy Spirit and live through Him. Too many Christians are struggling to work for God in their own strength and power.

The heart is the center of our physical lives, and as far as our spiritual lives are concerned, it is the core of our spiritual experience. The heart provides the motivation for all we do. If the heart is damaged, we will be thwarted in our motivation for spiritual things. Our desires and interests will be diverted from God's purposes.

If you wear the bulletproof vest of God's righteousness, however, you can ensure that your heart and emotions are securely guarded and adequately protected against attack. When we count on our own righteousness, we often begin to feel unworthy of God, or that we have failed in the Christian life and God will surely reject us. The enemy builds on this sense of unworthiness because his aim is to make us think that God has not really forgiven our sins. He wants us to forget that it is not our own righteousness that counts, but Christ's righteousness in us. This is simply the devil's means of opposing and destroying what God intends to do through believers who put their trust in His forgiveness and power.

Again, when we come to Jesus Christ and accept Him as Lord and Savior, our sins are forgiven, and we are granted the very righteousness of Christ Himself. The Greek word for "putting on" the breastplate of righteousness means "to clothe or be clothed with (in the sense of sinking into a garment)."[10] Jesus clothes us with the garment of His righteousness. In this sense, we don't so much put it on as allow it to be placed on us. To use the metaphor of "sinking into a garment," such as a robe, we lift up our hands to receive God's grace, and it flows over our heads and then covers our whole selves. When God the Father looks at us, He sees us as righteous because we are wearing the righteousness of His perfect Son.

> *I will greatly rejoice in the* Lord, *my soul shall be joyful in my God; for He has clothed me with the garments of salvation, He has covered me with the robe of righteousness.* —Isaiah 61:10

> [God] *made* [Jesus] *who knew no sin to be sin for us, that we might become the righteousness of God in Him.*
> —2 Corinthians 5:21

You cannot stand on your own merits. You have to come to Christ on the grounds of His imputed righteousness. I believe that, no matter what the circumstances, Paul knew he was secure in Christ because he had *"put on the breastplate of righteousness"* (Ephesians 6:14), which would deflect any weapon or ammunition with which the enemy would assault him.

10. *Strong's*, #G1746.

The only righteousness worth anything in the eyes of God is the righteousness of Jesus. The only way in which God can look on us as righteous is when He sees us in Christ, clothed in the garments of His righteousness. We must discard any robes of self-righteousness and put on the protective breastplate of the righteousness of Christ.

We need this protection because, again, the devil will try to cause us to become discouraged and depressed. He uses every wicked device he has in order to attack our hearts and emotions. He attacks Christians with confusion, doubt, uncertainty, strife, discord, and arguments. He tries to get us to feel sorry for ourselves. He tries to get us to doubt the love of God. One of his favorite schemes is to attack us with a spirit of indifference, cynicism, callousness, coldness, and bitterness toward one another and God. He approaches us through our circumstances, our feelings, and our thought life.

We must be sure to guard our emotions, as they can often give the devil an entry into our lives. The fourth chapter of Ephesians gives us an example of the relationship between our emotions and spiritual warfare:

> *"Be angry, and do not sin": do not let the sun go down on your wrath, nor give place to the devil.* —Ephesians 4:26–27

Failing to control your anger grants the devil an opportunity to get a foothold in your life. Then he can use it as a base of operations to launch more spiritual attacks against you. Many Christians are suffering today because of anger that has not been resolved. Still, anger is just one of many human emotions. If Satan can get a grip on our feelings, he can destroy our ability to function by crippling us emotionally or leading us into all manner of destructive and addictive behavior.

God has shown me many people who are wounded in soul and spirit. As I look into their faces, I can see the results of Satan's attacks on them. This doesn't mean they were necessarily doing something really *bad* in their lives, but that they listened to the wrong voice, and it resulted in wrong and ultimately painful choices.

Jesus protects us with an impenetrable vest against anything the devil may throw at us. Knowing that we are covered by the righteousness of Christ will guard our hearts and emotions and enable us to live the Christian life with security and joy regardless of the attacks of Satan. When we get weary in the battle, we must remind ourselves that Christ is the Truth, and that He is our righteousness.

THE SHIELD OF FAITH

"Above all, taking the shield of faith with which you will be able to quench all the fiery darts ["flaming arrows," NIV*] of the wicked one"* (Ephesians 6:16). The shield of a Roman soldier was several feet in height and was carried with one hand. It would protect him from an onslaught of rocks and flaming arrows. The shield was also used to ward off the blows of an enemy's sword. In addition, it enabled the Roman soldier to get near to an enemy soldier so that his short sword could be effectively used, while the enemy's longer sword would be useless in such close quarters. Similarly, our *"shield of faith"* can ward off the *"flaming arrows"* and other assaults of the evil one while enabling us to effectively counterattack using the sword of the Spirit.

It is of the utmost importance that we take this shield with us wherever we go because *"it is impossible to please God without faith. Anyone who wants to come to him must believe that God exists and that he rewards those who sincerely seek him"* (Hebrews 11:6 NLT). The faith that will deflect and extinguish the flaming arrows of the evil one is simply trust in God. We must live a life of faith, *"for in the gospel a righteousness from God is revealed, a righteousness that is by faith from first to last, just as it is written: 'The righteous will live by faith'"* (Romans 1:17 NIV).

The word Paul used for *"shield"* in Ephesians 6:16 is *thureos,* which refers to "a large shield."[11] Since a Roman shield covered much of the soldier, it also covered the other pieces of his armor. In a similar way, there is a connection between the shield of faith and all the other pieces of armor for spiritual warfare. Let's examine some of those connections.

When Paul referred to *"faith"* in Ephesians, he was speaking of faith in Christ. The Scripture says that *"faith comes by hearing, and hearing by the word of God"* (Romans 10:17). By faith, we who believe in Jesus through the testimony of the Word are "in Him." Paul used the phrase *"in Christ"* twelve times in the first three chapters of the book. An understanding of our position in Christ through faith renders all of Satan's lies ineffective; all the pieces of armor mentioned in Ephesians 6, as well as our prayers, involve aspects of our being in Him:

- *Belt of Truth*: The truth is in Christ. (See, for example, Ephesians 4:21.)
- *Breastplate of Righteousness*: We are righteous in Christ. (See, for example, Romans 3:22.)
- *Feet Shod with the Preparation of the Gospel of Peace*: We have peace with God in Christ. (See Romans 5:1.)
- *Helmet of Salvation*: We will spend eternity with God in Christ. (See, for example, Ephesians 2:6–7.)
- *Sword of the Spirit*: We apply the Word of God in Christ. (See, for example, 2 Corinthians 5:19.)
- *Praying Always:* We have access to God the Father through Christ. (See, for example, Ephesians 3:11–12.)

11. *Strong's*, #G2375.

If you understand the implications of being in Christ through faith, you will be able to *"extinguish all the flaming missiles of the evil one"* (Ephesians 6:16 NASB). Again, the imagery here is of flaming arrows launched with the intention of starting a destructive fire—a fire that quickly spreads out of control. This is a vivid metaphor for Satan's lies. With his deception, he attempts to light fires in our minds by impressing on us an incendiary idea that can ignite a series of destructive thoughts. This causes our imaginations, our impressions, and our questions to run wild. Moreover, this wildfire of the mind feeds on fear. *"Your adversary the devil walks about like a roaring lion, seeking whom he may devour"* (1 Peter 5:8). A lion roars to intimidate its rivals and to paralyze its prey with dread.

For example, worries about the future can rage out of control if we don't believe that God is both all knowing and good. Fear of being hurt emotionally consumes us if we don't believe that God will meet our relational needs. However, if we understand the truth of our position in Jesus and bring *"every thought into captivity to the obedience of Christ"* (2 Corinthians 10:5), we can recognize such fears as invalid, since they are based on false ideas.

Note that there is also a strong connection between faith and recognizing our position of being righteous in Christ (which enables us to wear the breastplate of righteousness.) In fact, in 1 Thessalonians 5:8, Paul said we are to put on the *"breastplate of faith and love."* Faith in Christ leads to Christ's righteousness being imputed to us, so that we no longer need to fear, but are *"made perfect in love"* (1 John 4:18).

THE HELMET OF SALVATION

"And take the helmet of salvation," Paul said in Ephesians 6:17. In 1 Thessalonians 5:8, he referred to this same headpiece as *"the hope of salvation."* This piece of armor concerns our eternal destiny and our assurance of salvation. Again, the enemy often calls into question the level of our loyalty and commitment to God. He tries

his best to cause us to doubt our safekeeping in Christ. As a result, we can be paralyzed by fear and insecurity.

If Satan is unsuccessful at causing us to doubt our salvation, then he'll attempt to convince us to downplay its importance. He doesn't want us to live with an eternal perspective in mind, but a worldly one. He wants us to be caught up in temporal things so that we won't spend time waging warfare against the powers of evil and on behalf of those who are lost.

How are we to "take" the helmet of salvation? The Greek word for "*take*" means to "accept, receive."[12] This provides an image of someone handing a helmet to a soldier for him to put on, or of a helmet being placed on a soldier. Similarly, we have to accept and receive salvation through Christ; He bestows his salvation on us. As Psalm 149:4 says, "*He crowns the humble with salvation*" (NIV).

The helmet of salvation protects the head, shielding it from deception and accusation. In addition, the head houses the brain. Our brains make decisions concerning how the rest of our bodies are going to operate. They are in charge of what we speak and how we speak it. They control what we listen to, as well as what we think. They enable us to experience emotions. Our minds are what we use to form positive or negative perceptions about other people, and to decide what we will or will not be content with.

Your mind is your consciousness. In this sense, it is *you*, and therefore it determines your future. With it, you make crucial decisions concerning your life's direction and destiny.

The Lord once brought to my mind a Scripture, which I immediately looked up. It says, "*We all once conducted ourselves in the lusts of our flesh, fulfilling the desires of the flesh and of the mind, and were by nature children of wrath, just as the others*" (Ephesians 2:3). I came to realize this means that we followed the sinful desires of our bodies and of our minds. We did what we felt like doing. We

---

12. *Strong's*, #G1209.

responded to so-called natural stimuli. We were under the direction of Satan and were, by nature, children of wrath, just as the rest of mankind is.

But now that we have been changed by Christ, we no longer live in that way. As children of the King, we follow the Prince of our Salvation as He leads us in warfare against the prince of darkness. When we put on the helmet of salvation, we receive the *"mind of Christ"* (1 Corinthians 2:16), and we are to renew our minds according to God's Word, through the Holy Spirit. In this way, our thoughts, actions, and words will be based only on God's thoughts and ways, for the purpose of glorifying Him. Jesus prayed to the Father regarding His disciples, *"Sanctify them in the truth. Your word is truth"* (John 17:17).

The Word accurately describes God as good, loving, kind, patient, and trustworthy. In contrast, Satan—just as he did to our first parents in the Garden of Eden—tries to convince us that God desires to withhold good from us and is not looking out for our best interests. He sometimes goes so far as to convince people that God's good gifts, such as marriage and certain foods, are bad. (See 1 Timothy 4:1–7.)

If we believe that God is good, however, we have nothing to fear. If God is good, we can be liberated from the self-defeating hell of worry, anxiety, and panic that we have created for ourselves—with a lot of help from our enemy and his forces of evil. The power of God will sustain us. The Bible says that we are *"kept by the power of God through faith for salvation"* (1 Peter 1:5).

Without the helmet of salvation securely on your head every day; without a focus on your future that is based on your redemption, the gift of the Holy Spirit, and the promise of eternity with God, you can only fall back on the world's system and culture to help you make important decisions. This will inevitably cause you to stumble into the deception of the enemy. *"There is a way that seems right to a man, but its end is the way of death"* (Proverbs 14:12).

PRAYING ALWAYS

After describing the specific pieces of spiritual armor, Paul concluded, "*Praying always with all prayer and supplication in the Spirit, being watchful to this end with all perseverance and supplication for all the saints*" (Ephesians 6:18). He revealed that the practice of prayer completes the whole armor of God. We will discuss this crucial spiritual weapon in a coming chapter, so that we may examine it more fully.

NO RETREAT

In the pieces of armor we have just discussed, have you noticed that there is one area of the soldier's body that is left unprotected? The armor wasn't designed to cover his *back*; Roman soldiers gave no thought to covering their backs because they did not believe in retreat!

Likewise, God's people should not believe in retreat because Christ has already won the victory! Thus, we see that we must take up the whole armor of God and *go forth* to spiritual battle. Sometimes, Satan will come with a full-scale frontal assault; sometimes he will choose guerilla warfare. This is why all the pieces of our armor must be utilized and cared for. We must ensure that they aren't laid aside, taken away, or knocked off by a wrong attitude or by apathy toward the very real warfare in which we are engaged.

Let us move forward, fully protected by the armor that God has provided for us. As Paul said, "*Forgetting those things which are behind and reaching forward to those things which are ahead, I press toward the goal for the prize of the upward call of God in Christ Jesus*" (Philippians 3:13–14).

7

THE LIFESTYLE OF A SPIRITUAL WARRIOR

I have been crucified with Christ; it is no longer I who live,
but Christ lives in me; and the life which
I now live in the flesh I live by faith in the Son of God,
who loved me and gave Himself for me.
—Galatians 2:20

Spiritual warfare is a lifestyle, not just an occasional event of rebuking the enemy or casting out demons. The believer must be spiritually prepared at all times. He must understand that since the enemy is continually on the prowl seeking whom he may devour, he must maintain an ongoing *warrior's awareness* of the spiritual battle that constantly rages around him. This understanding must become a natural part of the life of a follower of Christ.

Spiritual warfare requires us to be spiritually on guard because skirmishes can take place even on the inner battlefields of our own minds and hearts. We battle not only the world and the devil, but also our sinful nature, which desires what is contrary to God. The apostle Paul reminded us of this truth:

> *For the weapons of our warfare are not carnal but mighty in God for pulling down strongholds, casting down arguments and every high thing that exalts itself against the knowledge of God,* ***bringing every thought into captivity to the obedience of Christ.*** —2 Corinthians 10:4–5, emphasis added

> *And do not be conformed to this world, but* ***be transformed by the renewing of your mind.***
> —Romans 12:2, emphasis added

Many of us are holding on to false mind-sets and even destructive attitudes that do not belong in a child of God, without realizing that they weaken us spiritually. In fact, holding on to them hinders our relationships with God, gives the devil a foothold in our lives, and decreases our effectiveness in spiritual warfare. In addition, Satan seeks ways to encourage and provoke the sinful nature in our lives. He would like us to be dominated by sinful desires, such as the following:

> *The acts of the sinful nature are obvious: sexual immorality, impurity and debauchery; idolatry and witchcraft; hatred, discord, jealousy, fits of rage, selfish ambition, dissensions, factions and envy; drunkenness, orgies, and the like. I warn you, as I did before, that those who live like this will not inherit the kingdom of God.* —Galatians 5:19–21 NIV

Notice that the acts of the sinful nature include such things as anger, jealousy, and selfish ambition, as well as sexual immorality and witchcraft. None of us can claim to be free from this battle just because we don't struggle with the "larger" sins. Let us look more closely at our war with the sinful nature so that we can increase our understanding of how to deal with it effectively.

WHAT IS THE SINFUL NATURE?

The primary characteristic of the sinful nature is that it is always trying to please itself, disregarding everyone else, including God. Living for yourself is a very easy trap to fall into. Outwardly, a person may appear to be living for God. Inwardly, however, he may be indulging in the sinful nature. Many people, working in the energy of the sinful nature, may even perform good deeds. They make themselves look good, but their inner motives are always aimed at advancing self. In effect, they are relying on their good deeds for their salvation, rather than on forgiveness through Christ. This is true even of some who appear to be waging spiritual warfare. Jesus warned,

> *By their fruits you will know them. Not everyone who says to Me, "Lord, Lord," shall enter the kingdom of heaven, but he who does the will of My Father in heaven. Many will say to Me in that day, "Lord, Lord, have we not prophesied in Your name, cast out demons in Your name, and done many wonders in Your name?" And then I will declare to them, "I never knew you; depart from Me, you who practice lawlessness!"*
>
> —Matthew 7:20–23

Inwardly indulging in the sinful nature may seem harmless, but Paul said that it leads to spiritual death. In the following passage, he described the results of living by the sinful nature:

Letting your sinful nature control your mind leads to death. But letting the Spirit control your mind leads to life and peace. For the sinful nature is always hostile to God. It never did obey God's laws, and it never will. That's why those who are still under the control of their sinful nature can never please God.
—Romans 8:6–8 NLT

HOW DOES THE SINFUL NATURE OPERATE?

Let's look now at how the sinful nature operates. To do this, we must understand how human beings were originally designed, and how this design became distorted when mankind rebelled against God.

SPIRIT

The Bible says, ***"God is Spirit**, and those who worship Him must worship in spirit and truth"* (John 4:24, emphasis added). It also says that mankind was created in the image of God. (See Genesis 1:26–27.) As God is Spirit, He created man as a spiritual being. Man was designed to communicate with and worship God through his spirit.

SOUL

Mankind was also given a soul, which was created as the site of man's consciousness and as the expression of his personality. The soul is made up of the mind, the emotions, and the will. It connects the spiritual and physical aspects of man's nature.

BODY

The body was created as the physical "house" in which man was to dwell and through which he was to interact with the physical world through his senses.

Adam and Eve were the first human beings whom God created. Originally, their spiritual nature was totally yielded to God's Spirit (the Holy Spirit) as they lived their lives, made decisions, and took care of the earth. Their spirits were the dominant aspect of their nature as they directed their souls and bodies to think and act in ways that pleased God. In this way, the three parts of their nature—spirit, soul, and body—functioned in harmony with one another.

However, Adam and Eve eventually rejected God's Word and the Holy Spirit's authority and instead followed the word of Satan. The result was that they became spiritually dead and lost the harmony with God and themselves in which they were intended to live. Because of their rebellion against God, their nature became corrupt, or sinful, and so sin entered the world. Since Adam and Eve were spiritually dead, their minds and bodies were no longer being directed by what God's Spirit desired; instead, they became dominated by the sinful nature and its passions. The same domination by sin is true of all people, if they have not been forgiven through the blood of Christ, which He shed on the cross.

Tragically, the soul of every fallen human being is reduced to being a follower of its sinful inclinations and Satan's schemes, both of which are opposed to God and His nature. The spirit of fallen man is dead, and the soul of every person who hasn't received forgiveness through Christ is now under the power of his own uncontrolled, ungodly desires. Paul wrote about this terrible state:

We all once conducted ourselves in the lusts of our flesh, fulfilling the desires of the flesh and of the mind, and were by nature children of wrath, just as the others. —Ephesians 2:3

To add to mankind's predicament, Satan knows people's weaknesses as fallen human beings, and he is continually tempting them to disobey God and indulge in every kind of sin against Him. So, not only did the enemy incite man to sin, but he also continues to promote sin in mankind.

Praise God that this is not the end of the story! The good news is that, when we receive salvation through Jesus Christ, our spirits are made alive again, as Paul wrote:

You He made alive, who were dead in trespasses and sins.

—Ephesians 2:1

When you were dead in your sins and in the uncircumcision of your sinful nature, God made you alive with Christ.

—Colossians 2:13 NIV

When our spirits are made alive, the Holy Spirit comes to dwell in us, and we are able to yield to God's Spirit once more. Our spiritual rebirth through Jesus Christ enables God's nature to be the dominant influence in our lives again rather than the sinful nature. The Bible says,

---

Clothe yourselves with the Lord Jesus Christ, and do not think about how to gratify the desires of the sinful nature.

—Romans 13:14 NIV

SPIRITUAL CIVIL WAR

The above verse refers to an entire change of mind-set. We're not even to think about ways to indulge in the sinful nature. Yet we must be aware that this evil nature still continually seeks to surface in the lives of Christians. Until we go to be with Christ, or until He returns to the earth, we will need to be on guard against the sinful nature. It fights against the Spirit of God within us; it still wants to gratify its desires. However, we can have the Holy Spirit living within us, and He wants us to live in a way that pleases God. Spiritual warfare is needed to win each battle with the sinful nature, and the Holy Spirit living within us gives us the power to overcome every evil desire and inclination.

The following scenario is an example of the battle between the sinful nature and God's Spirit in the life of a Christian, and how our spirits, souls, and bodies are involved in the conflict:

1. Through the bodily senses, a person sees, hears, tastes, smells, and touches the world around him.
2. The sinful nature, through the senses, can be stimulated to desire certain forbidden things or experiences that are contrary to God's wishes, and our emotions can be affected by these desires.
3. The mind, or the mental part of man, evaluates, *Is this desire good or evil according to God's Word? Is it productive or nonproductive? Will it help me or hurt me in the long run?* Jesus said that when we receive the Holy Spirit, *"He will guide* [us] *into all truth"* (John 16:13). Believers have the witness of the Holy Spirit within them, as well as the Bible, to enable them to discern what is right.
4. The will must then make a decision. It must decide whether to obey the Spirit and therefore remain united with God and His purposes—or listen to the sinful nature and yield to temptation, choosing what is hostile to God.

Because of the ongoing conflict between the sinful nature and God's Spirit within us, each believer is, in effect, a walking "civil war." As ungodly thoughts and desires come up, we must learn to "[cast] *down arguments and every high thing that exalts itself against the knowledge of God, bringing every thought into captivity to the obedience of Christ"* (2 Corinthians 10:5). We do this by living by the Spirit and not for our selfish desires. *"For as many as are led by the Spirit of God, these are sons of God"* (Romans 8:14).

LIVING BY THE SPIRIT

Galatians 5:16–18 says,

> *So I say, live by the Spirit, and you will not gratify the desires of the sinful nature. For the sinful nature desires what is contrary to the Spirit, and the Spirit what is contrary to the sinful nature. They are in conflict with each other, so that you do not do what you want.* NIV

Here is how the *New Living Translation* expresses the same passage:

> *So I say, let the Holy Spirit guide your lives. Then you won't be doing what your sinful nature craves. The sinful nature wants to do evil, which is just the opposite of what the Spirit wants. And the Spirit gives us desires that are the opposite of what the sinful nature desires. These two forces are constantly fighting each other, so you are not free to carry out your good intentions.*

We have to be thoroughly convinced that what the sinful nature wants and what the Holy Spirit wants are totally opposite. We cannot "peacefully coexist" with the sinful nature. It is our enemy; it will lead us to our deaths, spiritually, if we let it be the ruler of our lives.

The Bible warns us about being sinfully minded rather than spiritually minded:

The mind of sinful man is death, but the mind controlled by the Spirit is life and peace. —Romans 8:6 NIV

Do not love the world or anything in the world. If anyone loves the world, the love of the Father is not in him. For everything in the world—the cravings of sinful man, the lust of his eyes and the boasting of what he has and does—comes not from the Father but from the world. —1 John 2:15–17 NIV

It is only by the power and guidance of the Holy Spirit that we can live as God wants us to, as these Scriptures testify:

The natural [unregenerate] *man does not receive the things of the Spirit of God, for they are foolishness to him; nor can he know them, because they are spiritually discerned.*

—1 Corinthians 2:14

[Jesus said,] *"He who believes in Me, as the Scripture has said, out of his heart will flow rivers of living water." But this He spoke concerning the Spirit, whom those believing in Him would receive.* —John 7:37–39

But you shall receive power when the Holy Spirit has come upon you. —Acts 1:8

Live by the Spirit, and you will not gratify the desires of the sinful nature. —Galatians 5:16

In Romans 8:3, Paul explained how we overcome the sinful nature: *"For what the law was powerless to do in that it was weakened by the sinful nature, God did by sending his own Son in the likeness of sinful man to be a sin offering"* (NIV). In other words, God gave the law of Moses to the Israelites, which provided God's commandments and instructions for righteous living. The law is good, but without the Spirit's help, we continually yield to the temptation to do what is wrong instead of what is right. God gave the law to convince and remind us of our inability to do what is right, so that we would see our need and turn to Him for help.

God the Father put into effect a different plan to save us and enable us to live righteously. He sent His own Son Jesus Christ to earth in a physical, human body that was like ours, except that He was without sin. Jesus did what no one else could do: He lived on earth in perfect obedience to God the Father, and then He died on the cross as our Substitute, taking our sins on Himself so that we wouldn't have to be punished for them. God made those who love Him and receive His offer of forgiveness and restoration through Christ spiritually alive. Then He sent His Spirit to live within them. In this way, God destroyed the sinful nature's control over us. He did this so that we would no longer have to *"live according to the sinful nature but* [could live] *according to the Spirit"* (verse 4 NIV). Galatians 5:24 says, *"Those who belong to Christ Jesus have crucified the sinful nature with its passions and desires"* (NIV). Living by the Spirit means living in obedience to the Father, just as Christ did.

WHAT IT MEANS TO BE SPIRITUALLY MINDED

Therefore, to be spiritually minded means to be occupied with what the Holy Spirit desires and not live under the influence of the sinful nature and its corrupt passions. To be spiritually minded is to make pleasing God and living by His Spirit our major aim and objective in life. It means to be supremely devoted to fulfilling

God's will. It means to follow the leading of the Spirit and to obey the Word of God.

Being spiritually minded enables us to put on the whole armor of God that is so necessary for spiritual warfare. It enables us to live in the fullness of our salvation, full of faith and strong in the knowledge of God and His Word. In this way, we can deflect both the attacks of the enemy and the temptations of the sinful nature.

If we are committed to Jesus, and if we are willing to continually renounce and repent of our sins so that we have a clear relationship with God, then we can have authority over Satan. We can command the devil to leave in the name of Jesus. Our enemy can be stubborn, and at times he may seem to delay his departure. However, we are assured that he *must* leave as we yield to God and exercise His authority over the enemy. James 4:7 says, *"Submit to God. Resist the devil and he will flee from you."*

VICTORY OVER THE SINFUL NATURE

Unfortunately, too many Christians have allowed themselves to be weakened and defeated by yielding to the sinful nature and neglecting to live by the Spirit. They have been rendered powerless and ineffective in spiritual warfare. Please understand that it is difficult, if not impossible, to win this war against the enemy of our souls without learning to overcome the sinful nature.

> *For if you live according to the flesh you will die; but if by the Spirit you put to death the deeds of the body, you will live.*
>
> —Romans 8:13

> *I have been crucified with Christ; it is no longer I who live, but Christ lives in me; and the life which I now live in the flesh I live by faith in the Son of God, who loved me and gave Himself for me.*
>
> —Galatians 2:20

The sinful nature can be dangerously subtle. Just when you think your spiritual life is going well, and that the war with your old nature is over, you need to watch out for a sneak attack on the perimeter of your life. In 1 Corinthians 10:12, Paul warned about becoming overconfident: *"If you think you are standing strong, be careful not to fall"* (NLT). Remember that, as a devouring enemy, Satan will try to prey on the weakness of our sinful nature and incite it.

In physical warfare, the infantry often calls in the superior firepower of the air force with its guided missiles and fighter jets to demoralize the enemy for the decisive assault. Likewise, you have superior power over the sinful nature through the power of prayer, the Word of God, and the Holy Spirit. This superior power enables you to prepare for decisive assaults on areas of the sinful nature that you need to conquer.

As we live the lifestyle of a spiritual warrior, we can also counteract the desires of the old nature by bearing fruit for God wherever we have been planted. How can you produce the fruit of the Spirit in your life? Recognize the things of the world that pull you away from God, and the things of the Spirit that draw you toward God. Learn to avoid the traps and minefields of the sinful nature. You can overcome them as long as you allow the Holy Spirit to guide and control your desires.

It may not always feel good to do battle with the sinful nature. Yet when we follow Christ, our Captain, we begin to bear the fruit of righteousness, which enables us to wage spiritual warfare even more effectively.

No discipline seems pleasant at the time, but painful. Later on, however, it produces a harvest of righteousness and peace for those who have been trained by it. Therefore, strengthen your feeble arms and weak knees. "Make level paths for your

feet," so that the lame may not be disabled, but rather healed.
—Hebrews 12:11–13 NIV

Your own force is never enough. To maintain your spiritual strength in your battle with the sinful nature, you have to be in constant touch with your "Commanding Officer," God the Father, and He always has to be able to get in touch with you. Keep praying. First Thessalonians 5:17 says, *"Pray without ceasing."* Yield to God the Father in prayer, and ask God's Spirit to fill you every day. Trust God to provide what you need, when you need it, to overcome the sinful nature. *"Live by the Spirit, and you will not gratify the desires of the sinful nature"* (Galatians 5:16). Don't neglect to fellowship with other believers who can encourage you in the Lord. *"Not forsaking the assembling of ourselves together"* (Hebrews 10:25). Learn how other believers overcame the same struggles you are going through. *"God...comforts us in all our troubles, so that we can comfort those in any trouble with the comfort we ourselves have received from God."*

SPIRIT-FILLED AND SPIRIT-LED

Seek to be Spirit-filled and Spirit-led in everything you say and do. *"He has shown you, O man, what is good; and what does the LORD require of you but to do justly, to love mercy, and to walk humbly with your God?"* (Micah 6:8).

Many things impact the Spirit-filled life we are reclaiming in Jesus' name. It is often directly related to the content and quality of our thought life. Inner righteousness produces outward peace, but sinful attitudes frequently produce sinful behavior. The enemy also seeks to nullify the blessings of a Spirit-led life by trying to keep us from being totally committed to God. Yet one of his greatest weapons is unforgiveness:

> *In this the children of God and the children of the devil are manifest: Whoever does not practice righteousness is not of God, nor is he who does not love his brother.* —1 John 3:10

I have found that one of the most effective ways of maintaining spiritual strength and releasing the power of God in your life is by forgiving someone who has hurt you. If you really want to defeat the enemy's plan to destroy your life, you have to forgive everyone who has ever wronged you, however seriously.

Bitterness and unforgiveness will eat away at you. If they are not conquered, they will destroy you. You will begin to feel the effects of unforgiveness in your physical body. I have heard countless people testify that, when they released their resentment toward someone and forgave the person who had hurt them, they began to get well physically. Nourishing hatred toward others can destroy you—spirit, soul, and body. This is exactly what the enemy hopes to accomplish. In contrast, forgiveness releases tremendous power. It brings healing and restores the joy of fellowship. It unbinds the tensions that tear you apart. Although a spiritual warrior is engaged in warfare with Satan, he is a person who is at peace with God and himself and who seeks to live in peace with other people. The Bible says, "*God has called us to peace*" (1 Corinthians 7:15).

Determine therefore to live in peace in all your relationships, because this is God's will. Jesus said, "*Salt is good, but if the salt loses its flavor, how will you season it? Have salt in yourselves, and have peace with one another*" (Mark 9:50). Hebrews 12:14 says, "*Pursue peace with all people, and holiness, without which no one will see the Lord.*"

In fact, we can experience the peace of God in all circumstances. "*Now may the Lord of peace himself give you peace at all times and in every way*" (2 Thessalonians 3:16 NIV). This peace is already at work in our lives. Jesus said, "*Peace I leave with you, My peace I give to you; not as the world gives do I give to you. Let not your heart be troubled, neither let it be afraid"* (John 14:27). These are the words of the Captain of our salvation, who wants us to take back what we, in negligence, have permitted Satan to take away from us. Our peace belongs to us. It does not belong to the devil.

If we are not experiencing peace, then we must discover how we have let it slip away, or how we have allowed Satan to steal it from us. Though we experience challenges and spiritual attacks in life, God's peace is available to us at all times. It is constant, never changing. The peace of God drives out all fears caused by the evils of the past or present: *"Great peace have those who love Your law, and nothing causes them to stumble"* (Psalm 119:165). *"You will keep him in perfect peace, whose mind is stayed on You, because he trusts in You"* (Isaiah 26:3).

TRANSFORMED INTO THE IMAGE OF CHRIST

In living the lifestyle of a spiritual warrior, we must realize that God desires for us to be continually renewed in our hearts and minds so that we have the same nature and mind-set as God Himself:

> *You were taught, with regard to your former way of life, to put off your old self, which is being corrupted by its deceitful desires; to be made new in the attitude of your minds; and to put on the new self, created to be like God in true righteousness and holiness.*
>
> —Ephesians 4:22–24 NIV

At the same time, Satan wants us to rebel against God's nature. He is a master at guerilla warfare, and he comes at us with subversion, deception, and intrigue. He attacks our thoughts when we least expect it and tries to provoke our sinful nature. We must always be on guard, and we must never give up our faith and trust in God during our battle against sin:

Jesus [is] *the author and finisher of our faith, who for the joy that was set before Him endured the cross, despising the shame, and has sat down at the right hand of the throne of God. For consider Him who endured such hostility from sinners against Himself, lest you become weary and discouraged in your souls. You have not yet resisted to bloodshed, striving against sin. And you have forgotten the exhortation which speaks to you as to sons: "My son, do not despise the chastening of the* Lord*, nor be discouraged when you are rebuked by Him; for whom the* Lord *loves He chastens, and scourges every son whom He receives."* —Hebrews 12:2–6

We are strengthened by the knowledge that Satan's final defeat will come from the hand of God—the same God who sustains us and trains us as we are daily transformed into the image of Jesus Christ, bearing fruit for Him:

The final outcome for a spiritual warrior is total victory over Satan and the sinful nature! A day is coming when, for the people of God, all questions will be answered and all the parts of the puzzle of life will fall into place. We will be complete in Christ, and we will be one with Him forever.

8

PRAYER AND FASTING: POWERFUL WEAPONS IN GOD'S ARSENAL

Praying always with all prayer and supplication in the Spirit, being watchful to this end with all perseverance and supplication for all the saints.
—Ephesians 6:18

How often have you thought of prayer as a weapon? Remember that, after describing specific pieces of spiritual armor in Ephesians 6, Paul added the above verse, revealing that prayer completes the *"whole armor of God"* (verses 11, 13).

When I was receiving the revelation of the man dressed in spiritual armor, the Lord gently placed His hand on me and said,

> When you have put on all the armor I have showed you, armor that is described in My Word, you are still not safe unless you utilize these two weapons in My arsenal—prayer and fasting. They are the most powerful resources I

have given to believers. They are the most powerful combat devices in your full arsenal of weapons. Regardless of your offensive or defensive armor, you need these in your own arsenal if you desire to effectively attack and defeat Satan and his cohorts.

I began to ask God to show me the advantages of prayer and fasting. Over the next several months, He opened up His Word and truth to me regarding the blessings of prayer and fasting. What I discovered is essentially this: Prayer enables us to hear from Jesus, the Captain of God's army. Fasting gives us entry into the resources of God's power to carry out His will.

THE ROLE OF PRAYER

Much of spiritual warfare takes place on a cosmic level between God's holy angels and Satan and his demons. (See Daniel 10; Jude 9.) There is no indication that believers are directly involved in this phase of warfare, however, except through prayer.

The Spirit of God spoke to me and said that men and women must be equipped to pray for families, churches, cities, and nations. They must guard and strengthen their own lives against the enemy's onslaughts. Every believer must be encouraged to enlist in an army of intercessors. Sometimes, we have to fight on our knees in order to win. God is calling men and women to warfare through prayer.

A SIX-FOLD MANDATE

Let's take a closer look at Ephesians 6:18 and the six aspects of prayer that it emphasizes:

Praying always with all prayer and supplication in the Spirit, being watchful to this end with all perseverance and supplication for all the saints.

In the *New Living Translation*, the verse reads,

Pray in the Spirit at all times and on every occasion. Stay alert and be persistent in your prayers for all believers everywhere.

In this significant verse, we learn that we are to...

1. Pray always
2. Pray with all kinds of prayers and supplications
3. Pray in the Spirit
4. Be watchful in prayer
5. Have all perseverance in prayer
6. Pray for all believers

1. PRAY ALWAYS

Colossians 4:2 echoes the theme of Ephesians 6:18, saying, "*Continue earnestly in prayer, being vigilant in it with thanksgiving.*" The *New International Version* reads, "*Devote yourselves to prayer, being watchful and thankful.*" We are to devote ourselves to earnest prayer, including warfare prayer. There is nothing that we can't take to God's throne. In all things, we can ask for His grace, strength, and power.

The basis on which we come to God in warfare prayer is the righteousness of Jesus Christ. Jesus gives us access to the Father, confidence in coming to Him, and the assurance of help in time of need:

To the intent that now the manifold wisdom of God might be made known by the church to the principalities and powers in the heavenly places, according to the eternal purpose which He

accomplished in ***Christ Jesus our Lord, in whom we have boldness and access with confidence through faith in Him.***
—Ephesians 3:10–12, emphasis added

Seeing then that we have a great High Priest who has passed through the heavens, Jesus the Son of God, let us hold fast our confession. For we do not have a High Priest who cannot sympathize with our weaknesses, but was in all points tempted as we are, yet without sin. ***Let us therefore come boldly to the throne of grace, that we may obtain mercy and find grace to help in time of need.***
—Hebrews 4:14–16, emphasis added

---

2. PRAY WITH ALL KINDS OF PRAYERS AND SUPPLICATIONS

Warfare praying includes many kinds of prayers and supplications to God. Paul wrote to Timothy,

---

Therefore I exhort first of all that supplications, prayers, intercessions, and giving of thanks be made for all men, for kings and all who are in authority, that we may lead a quiet and peaceable life in all godliness and reverence. For this is good and acceptable in the sight of God our Savior, who desires all men to be saved and to come to the knowledge of the truth.
—1 Timothy 2:1–4

When we come before the throne, we are to pray to the Father, through the Son. We must also come with a humble attitude. This does not negate the boldness with which we are to come. To be humble does not mean to be passive. We must realize, again, that our boldness is based on the work of Christ, not our own efforts. Without Christ, we are nothing, and we can do nothing. (See John

15:5.) Peter wrote, "*Therefore humble yourselves under the mighty hand of God, that He may exalt you in due time*" (1 Peter 5:6). We can rely completely on God as we live and work in obedience to Him, knowing that He will take care of everything that concerns us.

In this section, I want to discuss five aspects of warfare prayer: forgiveness, supplication, intercession, thankfulness, and praise.

Warfare praying includes forgiveness. As we saw in the previous chapter, one of the most effective ways of releasing the power of God is by forgiving those who have offended or hurt us. Forgiveness provides clear access to God's grace and power. Jesus said,

---

> *If you bring your gift to the altar, and there remember that your brother has something against you, leave your gift there before the altar, and go your way. First be reconciled to your brother, and then come and offer your gift.*
>
> —Matthew 5:23–24

> *For if you forgive men their trespasses, your heavenly Father will also forgive you. But if you do not forgive men their trespasses, neither will your Father forgive your trespasses.*
>
> —Matthew 6:14–15

Not only does forgiveness bring healing and restoration, but it also connects us to God the Father and Jesus our Captain, enabling us to hear divine instruction and guidance in warfare praying.

Warfare praying includes supplication and intercession. Supplication involves entreaties, requests, or petitions.[13] Intercession involves requests made on behalf of others[14] or in

13. See *Strong's* and *NASC*, #G1162.
14. See *Strong's* and *NASC*, #G1793, #G5241.

response to others' actions. In the New Testament, there are many examples of believers offering supplication and interceding to God. In addition, in the only places where the actual word *intercession* appears in the New Testament, it describes the prayers of Jesus and the Holy Spirit on our behalf. (See, for example, Romans 8:26–27, 34.) We read in Hebrews 7:25, "[Jesus] *is also able to save to the uttermost those who come to God through Him, since He always lives to make* ***intercession*** *for them*" [emphasis added]. We can follow the example of Christ's continual, earnest prayers as we intercede for others.

Warfare praying includes thankfulness. When we have thankful hearts, we are attributing everything that happens in our lives to God. The devil attributes evil to God, but the believer knows that God is good: "*Every good gift and every perfect gift is from above, and comes down from the Father of lights, with whom there is no variation or shadow of turning*" (James 1:17). "*And we know that all things work together for good to those who love God, to those who are the called according to His purpose*" (Romans 8:28). In addition, when we express our gratitude to God for His mercy and love, we are lifting up His holy name. God responds to the prayers of those who truly honor Him from their hearts.

Warfare praying includes praise. "*Therefore by* [Jesus] *let us continually offer the sacrifice of praise to God, that is, the fruit of our lips, giving thanks to His name*" (Hebrews 13:15). Praise is a vital part of prayer because it ushers us in to the presence of God, who inhabits the praises of His people. The psalmist said, "*You are… enthroned in* ["*inhabitest*" KJV] *the praises of Israel*" (Psalm 22:3). God is worthy of our praise. The notion that our praise pleases God is an awesome thing to think about.

Praise also gives *us* strength as we place our trust in Him. Job's wife told him to curse God and die. (See Job 2:9.) Instead, he praised God and lived. (See 1:21–22; 2:10; 42:10–16.) Again, the Lord has control over all the circumstances of our lives and uses them for our benefit. He is with us during our adversities, and He fights for us in the battles of life. When we glorify God, we are enabled to put the things, people, and events of our lives in eternal perspective.

3. PRAY IN THE SPIRIT

You and I were created to be the vessels and instruments of the Spirit of God. Humanity's rebellion slammed the door in God's face, but Jesus came to create a new race of human beings in whom God could dwell and through whom God could work. When we are in Christ, we live in the Spirit, walk in the Spirit, and pray in the Spirit!

To pray in the Spirit generally means to speak in a heavenly language or an earthly language unknown to you, through the power of the Holy Spirit. In Mark 16:17, Jesus said, "*And these signs will accompany those who believe: In my name they will drive out demons; they will speak in new tongues....*" Believers first spoke in tongues on the day of Pentecost, after Jesus' ascension to heaven, when the disciples received the promised gift of the Spirit: "*All of them were filled with the Holy Spirit and began to speak in other tongues as the Spirit enabled them*" (Acts 2:4).

The apostle Paul said that when a person prays using a heavenly language, "[he] *does not speak to men but to God.*" Praying in the Spirit is crucial for warfare prayer because there is so much about what is happening in the spiritual realm that we are not aware of. Job didn't know the drama involving God and the devil that was going on behind the scenes of the cataclysmic events occurring in his life. (See Job 1–2.) Daniel didn't know that the "*prince* [evil spirit] *of the kingdom of Persia*" was attempting to hinder the answer to his prayers until the angel came and told him. (See Daniel 10:12–14.)

The gift of the Holy Spirit therefore, given to us through Jesus, enables us to pray for needs that are important to God and for needs of which we are unaware: *"In the same way, the Spirit helps us in our weakness. We do not know what we ought to pray for, but the Spirit himself intercedes for us with groans that words cannot express"* (Romans 8:26 NIV). Praying in the Spirit gives us the assurance that God is taking care of whatever is needed, and it gives us peace in trying times.

4. BE WATCHFUL IN PRAYER

The Greek word for *"watchful"* in Ephesians 6:18 means to "be vigilant" and comes from the word for "keep awake."[15] It means to be alert.[16] This admonition is similar to Galatians 6:9, which says, *"Let us not grow weary while doing good, for in due season we shall reap if we do not lose heart."* We cannot allow ourselves to grow weary of engaging in warfare prayer or to become lackadaisical about it. We are called to pay attention to the needs of the body of Christ and to earnestly focus on what we are praying for. As we read earlier, *"Devote yourselves to prayer, being watchful and thankful"* (Colossians 4:2 NIV).

5. HAVE ALL PERSEVERANCE IN PRAYER

If you desire to be a triumphant believer who lives in the victory of Christ, you cannot expect to walk with the Lord without a fight for your faith. A life of faith in Jesus Christ is a life of conflict. Spiritual warfare is intense. It involves fierce battles that may seem unrelenting. The devil will oppose you. At times, it will seem as if the whole universe is against you.

Victorious spiritual warfare is possible as the Holy Spirit empowers you to fight through prayer. One mark of a truly spiritual warrior is that the tougher the battle gets, the more he keeps fighting. He is persistent, not passive. He is a victor, not a victim. The believer who wants to be an overcomer in spiritual battles

---

15 See *Strong's*, #G1127.
16. *NASC*, #G1127.

wrestles until he wins the war. He understands that spiritual battles require spiritual tactics. He wields God's mighty spiritual weapons of prayer and fasting.

Godly women and men are a source of constant frustration to the enemy. They understand that Satan uses human weaknesses to try to destroy them and their loved ones. Godly women will fight for their children, their husbands, and their extended families with the Word of God. They are sensitive to the Holy Spirit. They will readily do what the Word says to do in difficult situations. Through prayer, they protect their homes from the enemy's destructive powers.

God's Word is a very strong weapon in your spiritual artillery. When you use the Bible in your intercession warfare, you can bind the evil one and declare God's promises and victory for your life and for the lives of your loved ones.

The struggle between the visible world and the invisible world, even in the realm of prayer, is illustrated clearly in the trials of the prophet Daniel, as we have seen. While Daniel was praying, an unseen evil spirit hindered the answer to his prayers. Yet Daniel was assured that, even though the answer was delayed, his prayers had been heard. Similarly, when we pray, there are "*principalities, powers,...*[and] *spiritual hosts of wickedness in the heavenly places*" (Ephesians 6:12) who will try to oppose us. Like Daniel, we can be assured that God hears and acknowledges our prayers the minute we pray them, and that sometimes we must persevere in order to receive the answers we seek.

An important thing to notice from Daniel's experience is that angels are very much involved in the affairs of men and nations. The godly angel came in response to Daniel's prayers, while ungodly demons opposed him. Moreover, the unholy angels seemed to be linked with political kingdoms and their rulers. The angel told Daniel, "*And now I must return to fight with the prince of Persia; and when I have gone forth, indeed the prince of Greece will come*" (Daniel 10:20). Yet, we can know that in spiritual warfare, all the resources of heaven are at our disposal. The power of political kingdoms or even of entire armies is no match for God.

For example, in 2 Kings 6, we read that the army of Syria was fighting against Israel. God revealed to Elisha, the prophet, all of the Syrian king's battle plans in advance. The prophet told the plans to the king of Israel, and all of Syria's attacks were nullified. The king of Syria heard that Elisha was the source of his troubles, so he sent his army out to seize him. The Syrian troops surrounded the city of Dothan, where Elisha was staying.

When Elisha's servant arose early and went outside his tent, he saw the vast Syrian army surrounding the city. Panic-stricken, the servant rushed to Elisha and told him what he had seen. Although the servant was terrified by the enemy that surrounded them, Elisha remained calm. He knew what his servant did not know. He knew that spiritual warfare was going on. He also knew that earthly armies are no threat when the host of heaven is on your side. So he prayed that God would open the eyes of his servant so he could see the "invisible army" on duty, protecting them:

> *And when the servant of the man of God arose early and went out, there was an army, surrounding the city with horses and chariots. And his servant said to him, "Alas, my master! What shall we do?" So he answered, "Do not fear, for those who are with us are more than those who are with them." And Elisha prayed, and said, "*Lord*, I pray, open his eyes that he may see." Then the* Lord *opened the eyes of the young man, and he saw. And behold, the mountain was full of horses and chariots of fire all around Elisha. So when the Syrians came down to him, Elisha prayed to the* Lord*, and said, "Strike this people, I pray, with blindness." And He struck them with blindness according to the word of Elisha. Now Elisha said to*

them, "This is not the way, nor is this the city. Follow me, and I will bring you to the man whom you seek." But he led them to Samaria.

—2 Kings 6:15–19

This heavenly army was sent to protect God's servant. Elisha prayed that the enemy armies might be struck with blindness. As a result, he was able to single-handedly lead the entire Syrian army into the hands of the Israelite army. Many times, God has allowed me to see His heavenly army. I believe it is ever present, and it responds to the prayers of believers.

God may send an army of angels, as He did for Elisha, or He may send just one, as He did for Daniel, but He will come through for you. Believe Him, and trust Him at all times.

In God is my salvation and my glory; the rock of my strength, and my refuge, is in God. Trust in Him at all times, you people; pour out your heart before Him; God is a refuge for us.

—Psalm 62:7–8

---

6. PRAY FOR ALL BELIEVERS

How can we pray for all believers? First, we need to be aware of the needs of believers in our own families, churches, and workplaces, and commit to praying regularly for them. We can also keep in touch with the needs of Christians around the world through missionary society updates and persecution alerts. The way we can truly pray for all believers is to pray in the Spirit, which we talked about earlier. We can intercede for others through the wisdom and power of the Holy Spirit. *"He who searches our hearts knows the mind of the Spirit, because the Spirit intercedes for the saints in accordance with God's will"* (Romans 8:27 NIV).

In addition to believers, we also need to pray for those who do not yet know the Lord and those who are opposing the things of God. The apostle Paul once strongly opposed the church, and he is now considered one of its foundational leaders. The Lord has wonderful purposes and plans that are beyond our imaginations. As we are faithful to pray, He will carry out His works of salvation, healing, and deliverance in the world.

PRAYER IS A BATTLEFIELD

As we engage in spiritual warfare, we must realize that prayer is not just a weapon, but it is also a theatre of war in itself! It is the battleground or arena where fierce spiritual conflicts occur. As I mentioned earlier, when we come before God in prayer, Satan may begin to accuse us, as he accused Joshua the high priest. (See Zechariah 3:1.) The devil may make a point of calling attention to our shortcomings and our *"filthy garments"* (verses 3–4). Once more, we must stand upon the fact that Christ has removed our sin and replaced it with His righteousness.

Satan readily attacks prayer because he knows that victories are won or lost on the battlefield of private prayer. They are not usually won in public; they are often won in the secret chamber of communion with God. On this spiritual battlefield, great men and women have reclaimed their faith, reestablished their confidence in God and in themselves, and won decisive spiritual battles.

The battlefield of prayer is also the arena where we conquer perhaps our greatest enemy—self. In this combat zone rages the conflict between a desire to please God and a desire to please people. If we want to live a lifestyle of obedience and fellowship with God, as we talked about in the previous chapter, we can gain this victory through prayer.

FASTING AND SPIRITUAL WARFARE

Fasting is also a mighty weapon of spiritual warfare. Fasting gives us entry into the resources of God's power. When God gave me the word about prayer and fasting in the revelation of the spiritual armor, the words of 2 Corinthians came to me forcefully. Through these verses, I received an additional perspective on the power of fasting to overcome spiritual strongholds:

For the weapons of our warfare are not carnal but mighty in God for pulling down strongholds, casting down arguments and every high thing that exalts itself against the knowledge of God, bringing every thought into captivity to the obedience of Christ, and being ready to punish all disobedience when your obedience is fulfilled. —2 Corinthians 10:4–6

In Matthew, we see an example of the kind of stronghold that fasting can break. Jesus' disciples were unable to cast a spirit of epilepsy out of a young boy. After Jesus cast the demon out, He explained to His disciples why they had not been able to do so themselves:

Because of your unbelief; for assuredly, I say to you, if you have faith as a mustard seed, you will say to this mountain, "Move from here to there," and it will move; and nothing will be impossible for you. However, ***this kind does not go out except by prayer and fasting.***

—Matthew 17:20–21, emphasis added

FASTING IN SCRIPTURE

The practice of fasting is taught prominently in Scripture. Fasting was engaged in for such purposes as repentance, drawing close to God, asking for strength, requesting healing, and seeking God's guidance and help.

- In Exodus 34:27–28, Moses fasted when he was communing with the Lord and receiving instructions for the people of Israel.
- In 1 Samuel 7:3–6, the people of Israel fasted for the glory of God to return to their nation.
- In 2 Samuel 3:30–35, David fasted when he was grieving over the death of a close friend.
- In Esther 4:15–17, Esther asked her friends to fast and pray with her when she needed favor with the king to protect the Jews from destruction.
- In Ezra 8:21–23, the prophet Ezra fasted for protection and guidance before he and other exiled Israelites journeyed from Babylon to Jerusalem.
- In Nehemiah 1:1–11, Nehemiah fasted in repentance for the sins of Israel and for favor and guidance in rebuilding the wall of Jerusalem.
- In 2 Chronicles 20:1–3, Jehoshaphat fasted when the nation of Israel was faced with a threatening situation.
- In Psalm 35:11–13, David even fasted for his unfaithful friends when they were ill.
- In Luke 2:37, we learn that fasting was a regular part of the spiritual regimen of Anna, a godly woman and a prophetess.
- In Matthew 4:1–2 and Luke 4:1–2, Jesus fasted for a prolonged period before beginning His ministry on earth.
- In Matthew 6:16–18, Jesus' statement, *"When you fast..."* showed that He assumed His disciples would fast, and gave specific instructions for them to follow.

- In Acts 9:1–18, Paul fasted for three days before he received the Holy Spirit.
- In Acts 13:1–3, as the church elders fasted and prayed, the Holy Spirit spoke to them and told them to commission Paul and Barnabas as missionaries.
- In Acts 14:23, Paul and Barnabas fasted before they appointed elders in the churches.

From the Scriptures, we learn that fasting played an important role in the lives and activities of God's people. It should also be an important part of our own spiritual lives, including our spiritual warfare. The Reverend T. L. Lowery experienced tremendous power and anointing when he emerged from forty days of fasting and prayer a few years ago. These mighty weapons are a vital part of our spiritual arsenal.

Let us now look at different types and examples of fasts.

TYPES AND EXAMPLES OF FASTS

A *total fast* means going without food or water. A total fast is the kind that Esther called on her friends to make for three days and nights. (See Esther 4:16.)

A *limited fast* is restrictive in that the person fasts from certain kinds of foods. This is the kind Daniel went on when he fasted for three weeks. (See Daniel 10:3.)

The purest and most traditional form of fasting consists of drinking only water. An adult needs three quarts of water daily. We normally get this amount from the foods we eat, such as fruits, and from the beverages we drink. During a fast, it is crucial to drink at least twelve cups of liquid a day. Nutritionists recommend a combination of various fruit and vegetable juices.

When you go on a one-day fast, your body will still be getting its energy from the foods you ate the day before, so it will result in minimal discomfort. However, instead of a boisterous schedule on the day of the fast, consider engaging in quiet, meaningful activities such as prayer and Bible study, if possible.

For several days before you fast, you should cut back on your intake of liquids that contain caffeine, such as coffee, tea, and sodas. This reduces the potential for headaches, lethargy, and irritability during the fast. Do the same with high-sugar foods. Gradually reducing them will keep your body from "crash-landing," which it might do if you stop them abruptly. Remember, however, that you should always seek medical advice before starting an extended fast if you have any health problems at all.[17]

NEGLECT OF FASTING

The Lord revealed to me that the devil tries to stop God's people from fasting with all kinds of enticements and temptations. Fasting seems to have "gone out of style" in today's church. Many Christians do not fast at all. Some consider it inconvenient, while others aren't willing to miss a single meal. This is one area in which the flesh is dominating the spirit in many believers' lives. If we are going to be effective in spiritual warfare, we need to make fasting a regular practice and perhaps even plan designated times of the year that we set aside for special prayer and fasting.

THE ATTITUDE OF FASTING

What attitudes should we have while fasting? First, all fasting should be accompanied by humility and a confession of sin that are more than mere pretense and words. In Isaiah, the Lord lamented, "*These people draw near with their mouths and honor Me with their lips, but have removed their hearts far from Me*" (Isaiah 29:13).

---

17. For further reading on fasting, see Derek Prince, *Shaping History through Prayer and Fasting* (New Kensington, PA: Whitaker House, 2002) and Arthur Wallis, *God's Chosen Fast* (Fort Washington, PA: Christian Literature Crusade, 1968).

Second, for our fasting and prayer to be effective, we must be generous and be in the habit of giving to and helping those in need. When the Israelites questioned why God seemed to be ignoring them when they fasted, God replied, "'*Why have we fasted,' they say, 'and You have not seen? Why have we afflicted our souls, and You take no notice?*'" (Isaiah 58:3). He went on to accuse them of exploiting their employees and of fasting "*for strife and debate*"; they were not fasting to draw closer to God. (See verses 3–4.) He reminded them that the purpose of fasting was not to make a person miserable and afflict his soul. (See verse 5.) Then He explained what it meant to fast in a way that was pleasing to Him:

> *Is this not the fast that I have chosen: to loose the bonds of wickedness, to undo the heavy burdens, to let the oppressed go free, and that you break every yoke? Is it not to share your bread with the hungry, and that you bring to your house the poor who are cast out; when you see the naked, that you cover him, and not hide yourself from your own flesh?*
>
> —Isaiah 58:6–7

A true fast is the surrender of self in willing service to God and man. Doing without food not only makes us more aware of the awesomeness of God, but it also makes us conscious of those who continually have to do without the necessities of life. God will teach you to share your bread with the hungry and to care for the homeless. He will inspire you to reach out with compassion to the poor and the disenfranchised. Fasting from the right motives gives you the approval of God and prepares you to engage in spiritual warfare on behalf of others.

WARFARE PRAYING: INTERCEDING WITH JESUS

Amy Carmichael, noted missionary to India, illustrated the effectiveness of warfare praying when she was diligently fighting to rescue the "temple girls" of India, young girls who were being forced into prostitution. Once she grew discouraged and wondered if she could carry on any longer. She said,

> At last a day came when the burden grew too heavy for me; and then it was as though the tamarind trees about the house were not tamarind, but olive, and under one of these trees our Lord Jesus knelt alone. And I knew that this was His burden, not mine. It was He who was asking me to share it with Him, not I who was asking Him to share it with me. After that there was only one thing to do; who that saw him kneeling there could turn away and forget? Who could have done anything but go into the garden and kneel down beside him under the olive trees?[18]

My "garden of prayer" with Jesus is many different places, but I always receive strength from Him when I intercede. When we pray and fast, we can claim the full victory that our Lord Jesus Christ won on the cross. He disarmed evil powers and authorities; He made a public spectacle of them and triumphed over them. (See Colossians 2:15.) Warfare praying is praying in unity with Jesus "*to bring all things in heaven and on earth together under one head, even Christ*" (Ephesians 1:10 NIV), freeing those held captive by Satan, and bringing honor and glory to God.

His victory is our victory!

---

18. Dennis Kinlaw, *Preaching in the Spirit* (Wilmore, Kentucky: Francis Asbury Press, 1985), 43–44.

9

THE NAME AND BLOOD OF JESUS

Now I saw heaven opened, and behold, a white horse. And He who sat on him was called Faithful and True, and in righteousness He judges and makes war. His eyes were like a flame of fire, and on His head were many crowns. He had a name written that no one knew except Himself. He was clothed with a robe dipped in blood, and His name is called The Word of God. And the armies in heaven, clothed in fine linen, white and clean, followed Him on white horses.

—Revelation 19:11–14

In this chapter, I want to discuss two other powerful weapons for spiritual warfare that I have used extensively in my ministry: the name of Jesus and the blood of Jesus.

THE AUTHORITY OF THE NAME OF JESUS

The effectiveness of spiritual warfare depends on authority and power. Jesus Christ has overwhelming authority and power over Satan, a created being who rebelled against the good and rightful rule of God. When we have been reconciled with God through Christ, understand spiritual warfare, and are living in a way that pleases Him, we have access to His authority and can command the devil and demons in His name.

Deliverance evangelist Christopher Alam told of a man in Argentina who took his daughter to the lobby of his hotel one afternoon during a crusade. Sobbing, the man told the evangelist that his seventeen-year-old daughter, Jacqueline, had become demon-possessed after visiting occult healers to seek a cure for her sick mother.

The girl had not slept for ten days. She screamed like a wild animal and was totally out of control. They had visited the crusade three nights in a row, but she was still bound. The evangelist promised to minister to her personally after the service that evening.

"When I met with her," Rev. Alam said, "the demons in her screamed blasphemies in my face for forty-five minutes. I sensed that I should not proceed any further, and decided to wait on the Lord's directions."

Rev. Alam was speaking in a church the next day when he spotted Jacqueline in the audience. She sat stone-faced and stared at him throughout the worship time. When the evangelist began to preach, she got up and ran outside. Her parents ran after her and dragged her back into the church. This happened two more times.

"When I gave the altar call," Rev. Alam continued, "Jacqueline, in an unexpected move, was the first to come forward. About three hundred people joined her. I began to pray from the platform and saw her fall on the ground under the power of God. Then something amazing happened. Her face seemed to glow—to literally emit light. This happened for about fifteen minutes, and then she woke up and stood to her feet, completely free."

Jacqueline's deliverance resulted in her whole family receiving Christ. They are now all serving God. Jacqueline later went to Bible school, and today she is a successful attorney. Families need deliverance from the oppression of Satan and of evil, and only the power of God through Jesus Christ can accomplish this.

Jesus' authority comes from His deity, His sinless humanity, and the honor given to Him by God the Father because of His perfect obedience and sacrifice:

> *God exalted him to the highest place and gave him the name that is above every name, that at the name of Jesus every knee should bow, in heaven and on earth and under the earth, and every tongue confess that Jesus Christ is Lord, to the glory of God the Father.* —Philippians 2:9–11 NIV

I believe there is a great move of God in the land accompanied by mighty miracles. People are being healed and delivered by the power of God, and souls are being won to the kingdom through those who understand and engage in spiritual warfare according to God's Word.

Recently, in my home church, an elderly lady came into our midweek service just as we started to conclude our altar ministry. Several people had gathered at the altar area for prayer when the woman walked up to one of the pastors. In a calm voice, she asked for prayer; however, when the believers started to pray, she became violent and out of control.

Although she was small in stature and probably weighed less than ninety pounds, the demons in her were so violent and destructive that it took several grown men to subdue her. Then, after about fifteen minutes of praying and intense spiritual warfare, God delivered her from the demonic influence that had her bound.

The glory of God came on the woman's countenance, and the believers began to rejoice with her. All her life, she had walked in darkness, but she was delivered by the power of God. Now she is enjoying the marvelous experience of fellowship in the family of God.

Satan and his demons can be rebuked and cast out only through the triumph of Jesus Christ by the power of the Holy Spirit. We are never to attempt to use magic, divination, bargaining, or ritual when dealing with evil spirits. Sacred objects, even holy water and crosses, are no substitution for the power of the Holy Spirit. In addition, they could be perceived by others as "Christian magic." This will confuse them about the truth of deliverance through Jesus Christ.

Most demons will leave when you give a direct command in Jesus' name. Others, however, can be cast out only by prayer and fasting, as we discussed earlier. (See Matthew 17:21.) We must rely totally on the name of Jesus Christ and on the powerful work He did at Calvary through His atoning blood.

A holy and anointed minister of God, the Reverend Byron Seymour, shared this story with me about spiritual warfare:

> One night in West Virginia, I was attacked by the devil in an unusual and unforgettable way. In the darkest hours of the night, I found myself still totally awake. The door to my bedroom opened and a creature that looked like a man walked in. He looked to be about 6 feet tall, weighing about 160 pounds. He wore a white shirt with a black suit and black tie.
>
> My first thought was that God had dispatched an angel to come and help me. The man walked over to the left side of the bed and started toward me with his hands outstretched. I thought he was going to lay hands on me and

> pray for me. Instead, he took both of his hands and put them around my neck. He began to physically strangle me.
>
> My whole body was totally paralyzed. The only parts of my body that would work were my eyes—I could still see. It seemed as though a big, black mass was hovering over me. The creature was literally strangling me to death! I could not breathe. I could not yell or make any sound. In desperation, I began to cry within me, *In the name of Jesus! In the name of Jesus!* but the sound would not come out of my mouth.
>
> When it felt as though I was going to be physically suffocated and lose consciousness, the anointing of the Holy Ghost was like a laser inside my inner being, piercing, touching, and overwhelming me. The creature that looked like a man immediately disappeared like a vapor! God then allowed me to go to sleep.

Several days later, Rev. Seymour was conducting some meetings in Tennessee when he experienced a similar attack that he perceived was connected to the previous one:

> I experienced some of the most severe warfare and pressure I have ever experienced. I felt as though I could not possibly conduct service that night. I told the pastor that I needed to cancel the service because of the pressure I was feeling—pressure that would not let up. He said he could not cancel the service because it was already advertised on the radio and we would have some special guests from Cleveland, Tennessee—miles away.
>
> As the service approached, I could not even pray. I felt as though God was miles away from me. During the first part of the service, I still could not get any relief. I felt I was standing alone. I was introduced to the congregation, and when I stepped into the pulpit, I felt as if I would

literally die. I felt paralyzed. I did not know if I could even open my mouth.

Suddenly, an overwhelming, powerful anointing fell on me. It sounded as if there was a voice coming into my ears, and I began to speak what I heard out of my mouth. I was preaching with tremendous power and anointing. I felt as though I was in another world.

In the middle of the sermon, a door behind me burst open onto the platform and a man in his late 20s or early 30s came into the sanctuary. This was in the wintertime, and he was wearing only a pair of old jeans. Both his hair and beard were very long and terribly matted. It looked as though he had been running in the mountains for weeks.

Someone in the congregation said, "Brother Seymour, this man needs deliverance!" (He was familiar to the congregation.) I said to the congregation, "Whatever anyone needs from God, come on up to the altar now!"

As the people were coming to the front, I walked over to this wild man, who was at the altar with people praying around him. When I reached to lay my hands on his head, he leaped to his feet and went for my neck with both of his hands. Immediately, I remembered the way the devil had gotten me by the neck some days before in West Virginia. When this happened, the people in the congregation jumped to their feet and ran to the back of the room.

As the man came toward me, I pointed my finger toward him and cried, "In the name of Jesus!" The man was stopped by the power of the Holy Ghost inside me. This happened several times. The man would come toward me again, and again I would cry, "In the name of Jesus!" The man would freeze momentarily, then regain himself.

Six men from the congregation rushed up and grabbed the man. Three would try to hold on to each arm, and he would fling them off as if they were nothing. He was growling and snarling at me like a lion. I realized I was going to have to cast the devil out of this man or he would kill me. People could not protect me, for humans could not bind or contain him.

Realizing the dangerous situation I faced, I mustered all the faith I could. By now the pastor and his nephew were by my side. As the power of the Holy Spirit rose up, I began to cast the demons out of the man. He fell limp and helpless to the floor and began weeping. He said, "Oh, my Lord! I'm naked." A man from the congregation put his coat around him.

After he was delivered, the man testified, "Today the devil let me know he was going to physically kill me tonight. You don't know how much I had to fight and struggle to get down the mountain to this building!" Then the power of God came on him and he was totally delivered that night.

Now I understood why God had let me have that experience in West Virginia.

God prepares us to fight against the forces of darkness. Not all believers will experience the kind of attack that Reverend Seymour did, but if you are a disciple of the Lord Jesus Christ, you will do battle with evil and with Satan.

THE POWER OF THE BLOOD OF JESUS

"Pleading the blood of Jesus" is more than just a catchphrase. It is, in a sense, a legal term. It means to invoke what Christ has done on the cross over a particular situation or person. A blood covering is provided through faith in God, prayer, and belief in the covenant of God. Thank God, we can overcome the temptation to sin, we can overcome the past, and we can overcome Satan—all enemies that try to destroy us.

When we say that we cover others with the precious blood of Jesus Christ, this means that we claim the blood that He shed, which enabled us to enter into the new covenant with God. The Scripture says, we can have *"boldness to enter the Holiest by the blood of Jesus, by a new and living way which He consecrated for us, through...His flesh"* (Hebrews 10:19–20). It means that almighty God will look down from heaven and watch over us and protect us. It means that we can also pray over our children and cover them with the covenant blood of Jesus Christ. Demons tremble at the name of Jesus, and they flee at the blood of the Lamb.

Pleading the blood gives us bold and confident access to God's power and providence. I have learned that when we are praying for people, and God impresses upon us to cover them with the blood, we should say, "I cover you with the blood of Jesus, the covenant of God!"

We can plead the blood for ourselves when the devil tries to torment us with the memory of past sins that have already been forgiven. Doing this reminds us and the devil that God has forgotten our sins because of Christ's sacrifice and His blood. He has shed His blood so that sin no longer has dominion over the believer who trusts completely in Him. The Word of God says, *"They overcame him by the blood of the Lamb and by the word of their testimony"* (Revelation 12:11). I believe that *"the word of* [our] *testimony"* simply means believing in the efficacy of the blood. A believer who pleads the blood in a time of dire circumstance or attack by the enemy is calling on the power and authority of Christ's blood. When we plead the blood, we acknowledge and testify to the overcoming power of the sacrifice of Jesus on our behalf.

To defeat the devil, you need to stand on the blood and proclaim its power! With that blood, we overcome Satan and the entire spiritual underworld. Demons are terrified by the blood. They cannot remain in the presence of the blood of Jesus Christ.

Don't let the enemy rob you of the truth of what defeats him. Jesus, our wonderful Lord and Savior, meets Satan, the flesh, and the world at the boundary of blood. Just as the Israelites did not have to fight if they trusted that God would fight for them—if they knew that *"the battle is the Lord's"* (1 Samuel 17:47)—so Jesus today fights our battles for us.

Whenever you speak the authority of the blood of Jesus Christ and actuate the power of the covenant of God, a battle will go on in the heavens and on the earth. When you stand boldly and proclaim the Word of the living God, therefore, know that in the name of Jesus, and through His blood, demons will flee and diseases will be healed. Many miracles, signs, and wonders will occur through the prayers of God's people. Let us look at some instances of healing and deliverance through the power of Jesus' blood.

Believers may encounter literal manifestations of evil spirits at times. I was awakened one night at about three o'clock in the morning, and I saw a large circle of light over my son's bed. Apart from the moonlight coming through the window, this was the only light in the room.

Then I saw an angel gazing at my son with a firm look on his face. His countenance mirrored strength. The angel drew a sword and started toward my son. Then I saw what looked like a large, black, caterpillar-like being wrapped around my son, who had been sick for several days with an intense fever.

The angel spoke in an authoritative voice and commanded the evil spirit to be loosed. The evil spirit obeyed the angel as he took the sword and removed that spirit of fever from my sick child. Then the angel and the evil spirit departed from the room.

Immediately, I rushed over to my son and picked him up. The power of God was on both of us, and my son was completely healed and delivered. Every bit of his fever was gone—for the first time in several days! I began to praise the Lord for delivering His people out of trouble.

Another time, I was in my room in intense intercession and earnest prayer. I was lying on my stomach, and suddenly I felt an evil presence enter the room. I cried out, "God, what is this?" Then I felt the evil force come nearer, and I felt a pressure on my back.

By now I could not move. It felt like I was frozen by some sinister, evil force. I could not even open my mouth and say aloud, "Jesus!" But in my heart, I was praying, *Jesus, Jesus. Help me.* I began to plead the blood of Jesus. I remember telling the devil, *When you let me go and turn me loose, I will tear your kingdom down!*

After a while, I felt the evil spirit move away from me. I felt the pressure let up. I was no longer frozen to the spot. I jumped up and said, "Jesus, I rebuke the devil in Your name. By Your blood, I am saved. I am Your child. I love You, Jesus." I was completely delivered and set free.

Roy Tucker, a very great pastor, described to me an encounter he had with demonic powers. It was a bizarre and terrifying experience that shows the ferocity and intensity of battling the forces of evil in spiritual warfare.

He said he first thought he was having a dream. He could feel something—it felt like a physical presence—pressing on his body. He felt weighted down, paralyzed. He could not imagine what was happening to him. He said it was as though he was screaming, but not a sound was coming out of his mouth. Roy knew an enemy from Satan had come to do something terrible to him. He knew in his spirit that this was a spiritual attack from the devil himself.

It was the middle of the night when he awoke; it was pitch dark. He could hear voices, as if someone was in the room with him, so he tried to open his eyes, but He could not. In fact, he could not move any part of his body. He tried to call out to someone for help but could not make a sound. He could not even move his lips.

The voices grew louder and louder. Soon they were close to him—right up next to him—screaming in his ears. He knew the voices belonged to evil spirits. With wild, raucous voices, they were scolding him for something he had or had not done—something that had offended them.

Then, he said, he felt his body floating upward; he was levitating from the bed. He found himself hovering against the ceiling, unable to move or speak or do anything. The screaming voices continued their relentless assault on his senses. He thought he was going mad. He actually thought he was going to die!

Gradually, his eyes opened and he could look around, but he could not do anything else. In addition to the voices, He sensed a malevolent presence in the room with him. Because of the pressure on his chest, he had difficulty breathing. As the evil spirit tormented him, he experienced sheer terror.

Finally, he had the presence of mind to realize that he could fight against this extreme spiritual attack of the devil. He willed himself to cry out, in his mind, *In the name of Jesus, and in the power of the blood of the Lamb, I resist the devil and all his evil spirits.* Immediately, he felt a lessening of the pressure!

Complete deliverance did not come immediately. But as he kept repeating the name of Jesus and calling on the blood of the Lamb, he became more free and more able to move and speak. By now, he could whisper, "Jesus, Jesus." His voice grew louder and stronger, and he was liberated from the oppressive power of the enemy by the precious blood of Jesus Christ.

Let me share one final testimony from a fellow believer:

Spiritual warfare means that you have the opportunity to defeat the devil through Jesus' blood and through His name. I was beginning my sophomore year of Bible college when I first experienced spiritual warfare. One night I was awakened from sleep by a noise in my room. Wide awake, I heard voices—threatening voices, frightening voices!

I can still hear them to this day. The frightening sound was unlike anything I had heard before or since. It sounded like many voices synchronized together into one blended tone. The voice said over and over, "I'm going to destroy you!"

I was paralyzed with fear. In terror, I tried to scream and call my parents, who were in the next room, but I was unable to make a sound. The only thing I could do was to whisper the name Jesus.

At first I could only say His name in my mind, but quickly my mind was at ease. Then I could whisper His name, and each time I whispered "Jesus," I gained more liberty and freedom. I noticed that as I said that powerful name, my voice became louder and louder until the evil presence that dominated the atmosphere left the room.

I fell asleep immediately; God had given His beloved sleep. The next morning I awoke refreshed. There were no side effects from the spiritual encounter the night before.

Not many weeks afterward, I had a second encounter. Again I was awakened out of sleep by the sense that some-one or something was in my room.

Because I didn't have the fear I had before, I passed it off and rolled over to go back to sleep. As I turned in my bed again, I noticed a shadow in the room. It was getting closer. Now I began to feel pressure around my throat and chest. The shadow didn't stop at the foot of the bed but came still closer. I experienced intense pain and had the sensation of being choked and smothered.

I called on the name of Jesus to break the hold of the enemy. The battle didn't last long, but it was intense. Afterward, I remember going in to the bathroom and looking into the mirror. My eyes were so bloodshot that I couldn't see the white in them at all. It seemed as though the veins in my eyes were about to burst from the pressure. Thank God, the name and power of Jesus delivered me.

I didn't understand what was happening, but the Lord revealed to me that the enemy was trying to keep me from going into the ministry. He was using his weapons of fear and intimidation. Thank God, I had already learned that the name of Jesus and the blood of Jesus are more than a match for the devil.

Yes, Jesus' name and blood are more than a match for Satan, sin, and the world. Jesus' authority is over heaven and earth and all that is in them, whether it be angel, demon, man, woman, nation, army, sickness, or act of nature. Whatever needs and difficulties you encounter, and no matter how fierce the enemy's attacks, you can rely on Jesus' love, power, and grace. He extends His authority to us so that we can minister alongside Him to manifest the power of the kingdom of God through His name and His atoning blood.

10

OCCUPYING ENEMY TERRITORY

Now thanks be to God who always leads us in triumph in Christ, and through us diffuses the fragrance of His knowledge in every place.
—2 Corinthians 2:14

One night, I was travailing in prayer, deeply engaged in intercession, when the Lord spoke to me,

> Mary, you are not alone in My work. I have an army of believers who are holding your hands up, who are standing with you, and who are praying with you and for you. Know that I am always with you, and you can find strength in My Word.

God began to show me a great army of His saints. There were millions, but they were divided into different groups. Each group was engaged in a separate, distinct mission. Some believers were in an army of liberation. Others were in an army of occupation. Still others were in an army that was busy rebuilding what had been torn down. Every individual, however, was engaged in a ministry of deliverance. I saw these armies, people from every nation, standing with Christ in His battle against evil.

THE MINISTERING ARMY OF GOD

In this concluding chapter, I would like to focus on the mission of the people of God on earth and what it means for us to have a vital role in the army of God. I will use the analogies of armies of liberation, occupation, and recovery to show the different ways in which God may call us to minister to others in Jesus' name in spiritual warfare. We should pray and ask the Lord which aspect of His army He wants us to fulfill at any given time.

AN ARMY THAT LIBERATES

Jesus began His ministry by proclaiming Himself as the Great Liberator:

> *And* [Jesus] *was handed the book of the prophet Isaiah. And when He had opened the book, He found the place where it was written: "The Spirit of the* Lord *is upon Me, because He has anointed Me to preach the gospel to the poor; He has sent Me to heal the brokenhearted, to proclaim liberty to the captives and recovery of sight to the blind, to set at liberty those who are oppressed; to proclaim the acceptable year of the* Lord*."...And He began to say to them, "Today this Scripture is fulfilled in your hearing."* —Luke 4:17–19, 21

Jesus followed this proclamation by calling men and women (His disciples and other followers) to join His army of deliverance. As they had received freedom in Christ, they were to liberate others in His name. This is how Jesus gave authority to the original twelve disciples:

> *And when He had called His twelve disciples to Him, He gave them power over unclean spirits, to cast them out, and to heal all kinds of sickness and all kinds of disease....* [Jesus commanded them,] *"And as you go, preach, saying, 'The kingdom of heaven is at hand.' Heal the sick, cleanse the lepers, raise the dead, cast out demons. Freely you have received, freely give."*
>
> —Matthew 10:1, 7–8

Jesus sends us forth today with the same authority. *"As the Father has sent Me, I also send you"* (John 20:21). We must see ourselves as a massive spiritual army of awesome deliverance! In this book, we have learned much about spiritual warfare and the weapons God has given us to defeat the enemy.

AN ARMY THAT BRINGS PEACE AND ORDER

Sometimes, the pressing need is for a spiritual army of occupation. At the end of World War II, the Axis armies of Japan and Germany had been thoroughly defeated, freeing much of the world from the control of invading armies. Yet, everyone knew that, left alone, these countries might recover their old strength, regroup, and cause strife again. The situation called for an occupying army to restore order to the chaos that existed in these countries, and to govern them until they could get back on their feet.

In Japan, General Douglas MacArthur was appointed Supreme Commander of the Allied Forces to lead the occupation army. The army governed the country and helped it through a very difficult time. When the United States ended the occupation six years later, they had helped a devastated Japan to rebuild itself, institute a democratic government, and chart a course that has made it one of the world's leading industrial powers.

The main goals of the occupation government were to end militarism in Japan, democratize the country, and repair its economy. The occupying armies did not fight pitched battles with an enemy, but they played a vital role in the fight for freedom.

Likewise, part of being God's army is to be an army of "occupation." This means we are to continue to intercede and to become channels for a peaceful, orderly, and stable society. We can do this in a number of ways, including providing wise counsel, godly examples, biblical principles, and positive solutions for the needs and problems of the world.

AN ARMY THAT REBUILDS AND RESTORES

General Lucius Clay was appointed Supreme Commander of the Allied Forces in Europe. The task of this army, however, involved more than occupying. The entire continent lay in ruins, ravaged by war and strewn with broken cities and despairing people. Homeless children whose parents had been killed and whose homes had been destroyed by bombs and artillery roamed the streets and scavenged for food.

A massive effort was needed for recovery and rebuilding. Europe had neither the manpower nor the resources to do the job. The armies of war had destroyed virtually all the continent's railways, roads, port facilities, communications, and basic infrastructure. In a speech to Congress outlining the Truman Doctrine, the president said that more than a thousand villages in Europe had been burned. Eighty-five percent of the children were tubercular. Livestock, poultry, and draft animals had almost disappeared. Inflation had wiped out practically all savings.

With the European Recovery Program, known popularly as the Marshall Plan, the United States led the continent in a massive rescue, recovery, and rebuilding program. United States armed forces carried the bulk of the load, furnishing manpower in rebuilding devastated infrastructures, conducting relief missions, and restoring confidence.

Likewise, being in God's army involves rescue, recovery, and rebuilding. More than anything else, the need of the hour is for God's people to rebuild what Satan has torn down and destroyed. Spiritual landscapes need to be rebuilt. There are lost souls and institutions that we can help put back on their feet through the power of God to save and restore.

To be a spiritual warrior means to be idealistic. However, it also means to be realistic by ministering to the whole person and giving practical help. Being a soldier in God's army includes fighting hunger, poverty, desperation, and confusion. We must help feed the starving and shelter the homeless.

More than anything else, spiritual warfare offers people hope—the hope that is in Jesus Christ. Therefore,

- let us offer hope to the devastated.
- let us restore confidence to the timid.
- let us rebuild what is shattered and in ruins.
- let us translate the claims and promises of the gospel into concrete actions to help others in need.

This is God's way of reclaiming what Satan has stolen and destroyed.

A MIGHTY WORK

There is a mighty work to be done in these last days. Spiritual warfare is vital to carrying forth the message of the gospel, and God needs all of us to help bring in the end-time harvest of souls. Leading people to salvation is one thing, but keeping them free is another. In order to do both, we have to live a lifestyle of spiritual warfare.

BE PERSEVERING

As we discussed earlier, this can take perseverance. Victory over Satan's attacks is not always obvious. Instead of his defeat and our success, sometimes it looks like our defeat and the devil's success. When Jesus died on the cross, it seemed as if the enemy had won. But by His death and resurrection, Jesus fully defeated Satan, brought about our salvation, and enabled us to be more than conquerors.

Similarly, what looks like defeat for believers is sometimes their greatest victory. The book of Revelation tells of a time when Satan and his subordinates will appear to triumph over the saints, but it will only be a momentary defeat that will accomplish the purposes of God and serve as a prelude to Satan's final destruction:

And when He broke the fifth seal, I saw underneath the altar the souls of those who had been slain because of the word of God, and because of the testimony which they had maintained; and they cried out with a loud voice, saying, "How long, O Lord, holy and true, wilt Thou refrain from judging and avenging our blood on those who dwell on the earth?" And there was given to each of them a white robe; and they were told that they should rest for a little while longer, until the number of their fellow servants and their brethren who were to be killed even as they had been, should be completed also.

—Revelation 6:9–11 NASB

Spiritual warfare takes its toll on people. We must always rely on God and His love to strengthen us for the task until Christ returns and brings the ultimate victory.

Who shall separate us from the love of Christ? Shall tribulation, or distress, or persecution, or famine, or nakedness, or

> *peril, or sword? As it is written: "For Your sake we are killed all day long; we are accounted as sheep for the slaughter." Yet in all these things we are more than conquerors through Him who loved us. For I am persuaded that neither death nor life, nor angels nor principalities nor powers, nor things present nor things to come, nor height nor depth, nor any other created thing, shall be able to separate us from the love of God which is in Christ Jesus our Lord.* —Romans 8:35–39

BE PREPARED

As we have learned, proper preparation is also necessary. An army cannot march into battle and expect to win without necessary provisions and support. We have to put on the whole armor of God and intercede in prayer. We must read and remember God's Word. We need to continually worship God and fellowship with other believers.

One night, when I was in deep intercessory prayer, God spoke to me about the mission and ministry to which He has called me. It gave me such peace.

> My child, the words you speak are not your own. My Spirit is within you, and you will know when to speak and when to refrain from speaking. The work you are doing is not your work; it is Mine. [Your] work is not done in your own strength and might; it is done in My strength and might.
>
> I am a God of judgment and a God of war as well as a God of love. You must continue to gather My children together. You must proclaim My Word and tell My people to continue to take back what the enemy has stolen from them. I will use you to rebuke those who rise up against Me, saith the Lord.

Call on My strength. When you encounter evil forces, go forth in boldness. Use the power of My name, My Word, and My blood. Rebuke every enemy in My name. Don't ignore the world, the flesh, and the devil. Overcome them by the word of your testimony and by the power of My blood that was shed for you. You must continue to give this message to My people!

This book is part of my commitment to fulfill this calling. God bless you as you move forward in spiritual warfare, *"strong in the Lord and in the power of His might"* (Ephesians 6:10)!

APPENDICES

APPENDIX A:

SPIRITUAL WARFARE & PERSONAL POTENTIAL

T. L. LOWERY INTERVIEWS DR. JEFF O'NEAL

When the enemy comes in like a flood, the Spirit of the LORD *will lift up a standard against him.*
—Isaiah 59:19

INTRODUCTION

Dr. Jeff O'Neal is CEO of Micah's Jewelry, Inc., of Atlanta, Georgia. He is a successful Christian businessman who has a heart for spreading the gospel in the marketplace. He also knows firsthand the reality of spiritual warfare. The following interview shows how the enemy often tries to detour us, or deter us, from reaching our maximum potential in Jesus Christ.

T. L. Lowery: Dr. O'Neal and I have both experienced great moments in our lives when we encountered the devil and the sinister powers of darkness. We have come against many strongholds that Satan has built up around us to try to keep us from reaching our destinies. In our varied experiences, we have witnessed some awesome deliverances. We have found that, as long as we try to fight the battle in ourselves, God turns the situation and its outcome over to us. But when we humble ourselves and turn the battle over to God, when we understand that the battle is the Lord's and not ours, then God sovereignly and divinely intervenes to show us His glory. He is faithful to give us peace and victory.

I have asked Dr. O'Neal to share with us one of the most difficult experiences he has gone through in spiritual warfare, so that we can gain additional insight into how to fulfill the purposes and potential God has ordained for our lives.

Dr. Jeff O'Neal: As a young businessman, at age thirty-eight, I discovered that God was in the process of defining who I was, including His plan, purposes, and destiny for my life. Little did I know then that my life was about to make a drastic change. God cast me into the "fire," just as Job was cast into the "fire."

One night, I was leaving a trade show in Gatlinburg, Tennessee, at about nine o'clock. Sleet and snow had come into the area, and when we left the convention center, I was detoured away around the mountain, a route that would take me an extra three hours to get home. Running low on fuel, I became concerned. Being in the jewelry business, I had to be careful and think about security issues. I knew the potential for danger because I was carrying large amounts of jewelry.

I said to my associate, "We need to get some gas. If we don't, we are going to mess around here and run out of gas. We could get robbed!" Not realizing the power of my own words, I spoke my fears, setting in motion the things that were about to take place. Literally, I spoke with my own words the very thing that was about to happen.

This experience has helped me to understand the principle of the power of the tongue to speak things upon our lives and our families. The wrong use of the tongue can set things in motion. But God was sovereignly in control as I stopped to get fuel there that night. Little did I know, as I stepped away to make a phone call to let everyone know we were safe and things were okay, that we were going to be several hours late. Little did I know that I was being followed by organized crime, as the FBI confirmed after an eighteen-month investigation. That night they took my truck, my trailer, and over $1.5 million worth of inventory and assets.

In just a few moments—in seconds—my whole life changed. Everything we owned was lost. Because I stepped away from the vehicle, even the insurance refused to pay what we had invested. Literally, we took a bottom-line loss of everything we had.

At that moment, God was defining who I was to become. You see, without a test, there is no testimony. The night we were robbed, I asked the man in charge of that facility, "Can I go to an office somewhere? I need to talk to my Father before I talk with the police." I wouldn't talk to the police until I first talked to my Father in heaven.

The man pointed to a door. I walked to the door, thinking he had identified with my pain. I struggled to get the door open; it was so dark I couldn't see. I flipped the light switch and found myself in a mop closet with a muddy floor and an old cast-iron sink. But I knew God was sovereign, so I said, "Well, if this is the way it has to be, so be it."

I fell on my knees, gripped the cast-iron sink, and began to cry out to God. First, I began to acknowledge God's sovereignty. I said, "God, I know You are sovereign. I know You rule and reign, and You are in control of all things. God, I know where I am with You. I acknowledge my covenant with You."

I went from God's sovereignty to the covenant I had with Him as His child, His son. I prayed, "God, I know that I am Your child;

and God, I know where I stand with You. Although I don't understand everything that is taking place in my life right now, I know You are sovereignly in control. I pray to You right now, Lord God, that You will touch me and help me to understand and trust You."

Romans 8:26 says that when you don't even know what to say, when you don't even know what to pray, the Spirit of God will begin to bring utterance. The Spirit within me began to moan and groan and cry out into my desperate situation. I began praying to the Lord through my spirit, not by my mind. I said things that didn't make any sense to my reason. Although the words were in English, they were supernaturally given. As prayed in the Spirit, I started off with these words: "Lord, I am not going to ask you to return our truck, trailer, and over $1.5 million worth of inventory." Something said to me, *What are you saying?* I said, "God, I am not going to ask You to return it because You knew it would be taken before the men ever did it."

I had to trust in the Lord. Proverbs 3:5–6, says, "*Trust in the* Lord *with all your heart and lean not on your own understanding; in all your ways acknowledge him, and he will make your paths straight*" (NIV). I had to accept the fact that God was sovereignly in control. So I prayed, "First, I will acknowledge the fact that You knew it would be taken. You sovereignly withdrew Your hand and allowed it to be taken, because the enemy cannot touch one hair on my head unless You allow it. So God, You have allowed this to be.

"God, give me the faith to trust in You. I need a greater measure of faith than I have ever had in my life. I need the faith to stand on Your Word and know that You're in complete control. God, I ask for Your strength because I cannot carry this burden within myself. I cannot do this within myself. I need to trust in You and lean on You.

"God, give me the wisdom to pick up the pieces and put things back together again."

I uttered this prayer, asking for faith, strength, and wisdom to move forward. While we lost everything we owned that night, little did I know that God was going to take me through a difficult course for about a year.

We did not file for bankruptcy. We stood on the Word of God and followed biblical principles. We diligently worked our way through. God gave us a plan, and He gave us a strategy. He also gave us the wisdom we needed to know what to do.

By the grace of God, He sent us enough business so that we could overcome. We paid back everyone what we owed them and continued to operate a business, which grew.

We are wholesalers, and we import and export quality jewelry. My suppliers from all over the world were amazed. Two Jewish men walked into my store a year later in January, expecting to see a man who was broken down, distraught, utterly destroyed. They came in January because they had let me have some merchandise. They thought that, by the time Christmas was over, and I had sold a little, they would come in and take what was left, cash out, and sell our accounts.

When they walked in the doors, rather than seeing someone broken, torn down, and destroyed, they saw a man standing out front, sharing the gospel of Jesus Christ. I was witnessing and preaching to my customers with a big smile and a glow on my face. Amazed, they walked over, looked at me, and said, "There's no doubt that God's hand is on this place and on your life, and we're proud to be associated with you, Jeff. It is an honor to work with someone like you. We have heard you testify of sharing and sponsoring mission work around the world, and we not only want to partner with your business, we want to partner with you in ministry."

Thus God began to take the wealth of Muslims, Jews, and Buddhists—our suppliers—and use it for ministry. They wanted to sponsor ministry we were affiliated with because of the testimony and the testing we went through, and they wanted to tap into that anointing. God touched these people and caused them to know that only a sovereign God could bring us through a situation like this.

Job 42:12–13 says that all that Job lost was restored to him. God cast me into the fire, but when we came out, we came out shining as pure gold. Little did I know then that the next test would be that, once God restored me, He would call me to leave Micah's.

When I told my employees that God had called me to leave Micah's and to go out and minister and preach, they said, "What do you mean, you're leaving? Who's going to run the company?"

I said to them, "Don't you know? Don't you understand? I told you that God runs this company. I have never run it; it has always been directed by His hand. He is the One who directs our thoughts, our ways, and everything we do. Since He has led me away to minister, He has put others in place who will continue the operation of Micah's."

I have now been gone three years, and Micah's continues to grow and expand. God honors our obedience. As He speaks to us, we must trust, submit, and obey. The testimony to our suppliers is the fact that they see the hand of God working through an entity created and breathed into existence through the Spirit of God for one purpose: to lift up the name of Jesus Christ and to share the gospel around the world.

God brought my wife, Okyon, and me into existence so that we would flow in the apostolic and the prophetic, so that we would stand in the marketplace, as Isaiah did 2,400 years ago, and speak His Word to the people He sent through those doors, and so we would challenge others to take their storefronts and turn them into mission fronts for the kingdom of God.

T. L. Lowery: Brother O'Neal, sometimes people find themselves in the heat of the battle. Like Joseph, they may be in prison.

Like David facing Goliath, they are going through a difficult time in their lives. It seems as if the forces of hell are rising up against them from every direction. When they try to climb out, it's like quicksand. They seem to sink deeper and deeper. When they take one step forward, they slide back two steps. Impossible, unbearable situations confront some people every day. Everything seems dark; they can't see any light at the end of the tunnel. Things continue to close in around them and come down upon them.

What would your counsel be to a person who is facing such circumstances as these?

Dr. Jeff O'Neal: Dr. Lowery, it didn't all just happen overnight. It took a year for us to overcome this. I had moments of depression, and I had moments when I struggled, but every day I would seek God in prayer and through His Word. God would give me what I needed for that moment. God would give me the revelation, the strength, and the wisdom I needed for the next step I had to take. You see, God gave manna to the children of Israel so that He could test them to see if they would walk in accordance with His instruction. (See Exodus 16:4.) But they had to gather it daily.

God will give you what you need for the moment. He told us to take no thought of tomorrow, for tomorrow will take care of itself. (See Matthew 6:34.) God clearly said in His Word that, if we will call out to Him, He will answer us. "*Call to Me, and I will answer you, and show you great and mighty things, which you do not know*" (Jeremiah 33:3).

I didn't have the wisdom to know what to do or how to win this battle, but God ordered my steps through His Word: "*The steps of a good man are ordered by the Lord, and He delights in his way*" (Psalm 37:23). God would direct my thoughts. He would direct my steps to know what I needed to know moment by moment. This kind of guidance comes through prayer and through the Word of God. The Spirit of God within you will begin to take over and begin to lead and direct you when you can't, within yourself, do the things you need to do.

T. L. Lowery: Brother O'Neal, going through such circumstances affects the sphere of your influence. It affects your family. You have to deal with the circumstances and the reverses in the spiritual warfare you are involved in, but your family is also involved. You have to guard your attitude and your demeanor in how you continue to minister to your family and be the priest of your household.

How were you able to really bring all these things together and keep a sound mind and a sound heart?

Dr. Jeff O'Neal: Again, it was through prayer. I began to cut off all influences that were not of God. I did not want to be associated with things and people and situations that were being poured into my spirit but were not positive and were not going to give me strength. God literally stripped me down until I was naked, in a metaphorical sense. As when Isaiah was stripped down to nothing (see Isaiah 20:2), my best friends, my family, and others did not understand. I've had Christian brothers say, "Well, God really has a way of getting your attention, doesn't He?" They would speak to me in a judgmental way, as Job's friends did to him.

In John 9, some people said that since a certain man was born blind, his parents must have sinned. They did not know that God, in His sovereignty, allows things to come about for different purposes and reasons. Rather than confer with flesh and blood, I conferred with my Father in heaven, and I conferred in the Spirit. I chose not to walk in the natural realm, and I began to isolate myself and insulate myself with the Word of God and prayer.

My wife and I were supposed to be yoked together in agreement, so together we stayed in Word of God and in prayer. The Spirit of God spoke to us, and God would divinely move on our behalf and do things that only He could do. Sometimes, He gave us mercy; sometimes, He gave us grace. For example, God would give us the wisdom to know how to structure payments to repay the people we owed and to honor our obligations.

You see, we had obligations. We had a covenant with these people, and we had to pay them back. I looked my creditors in the face because my life is a testimony to my Father. I am a reflection of Him. I said to those we owed, "I want you to understand, I have full intentions of honoring my covenants with you. You will be paid. I don't know how God's going to bring this about, but if you'll just give me a chance, by the grace of God, He will direct me."

I told my friends, "God is the same yesterday, today, and forevermore. God is going to direct me and show me what I need to do. Nothing has changed. I am the same man I was yesterday before this robbery, and God is the same God."

Although all my resources had been taken away, I looked at my suppliers and said, "The Lord giveth and the Lord taketh away, blessed be the name of the Lord." (See Job 1:21.) I stood on the Word of God, knowing that if He restored Job of old, He would do the same for me, because He is no respecter of people.

T. L. Lowery: Do you believe that God allows testing to come in each person's life to prepare the individual for a higher place in God? Do you believe that every person who amounts to anything significant in the kingdom of God must go through the refiner's fire to be purged and tested to see what kind of metal he really possesses?

Dr. Jeff O'Neal: No doubt, Dr. Lowery. Just as the Word of God says, "Everyone to whom much is given, has been committed, of him they will ask the more." (See Luke 12:48.) We don't understand the fullness and the context of that Scripture, but God is going to prepare us in advance for what lies ahead in our lives and our destiny, just as he did with Joseph, who was cast into the pit and the prison to prepare him for the palace.

"Being confident of this very thing, that He who has begun a good work in you will complete it until the day of Jesus Christ" (Philippians 1:6). He shall bring to pass what the Word of God says. God is working all things to the good for them that love the Lord and are called according to His purpose, as Romans 8:28 says. God is working everything and intricately networking it to bring about His purposes and His sovereign will, in order to spread the gospel around the world and establish His kingdom on earth as it is in heaven.

T. L. Lowery: What is happening at Micah's now? What is happening in your ministry? Can you see the hand of God in what He allowed you to experience during this time of spiritual conflict?

Dr. Jeff O'Neal: Dr. Lowery, the first thing I praise and thank God for in this struggle is for the salvation of souls. This is the first priority in all that we do. I have prayed for years that God would touch the hearts and lives of individuals who were in our inner circle and in our extended family. When I had tried to talk with them and share with them, the things I would say didn't seem to fall on open hearts and open minds. In this spiritual conflict, the Word was sown. God said His Word would not return void. The suffering that Okyon and I went through birthed their salvation. We have to be willing to suffer if we want to see the salvation of souls.

Another thing that we realized is that we have to be willing to wait on God as He is working in our lives and fulfilling a greater purpose and greater plan than we know. Sometimes, the answer doesn't come in the time frame we desire. But we have to understand that God's ways are higher than our ways and His thoughts are higher than our thoughts. (See Isaiah 55:9.) As God continued to move, I prayed, "O God, allow spiritual maturity and growth to come to certain individuals' lives."

As God was fulfilling His purpose in my life, He had to move me out of this situation and this assignment to go to another assignment, so these individuals could grow. At Micah's, I was literally overshadowing the growth of those around me. Another great joy that I have is noting the spiritual maturity I see in the people that I have mentored and discipled. As I moved out, they began to have the room to move up.

And third, God took me into other areas of ministry because I walked in obedience and I was willing to humble myself. When He moved me from Micah's as the President and CEO of a large corporation, He sent me to a little Christian bookstore that was literally seven days from closing—dying—going out of business. The Lord said, "I want you to buy this store." He spoke to me clearly and confirmed it by His Word.

Little did I know that He was going to make me sit there and wait! I had to wait for forty-two months. I had to stay there and be obedient. It was humbling. Who would want to wait in a small, run-down Christian bookstore that was struggling to stay afloat? God said, "I want you to take this and resurrect it. I want you to stay here until I give you the next assignment."

It required a great amount of financial resources for us to do this, but we went in and resurrected this bookstore. We stayed there for that time period, and God surrounded me with His Word so that He could continue to allow me to grow.

Again, it goes back to the Word of God. In designing a building, the foundation ultimately dictates the building's size. The foundation we have in God's Word ultimately dictates where and what we're able to accomplish for the kingdom of God. We must continue to expand our foundation in the Word of God through study and prayer.

Thus, God put me in this bookstore so He could increase the foundation of what He wanted to do in my life. He gave me an outlet to speak—not just to one church, but to all the churches in that area. I began to minister there in the bookstore. I was obedient for forty-two months, and then He released me. When the fullness of time had come and I had obeyed God, we sold the bookstore and I was released to go forward.

Little did I know what He was about to do! He opened the door for me to begin to minister around the world with Dr. T. L. Lowery. Just recently, God opened the door, without any effort on my part, to begin to minister to six million people weekly on Christian television in the Atlanta area.

I knew no one there; God sovereignly opened these doors. He gave me the divine appointments by sending Dr. Lowery to where I was. You don't have to do anything to make it happen. God has spoken it, and the Word of God says that all your days are ordained by Him. Before any of them existed, they were all written in the book. (See Psalm 139:16 NIV, NASB.)

God has a plan for your life. He has a destiny; He has a purpose. As you walk forward in faith and obedience, and humble yourself before God, and say, "God, not my will, but thine be done," God will set things in order in your life. He will set His plan in place, and it will begin to be fulfilled as you walk in obedience to the leading of the Spirit.

Appendix B:

Spiritual Warfare & Finances

T. L. Lowery Interviews Dr. Michael Chitwood

For I know the thoughts that I think toward you,
says the Lord, *thoughts of peace and not of evil,*
to give you a future and a hope.
—Jeremiah 29:11

Introduction

Dr. Michael Chitwood, CEO of Church Management & Tax Conferences (CMTC), is an expert in the area of finances and an outstanding Christian businessman. The following interview reveals the way the enemy works to attack us in the arena of our finances, and what we can do to counteract him.

T. L. Lowery: Dr. Chitwood, does spiritual warfare affect the area of finances in a Christian's life?

Dr. Michael Chitwood: Yes. Any area where there is a lack of faith (believing what God said) is a prime target for Satan. Finances is usually a common area of attack because most people are lacking in faith in that area. If Satan senses even a hint of doubt or insecurity, he will attack. He knows the power and the proof of biblical principles. If he can convince you to doubt, he can convince you to disobey. Once you disobey, you have cut off your supply line from the Lord. If we can believe God for our eternal security, why can't we believe Him to provide for our needs? Things that are more abstract in nature are easier to believe for because we have less control over them. Once we have any level of control or say so in a matter, it becomes subject to our pride and selfishness. Once our flesh has access to it, we want to take the control out of God's hands.

T. L. Lowery: What are some of the tactics the devil uses when he comes against believers in the arena of their finances?

Dr. Michael Chitwood: Being self-centered (displaying selfishness) instead of being God-centered is a major tool of the enemy. For men especially. Our ability to earn a living and be a provider is deeply rooted in our identity. This is a foundational issue for men that is linked to our masculinity and pride. If we can't provide an "acceptable" standard of living for our family, we feel like a failure. If we aren't meeting a standard, our nature is to find a way, in our own strength, to rise to that level.

Security is another area. Money has replaced God as our security. We have a sort of temporal, shallow feeling of security when we have money in our pockets. We feel as if we can handle any situation as long as we have money. If we don't have money, we feel we are in need. Once our faith and security in God is weak, Satan has an open door to play havoc with our minds.

T. L. Lowery: Why are finances such a critical area for Satan to use to come against believers?

Dr. Michael Chitwood: Because we are so closely involved with our finances, we become attached to and possessive over the money we receive. We work to earn it, we discipline ourselves to save it, and we stretch it out to cover expenses.

Money has become our god, in many cases. If we allow Satan to talk us into letting anything become an idol, he has a stronghold in our lives. We become involved in the "love of money" that the Bible warns us about. It's not so much that we love money itself; it is that we love the feeling of security. We love the feeling of control, power, and pride that money produces. These feelings replace our need for and dependence on God, and give way to the controlling power of greed.

I believe our society's idolatry of money is a generational curse that spreads farther than any curse of substance abuse or sexual addiction and perversion. The Lord said to the Israelites, "'*Do not forget the covenant I have made with you, and do not worship other gods. Rather, worship the* LORD *your God; it is he who will deliver you from the hand of all your enemies.' They would not listen, however, but persisted in their former practices. Even while these people were worshiping the* LORD*, they were serving their idols. To this day their children and grandchildren continue to do as their fathers did*" (2 Kings 17:38–41 NIV). Previous generations had that mentality and have raised children and grandchildren to think in the same way.

I believe this curse has as strong, or a stronger, hold on the church than it does the rest of society. The church has adopted a mentality of lack and poverty. We have believed the lie of the enemy that we are less than those in the world, that we should live meager, deprived lives so that we can show our humility, and that we should not draw attention to ourselves by living in plenty.

Instead, we should believe that we are the head and not the tail, that we are supposed to be the lender and not the borrower (see Deuteronomy 28:12–13), and that, by standing out from the crowd, we draw attention to God because we are His representatives in this world. Who wants to follow a God who demands that you lose more than you gain?

T. L. Lowery: Can you relate a particular experience you or someone you know has had in this area?

Dr. Michael Chitwood: A minister friend tells of a time when he had it all. He had both an active ministry and a great family. Then his wife left him, taking their child and all their possessions with her. He found himself living in a one-room apartment with no furniture, all the while still preaching the gospel. He prayed continually for his financial circumstances, but nothing changed until the day he finally obeyed God's instructions.

One day, he received $100 for preaching a service. God directed him to give it away. He reluctantly gave it to the person the Lord directed him to. At his next meeting, someone gave him $1,000. He thought of all the important and necessary things he needed to do with the money, but the Lord directed him to give that away, too. He knew that if he gave it away, he would go without food and possibly lose his apartment. He approached the person the Lord had led him to and gave him $200.

After much conviction, he went back to that person and gave him the remaining money. Shortly afterward, he was blessed with a check for $10,000 and a car. Today, he has a prosperous, worldwide ministry, teaching others the financial principles of God and seeing people blessed immeasurably.

T. L. Lowery: Thank you, Dr. Chitwood. God has blessed you with spiritual wisdom and financial acumen; and you, in turn, bless the kingdom of God with your dedication to Him.

CONCLUSION

In His Word, God has declared, "*No weapon formed against you shall prosper, and every tongue which rises against you in judgment you shall condemn. This is the heritage of the servants of the* L*ORD*, *and their righteousness is from Me*" (Isaiah 54:17).

In His power and supernatural anointing, God speaks life into every dead situation. He gives promise and hope when all expectations have been shattered. I thank God that nothing is over until *He* says it is over! God is planning great things for you. He will open supernatural doors in your life today. He will break the chains that have bound you for years and will set you free!

It is my sincere prayer that, as you read this book, God will reach down His mighty hand and cancel every plot, plan, and scheme that the enemy has devised against you. I am praying for your household. I am praying for your health. I am praying for your marriage. I am praying for your job. I am praying for your children, your parents, and your siblings.

I am praying especially for your financial situation. Dr. Chitwood has given us insights we all can follow with great profit. God wants to bless your ministry. God wants to bless your decisions. He wants your debts to be paid and your mortgages to be canceled. He wants to give you your heart's desire.

I am praying for God's perfect will to be done in your life, in Jesus' name!

ABOUT THE AUTHORS

ABOUT DR. MARY K. BAXTER

Dr. Mary K. Baxter has been in full-time ministry for more than thirty-five years, ever since she was taken by God into the dimensions and torments of hell, as well as the streets of heaven, for over forty nights in 1976. God commissioned Mary to record her experiences and tell others of the horrific depths, degrees, and torments of hell, as well as the wonderful destiny of heaven for the redeemed of Jesus Christ. There truly is a hell to shun and a heaven to gain!

Throughout her life, Mary has experienced many visions, dreams, and revelations of heaven, hell, and the spirit realm. She has been sent by God to minister in over 125 nations, and she has seen her books translated into more than twenty languages. Salvation springs forth as she walks in the miraculous power of God on her life. Signs and wonders follow her, and testimonies of God's saving grace abound in her ministry. She has a mother's heart to see all people come into the kingdom of God and become all that God has created them to be. She has birthed numerous other ministries and pours into the lives of others to see the kingdom of God expand into the emerging generations of the earth.

Mary K. Baxter was ordained as a minister in 1983 and received a Doctor of Ministry degree from Faith Bible College, an affiliate of Oral Roberts University. She continues to travel the world and minister in power. Mary's book *A Divine Revelation of Hell* has sold 1.4 million copies. In addition to that work, her books published by Whitaker House include *A Divine Revelation of Heaven, A Divine Revelation of the Spirit Realm, A Divine Revelation of Angels, A Divine Revelation of Spiritual Warfare, A Divine Revelation of Deliverance, A Divine Revelation of Healing, A Divine Revelation of Prayer, A Divine Revelation of the Powerful Blood of Jesus,* and *A Divine Revelation of Satan's Deceptions.*

For speaking engagements, please contact:

Dr. Mary K. Baxter
marykbaxter1@yahoo.com
www.marykbaxterinc.com

ABOUT T. L. LOWERY

T. L. Lowery (1929–2016) was born in Eastman, Georgia, and was converted to Christ in 1943. He served as a pastor and evangelist until 1969, preaching in massive tent crusades nationwide—his tent seated ten thousand—and in numerous foreign countries. His evangelism ministry was marked by testimonies of thousands of converts, reports of frequent divine healings, and unnumbered people filled with the Holy Spirit.

T. L. Lowery served as pastor of two Church of God congregations, North Cleveland, Tennessee (1969–1974) and National, Washington, D.C. (1981–1996), where he led both churches in significant growth and major building programs. Part of his pastoral legacy was an emphasis on ministries to all strata of society. His pastoral leadership helped awaken the consciousness of the denomination to personal evangelism, lay ministry, and local church outreach. In both pastorates, he provided housing for the elderly. In Washington, he founded an outstanding private Christian school, a Bible school, and a seminary.

Lowery may be best known as a denominational leader, serving sixteen years on the Church of God Executive Committee and thirty-four years on the Executive Council. He also acted interdenominationally on the boards of the National Association of Evangelicals (NAE), National Religious Broadcasters (NRB), and Pentecostal Charismatic Churches of North America (PCCNA).

He was the author or coauthor of over 85 books, most of which have been translated into numerous languages. He also edited three magazines and wrote many teaching booklets and articles.

Lowery's passion in personal ministry and in mentorship activities was the active preservation of apostolic ministry in the Church of God and the wider Pentecostal-charismatic community. He had numerous spiritual sons and daughters who were saved, called into ministry, and mentored under his spiritual leadership.

Lowery served more than seventy years in ministry, and the T. L. Lowery Global Foundation, Cleveland, TN, continues his legacy. Stephen Lanier Lowery, the son of Lowery and his wife, Mildred, followed his father as the pastor of the National Church of God, where he continues to serve.